Intimate Partner Violence in New Orleans

New Orleans Criminal Court Building, 1895. Louisiana Division/City Archives, New Orleans Public Library.

Intimate Partner Violence in
NEW ORLEANS

Gender, Race, and Reform, 1840–1900

Ashley Baggett

University Press of Mississippi / Jackson

www.upress.state.ms.us

The University Press of Mississippi is a member
of the Association of American University Presses.

First printing 2017
∞

Library of Congress Cataloging-in-Publication Data

Names: Baggett, Ashley, author.
Title: Intimate partner violence in New Orleans : gender, race, and reform,
1840–1900 / Ashley Baggett.
Description: Jackson: University Press of Mississippi, [2017] | Includes
bibliographical references and index. |
Identifiers: LCCN 2017023657 (print) | LCCN 2017025890 (ebook) | ISBN
9781496815224 (epub single) | ISBN 9781496815231 (epub institutional) |
ISBN 9781496815248 (pdf single) | ISBN 9781496815255 (pdf institutional)
| ISBN 9781496815217 (cloth : alk. paper)
Subjects: LCSH: Spousal abuse—Louisiana—New Orleans—History—19th century.
| Women—Abuse of—Louisiana—New Orleans—History—19th century. | Family
violence—Louisiana—New Orleans—History—19th century. | New Orleans
(La.)—Race relations—History—19th century. | African
Americans—Louisiana—New Orleans—Social conditions—19th century.
Classification: LCC HV6626.22.N66 (ebook) | LCC HV6626.22.N66 B34 2017
(print) | DDC 362.82/92097633509034—dc23 LC record available
at https://lccn.loc.gov/2017023657

British Library Cataloging-in-Publication Data available

To my husband and children—in the countless hours spent writing this,
you were always in my thoughts and gave me purpose.

To survivors of intimate partner violence—your voice matters.

Contents

Contents

Acknowledgments

Many people contributed to the creation of this work, and I am thankful for each and every one. For the women in my book, I hope I do justice to their lives and am grateful for the opportunity to give voice to those who were previously neglected in the historical record.

I began my research in nineteenth-century intimate partner violence at Louisiana State University. I ran into dead end after dead end and considered abandoning the project after finding scant references to the topic. Charles Shindo, Gaines Foster, and Alecia Long provided valuable feedback, guidance, and support during the early stages of research. Without their dedication and mentorship I could not have written this book. Other faculty members offered important insights at different points during my graduate career, including Kodi Roberts, Rand Dotson, and Carolyn Lewis. LSU's History Department and Women's and Gender Studies program made me the scholar I have become today, and I am immensely thankful for the guidance I received there.

My colleagues at North Dakota State University helped me build upon my earlier work through suggestions and funding for travel. The Northern Plains Ethics Institute and the Department of History, Philosophy, and Religious Studies generously provided funds allowing me to continue my research across the country. Moreover, everyone in my department created a warm and welcoming atmosphere, easing my transition into a new institution. They offered advice and support, and I am grateful for such a group of colleagues.

This project required countless months in the archives, particularly in Baton Rouge and New Orleans. The New Orleans Public Library's Louisiana Division/City Archives became a second home to me. In the care of the library's staff, I poured through more than twenty-five thousand cases, and they tirelessly worked to ensure that the court records were pulled when I needed them. Knowing that I faced time constraints with my travel, they would quickly keep me supplied with a steady stream of cases, working up to the last minute. Everyone remembered my methods for pulling cases and how many I could get through in a day, even with a year between visits. Often,

I didn't take a break more than once or twice in an eight-hour stretch, and always I was greeted with the smiles of helpful staff members, who rotated shifts and were prepared to keep my nose to the grindstone. Moreover, they generously waived permissions fees for images. To each and every person at the City Archives, thank you. I also had the pleasure of working with archivists at the Hill Memorial Library at LSU and the Historic New Orleans Collection. THNOC is a top-notch institution, and I am incredibly grateful for their quick responses and willingness to work with me from across the country to acquire permissions to items in their impressive collection.

The University Press of Mississippi also deserves many thanks for making this work into a reality. Craig Gill contacted me about an article I had previously published and encouraged me to submit my prospectus to the press. Both he and Emily Bandy answered countless emails, ensuring that the process continued without issue. Norman Ware diligently copyedited my book, and for that I am immensely grateful. All of their positivity and interest made working with them a pleasure, and I appreciate their hard work in making this a much better book than I could have imagined.

Above all, I could not have researched or written this book without the help of good friends and family. Ashley Heyer Casey, Alan Forrester, Mona Rocha, and Jason Wolfe have offered important suggestions and provided unfailing emotional support over the past several years. Countless times I bounced ideas off them or asked for edits, and they continued to encourage me even in the most difficult moments. My parents, Jim and Deborah Allen, sparked my interest in history and have enthusiastically supported my goals.

It is to my husband and children that I owe the largest debt, however. They endured endless hours of me being immersed in my research and patiently supported me during the process. Kevin worked to ensure that my goals were achievable. Throughout the entirety of this project, he provided help—including finding obscure materials, accompanying me to the archives, listening to my frustrations, and reading my work in every single version. I couldn't ask for a better friend or partner in life. From the bottom of my heart, thank you for your love, support, and companionship.

Intimate Partner Violence in New Orleans

Introduction

In the early evening of August 6, 1852, Peter Molloy attacked his wife, Elizabeth, in their home on Julia Street in New Orleans. He dragged her by her hair through the house, down a flight of stairs, and into the backyard, after which he hit her twice before picking up an ax and threatening to kill her if she tried to come back inside. The couple—both white and illiterate—went before the local Recorder's Court before the case made its way to the First District Court. In the case records, neither one's testimony was preserved, but the documents stated that Peter Molloy "unprovokedly assaulted and violently and barbariously" beat his wife.[1] Despite the apparent severity of the crime, the case was dropped, and Peter Molloy went unprosecuted.

After the Civil War, a similar case involving intimate partner violence with a white couple resulted in a different verdict. On July 8, 1886, Martin Johnson followed his wife, Louisa, into an alley on Poydras Street in New Orleans, kicked her, and then continued to beat her to the point at which she had to be carried to a nearby hospital. Louisa pressed charges for assault and battery, and a patrolman arrested Martin and brought him before the local magistrate. When Louisa gave her testimony, Martin cross-examined her, saying, "You got frightened. You ran into the alley ... [and] you fell."[2] Claiming that it had been an accident, the husband pressed his wife to recant, but she did not. Instead, the case went on to the Criminal District Court, and the judge found Martin Johnson guilty, sentencing him to four months in jail.

By the 1890s, however, the direction of the legal response to intimate partner violence again shifted. On September 1, 1891, James Reynolds, a white man, came home drunk and pulled a penknife on his wife, Harriet. When she knocked it out of his hands, James punched her in the face and choked her. Harriet managed to escape from their home on Constance Street in New Orleans and take refuge in her daughter's house, where she filed a complaint with a patrolman. Despite showing bruises and providing testimony from a neighbor, the judge found James Reynolds not guilty.[3]

In the same year, Jefferson Green attacked his wife, Alice, in their home on Dryades Street in New Orleans. Alice testified that they had argued two

3

days previously, and she had refused to sleep in the same bed with him since then. Instead, she went to her mother's home, where he also went and insisted on talking with his wife. Alice ran as her mother held the door against him, but eventually Jefferson broke through and cut Alice's mother on the arm, a wound that required stitches. In the cross-examination, the defense attorney claimed that Alice's mother had attacked him first, but she denied it. The key difference here was race. Jefferson and Alice Green were both black. The judge found Jefferson Green guilty and sentenced him to thirty days in jail or a twenty-five-dollar fine.[4]

Each of these four cases—*Molloy, Johnson, Reynolds,* and *Green*—illustrates a response to intimate partner violence from New Orleans courts spanning the antebellum period to the late nineteenth century, and each portrays a different reaction from the legal system at a different point in time. Throughout the history of intimate partner violence, courts have interpreted and reinterpreted old assault and battery criminal statutes as social attitudes toward the male privilege of chastisement fluctuated, allowing for periodic shifts in the courts' stance on privacy, abuse, and a woman's right to be free from violence. But what exactly prompted the courts to revoke their sanction of the male privilege of chastisement after the Civil War? Why did southern courts racialize intimate partner violence to control African Americans politically and socially in the 1890s and not earlier? These four introductory stories point to a complex sociolegal process.

Historians have looked at the development of the law and intimate partner violence through the lens of family and shown the family to have gradually lost its status as a private entity. As the public has felt the drive to perfect humankind, it has also become invested in fixing relationships within the family, particularly parent to child and husband to wife. Elizabeth Pleck in *Domestic Tyranny* and Linda Gordon in *Heroes of Their Own Lives* both focus on understanding shifts in family relations and their implications for public policy on family violence. Spousal abuse is the focus of only a chapter or two of those works, and their sources rely more heavily on Societies for the Prevention of Cruelty to Children and civil court cases rather than on criminal court cases. The family approach to intimate partner violence in the late 1800s has definite merits, because indeed family dynamics changed during that period.[5] But what about viewing intimate partner violence—a gender-based problem—through the lens of gender? How did the construction and reconstruction of gender expectations influence the shifting legal views of intimate partner violence? Depending on social attitudes, the courts provided or denied women legal assistance.

Like other criminal cases in the first half of the 1800s, the New Orleans case *State v. Molloy* ended up protecting the male privilege of chastisement and denied Elizabeth Molloy the right to be free from violence. The separate spheres ideology that dominated in the antebellum period created a zone of privacy for the family, and judges emphatically defended a man's prerogative to control his family apart from the prying eyes of the state. In a landmark 1836 case, the Louisiana Supreme Court ruled that domestic quarrels were not the domain of the courts. After all, the opinion stated, "[h]usbands are men, not angels."[6] Women could only seek legal assistance against their abusive husbands if the abuse was extremely violent, if the attacks were unprovoked, and if the beatings were habitual. The definitions of "extreme" and "habitual," of course, rested on the court's interpretation, and courts typically issued decisions that reinforced male privilege.[7] Legal and social attitudes toward intimate partner violence either dissuaded women from pressing charges or simply encouraged abused women to accept their situations. For both reasons, women sought legal help infrequently.

By the antebellum period, however, the temperance movement had reached most of the country, including New Orleans. Temperance advocates' attention to intimate partner violence generated a response. Some court cases mentioned "wife beating" and featured men who had become publicly intoxicated and disturbed the peace while abusing their spouses. Generally, though, the abuse had to be extreme, it had to involve alcohol, and it had to be a public act with a witness in order to attract the attention of the courts. Only when these conditions were met did some of these men face criminal prosecution. The cases did not mark a radical shift in gender relations by any means. Women's voices in the cases remained muted, and they were not allowed to testify about the abuse. More often than not, patrolmen or adult sons pressed charges when the violence spilled out into public view. The state remained largely uninvolved. Only two states nationwide went so far as to pass legislation criminalizing wife beating in the 1850s, namely the southern states of Georgia and Tennessee. Louisiana courts—and most other courts—tended to discourage charges of assault and battery against a husband because judges feared the impact on gender roles. If a wife could issue a complaint against her husband, then she challenged his authority. Charging a man for hitting his wife undermined the status of men, and courts recognized the possible risks associated with a such a transformation.

After the Civil War, the country developed a concern for intimate partner violence that arose from a complicated view of changing gender expectations.[8] While the postbellum period attempted to resurrect antebellum notions of white womanhood and confine women to the domestic sphere, changes resulting from the Civil War made a return to previous gender expectations of the nineteenth century impossible, at least in the short term.[9] Many southern women, for instance, witnessed firsthand the pitfalls of being a "lady." Men could not always protect women, as evidenced on the home front during the war, which necessitated the development of self-reliance. This reality made resurrecting antebellum white womanhood problematic. In assault and battery cases involving intimate partner violence, the new sensibilities increasingly led women to demand legal redress and validation of the right to be free from violence. In New Orleans, the rhetoric of civilized men versus savages also entered into the public discourse.[10] Men who beat their wives were labeled "brutes," "inhuman fiends," and "unmanly" by the press, the courts, and neighbors.[11] In a marked difference from the antebellum period, New Orleans courts in the postbellum period permitted the wife's testimony—without witnesses—and prosecuted cases, even if the abuse took place within the home. By the 1870s, gender expectations shifted from ignoring the problem of intimate partner violence to criminalizing it. Both black and white manhood required relinquishing the privilege of chastisement, and womanhood included the right to be free from violence.

In the fluid period of the 1870s and 1880s, the new attack on intimate partner violence extended legal and social protections to black as well as white women. Newspapers throughout the period condemned wife beating among all couples and described battered African American women similarly to white women who were abused with the words "pitiful" and "fearful."[12] This portrayal of black women as women in need of legal protection was limited to incidents of intimate partner violence, but the application of personhood in these cases suggests the country's attempt (as contradictory as it may have been) to define masculinity, femininity, and restraint.[13]

By the 1870s, courts similar to the New Orleans Criminal District Court in the *Johnson* case above regularly prosecuted men with assault and battery for abusing their wives. They also allowed the testimony of wives as evidence against a husband and recognized the consequences of mental as well as physical abuse.[14] In a precedent-setting case involving an African American couple, *Fulgham v. the State of Alabama*, the chief justice "charged that the proposition that a husband could moderately chastise his wife was a relic of barbarism."[15] Other southern courts quickly followed *Fulgham* by abolishing legal protection of the antebellum male privilege of chastisement (see table A.1 in the appendix).[16] Wife beating was no longer compatible with American conceptions of civilization, masculinity, or femininity, and courts nationwide started punishing abusive husbands under the misdemeanor of assault and battery.[17] This was a marked change from the antebellum period in which family violence was viewed more as a private matter and a man's "right" to chastise his wife went largely unchecked.

Admittedly, intimate partner violence, then as now, often went unprosecuted. While I argue that social and legal reform empowered women in New Orleans to demand freedom from violence, I also strive to convey the complexity of intimate partner violence during the postbellum period. Sometimes women dropped charges or refused to testify when the state sought to press charges against their husbands. A few cases, for various reasons, had the words "nolle prosequi" written on their covers, denoting that the accused would not be prosecuted further.[18] Despite the dropped cases, husbands could face legal and social consequences for spousal abuse, and the growing number of cases successfully prosecuting male abusers from the antebellum period to the postbellum period demonstrates this. Perhaps more importantly, extralegal violence by the community showed that society did not wholeheartedly condone this gendered violence.

By the 1890s, reform designed to help victims of intimate partner violence lost ground largely because race dominated social concerns in the South. Without northern oversight or concern among white southerners about race relations, southern states devised loopholes to impose segregation, disenfranchise black men, and deny African Americans civil rights. This shift in relations had implications for intimate partner violence, as shown in the contrast between the *Reynolds* and *Green* cases described above. From New Orleans, Louisiana, to Charlotte, North Carolina, politicians and broader society viewed wife beating as a problem peculiar to the black community, and intimate partner violence became racialized. Newspapers would describe an African American man who abused his wife as a "bad nigger" or "a blood thirsty negro."[19] Successful prosecutions were made more often against black men than white men during this period, and punishing intimate partner violence became a method of white elite control over African Americans.[20]

Given the major shifts in legal responses to intimate partner violence, the interplay between the complex social and legal attitudes begs further analysis. This book examines the changing public policies concerning intimate partner violence in heterosexual relationships through the lens of shifting gender roles in New Orleans from 1840 to 1900. In those sixty years, the concept of masculinity and femininity changed, fueling social and legal responses to abuse. The subjective and unequal distribution of power between the sexes, the social construction of race, the cultural influence of society on the legal system, and location drove responses to intimate partner violence.

Gender

Gender—and its constant definition and redefinition—is at the center of this study. Gender is a social and ideological process that has changed over time, and to understand gender expectations, the social values and customs of the period under consideration must be scrutinized.[21] Definitions of masculinity and femininity are not constants but rather shift according to time, location, socioeconomic status, religious faith, race, and ethnicity. Distinct from biological sex, men are not automatically masculine any more than women are predestined to be feminine. Masculinity and femininity are behavioral performances influenced by expectations in society, since, as feminist author Judith Butler states, there is no "right" gender.[22]

The expectations for socially accepted gendered behaviors manifest themselves in intimate relationships, discussions, courtrooms, and families, just to name a few venues, and those in power seek to maintain these expectations. The war's shattering of the South's slave society altered the power structures briefly, and this fluidity in gender expectations led to women demanding the right to be free from violence. Women of the nineteenth century were perceived to fall short of the ideals of womanhood if they were physically violent, but in intimate partner violence cases, women frequently utilized physical force, unabashedly admitting as much to the judge while still expecting the courts to fulfill their right to be free from violence. Historian Victoria E. Bynum notes: "Nor should viewing women as active agents of their own lives suggest that they were to blame for their own oppression."[23] Orleans Parish courts, particularly after the Civil War, seemed to uphold such a view, refraining from labeling women "mutually violent," deviants, or aggressors in physical assaults, further testifying to the fluidity of gender during the 1870s and 1880s. The dynamics of power and the voices of disempowered groups are central to history in general and intimate partner violence in particular.[24] The connections between gender, power, and battering are not inevitable, but the links are clearly present from 1840 to 1900. More importantly, they are crucial to past understandings of responses to and reform of intimate partner violence.

Gender expectations and power dynamics in any sort of relationship—whether a marriage, engagement, courtship, or cohabitation—matter. Since this book does not exclusively focus on marriage or incorporate familial relations outside of intimate partners, the phrases "family violence" and "domestic violence" are not the most appropriate terms for describing the scope of this book. These phrases are commonly used as umbrella terms to incorporate incest, molestation, patricide, matricide, femicide, infanticide, child abuse, child cruelty, child neglect, and intimate partner violence. Essentially, the phrase "family violence" is not specific enough because this again includes relationships outside of intimate partners. Moreover, family violence avoids placing blame. In a family-centered approach to identifying and correcting intimate partner violence, the violence precipitating the need for treatment is not given a high priority because courts and social workers often seek to maintain the marriage; instead, these professionals search for other difficulties within the couple's relationship. Taking a family-focused method, then, affirms the importance of power dynamics and spreads the blame to the victim as well as the batterer. Even the term "spousal abuse" and the contemporary "wife beating" are too limited for the purposes of this book, since the violence examined does not exist solely within the confines of legal marriage. "Wife beating" or "spousal abuse," like "family violence" and "domestic violence," are not inclusive enough and are infrequently used here.[25]

Although in recent decades women have empowered victims of intimate partner violence by using the term "survivor," "victim" is better suited for this project. Not all the women discussed in this work ultimately survived, and those who used the court systems and Progressive Era organizations for help called themselves victims. This is not to diminish the strength of anyone who has lived through intimate partner violence, nor is this to paint women as weak. Rather, the term "victim" serves to designate, as most courts define, the individual harmed as a result of violence against their person.

Race

Race forms another key element in the sociolegal response to intimate partner violence. From 1840 to 1900, social understandings of race, like gender, underwent significant change. As Evelyn Brooks Higginbotham writes, "race must be seen as a social construction predicated upon the recognition of difference and signifying simultaneous distinguishing and positioning of groups vis-à-vis one another."[26] The destruction of slavery necessitated redefining blackness in the South both socially and legally.

In New Orleans, race involved a more complex social understanding. During the antebellum period, *gens de couleur libres* (free people of color) traced their roots to Europe and Latin America and had a lighter skin color than most enslaved African Americans. They utilized this whiter skin tone and different heritage to maneuver in society and gain a level of respectability. Free people of color could and did acquire some respectability, but the Civil War altered the dynamics. While race consciousness already existed on some

spectrum in New Orleans before the war, the new status of four million freedmen and freedwomen led to changes for all men and women of color in the
postbellum period.

Until the 1890s, a period of fluidity existed in social conceptions of race
and power, as C. Vann Woodward, Grace Elizabeth Hale, and others have
observed, and this led to different social and legal responses to shifting ideas
of black manhood and black womanhood.[27] One way to identify views of race
lies in census records. Censuses for most of the nineteenth century used two
major categories for African Americans: black and mulatto.[28] The 1880s, however, saw remarkable changes, requiring further differentiation. As indicated
by this census, people delineated a spectrum of blackness, and certain rights
depended on the lightness of one's skin color. Mixed-race individuals were
tangible examples of race being fluid rather than polarized. Those who had
held freedom before the war sought to maintain some distance from those
formerly enslaved in an attempt to hold onto their prior status, but generally,
the city of New Orleans and the broader South faced obligations under the
new Fourteenth Amendment to recognize the citizenship, including the associated rights and privileges, of all people of color. With the newly acquired
rights of citizenship, formerly enslaved black women demanded legal redress
in cases of intimate partner violence, and courts acquiesced.

Social conceptions of race in the 1890s, however, again shifted, leading
to different views of black manhood, black womanhood, and responses to
intimate partner violence. All African Americans, including those formerly
identified as free people of color in New Orleans, found their status in the
city declining. Louisiana passed laws to differentiate black and white without
particular attention to degree of blackness. In 1890, for example, the Louisiana Railway Accommodations Act mandated "separate accommodations
for white and colored" customers.[29] No "in between" category or spectrum
of color existed, as the state forged ahead in its attempt to segregate the
races. Those who refused to obey the new laws faced a misdemeanor criminal charge and twenty-five-dollar fine (or twenty days in jail). In 1896, the
Supreme Court in *Plessy v. Ferguson* not only upheld segregation but, in doing
so, classified people who were only one-eighth black and formerly considered "octoroon" as "colored." The perceived need to polarize white and black
emerged in the 1890s in the wake of social and labor unrest, and segregation
issues dominated the decade. By defining all African Americans as "black,"
lawmakers made them the opposite of white, which facilitated racial control.
This revised classification tended to reinforce white conceptions of black men
as barbaric and violent, and prosecuting intimate partner violence among
black couples served to disempower African American men. The subjectivity

and the definition and redefinition of race, then, serve as a critical component in understanding the legal responses to intimate partner violence.

Court Cases as Culture

Legal intervention at first may seem a top-down method of control, but such a perspective overlooks critical social factors, particularly the changes in gender expectations.[30] In his book *Local Knowledge*, Clifford Geertz writes, "ordinary people shaped legal meanings, and to view law as one of the great cultural formations of human life."[31] And it is. Understanding the shifting social conceptions of gender and rights for men and women matters because it crafts definitions of legal personhood, duties, and individual rights. Without such beliefs, the law would remain static and divorced from the goals of its citizens. Many historians analyze the influence of culture on law in local courts, and that is the approach taken in this book.[32]

The majority of the women's testimony used in this book attests to a distinct transformation in people's attitudes after the Civil War. The courts did not create the shift in treatment of intimate partner violence but rather enforced a new social norm by reactively punishing abusive partners. Politicians did not, in most states, pass laws criminalizing intimate partner violence. Rather, judges began reinterpreting assault and battery statutes on the books and started finding abusive husbands guilty of assault and battery when they beat their female partners. The fact that the change took place in case law subtly, informally, and unevenly throughout the country indicates that judges responded to shifts in social expectations. Courts used their position to teach men the new restriction on male power. Case law, not legislation revising criminal statues, served as legal precedent, and the redefinition of gender expectations drove case law to repudiate the antiquated male privilege of physical "correction" in the 1870s and 1880s.

In case law history on abuse, people and the courts interpreted and reinterpreted old assault and battery criminal statutes but not in a neat, linear progression toward solving the problem of intimate partner violence. No clear evolution existed because the male privilege of chastisement was socially constructed, which allowed for periodic shifts in the courts' stance on privacy, abuse, and a woman's right to be free from violence. Instead, a cyclical pattern of reform emerged during the nineteenth century when solutions to the problem gained ground but then waned. Gender and society's definition of manhood and womanhood ultimately determined responses to intimate partner violence. Essentially, society drove reform as well as the decline of reform. The Civil War created a fluid moment for gender and race, and in that moment, the partial personhood of women and their right to be free from violence were recognized. The solidification of gender through race in the 1890s, however, meant the loss of legal rights for women and African American men. Reform to combat intimate partner violence was perverted as a means of racial control, and in white homes, the courts again recognized the veil of privacy, resurrecting the legally protected male privilege of chastisement. Rather than advancing in small steps toward eradicating the problem of intimate partner violence, reform for women's right to be free from violence had rolled back, like a wave, by the turn of the twentieth century.

Location

Location also matters. More than an abstract argument for regional distinctiveness, location is critical to the social and legal responses to intimate partner violence in the nineteenth century. This work seeks to inject postbellum New Orleans and, to some extent, the urban South into the narrative—locales that are absent in most works on intimate partner violence. Although the North and the South followed similar trajectories in criminalizing intimate partner violence in the 1870s and 1880s, definite differences existed, particularly in the reasons for the decline of intimate partner violence reform.

A few scholars, such as Laura Edwards, Reva Siegel, Jerome Nadelhaft, and Robin Sager, have examined select southern court cases, but most published their findings as chapters in anthologies or journal articles. Edwards's many works address intimate partner violence but only in the context of the legal system in the Carolinas. Her chapter in Michael Bellesiles's edited volume *Lethal Imagination*, moreover, argues that criminalizing spousal abuse in the postbellum South was a form of racial control, which it undoubtedly became by the 1890s, but she bases her assessment of southern courts' treatment of intimate partner violence in the early postbellum period on the 1867 US Supreme Court ruling in the *Rhodes* case alone rather than on a closer examination of multiple lower court records in the 1870s and 1880s.[33] Siegel, a legal scholar, published "'The Rule of Love': Wife Beating as Prerogative and Privacy" in the *Yale Law Journal*. Her article looks at intimate partner violence in the 1800s but focuses on the issue of privacy in cases from the US Supreme Court and some state supreme courts without much attention to regional differences. Nadelhaft, another legal scholar, published an article, "'The Public Gaze and the Prying Eye': The South and the Privacy Doctrine in Nineteenth-Century Wife Abuse Cases," in the *Cardozo Journal of Law and Gender*, again focusing on a few high-level cases in North Carolina and the role of privacy.[34] The only major regional studies that have been published are *What Trouble I Have Seen* by David Peterson del Mar and *Marital Cruelty in Antebellum America* by Robin C. Sager.[35] Del Mar, however, focuses only on the West. Sager, on the other hand, concentrates her analysis on divorce cases in Wisconsin, Texas, and Virginia between 1840 and 1860. While Sager explores southern intimate partner violence in more depth than prior works, *Marital Cruelty*, by the nature of its focus—legal marriage in the antebellum era—does not include the postbellum period, changes in the criminal courts, intimate partner violence among interracial couples or people of color, or intimate partner violence in relationships other than legal marriage. As such, the field still has a definite need for a monograph with a close historical analysis of gender and intimate partner violence in lower criminal courts, particularly in a southern state during the postbellum period.

The South, then, needs to be examined, but far from homogeneous, the diverse South needs to be understood in all its complexity with closer analyses that take into account the region's variations. This study of New Orleans and to an extent Louisiana is a beginning step toward filling that gap. New Orleans—the most densely populated settlement in Louisiana—lends itself to a rich and manageable analysis of the shift in social awareness and public policy. Much of Louisiana's population was clustered in the port city of New Orleans and its vicinity. In 1870, Orleans Parish was home to 27 percent of Louisiana's population. Even by 1900, 21 percent of the state's population resided within Orleans Parish, making it more than five times the size of the next largest parish, St. Landry.[36] Examining Orleans Parish consequently provides a good portion of the court cases tried in Louisiana. Also of important note, Orleans Parish and the City of New Orleans have maintained the best archives in Louisiana for court cases during the period.

New Orleans has sometimes been said to be *in* but *not of* the South (a perspective encouraged by those seeking to recover economically from the war and boost tourism in New Orleans during the second half of the nineteenth century).[37] The city and some of its distinctiveness is owed to its French and Spanish origins and to its diverse population as a port city. The division of civil and criminal law also earmarks Louisiana as a southern state in need of additional attention when analyzing the legal response to intimate partner violence. The state's Civil Code is particularly important for Louisiana civil cases addressing intimate partner violence. Since this is a case study of New Orleans, the city's vibrant culture, racial background, and social system consequently provide the context for a close examination of the issue.

In spite of differences, however, an analysis of New Orleans cases still offers some insight into other southern social and legal trends in intimate partner violence. The city's distinctive racial dynamic with its *gens de colour libres*, although not completely differentiated along socioeconomic class lines, can be a window into issues involving class and race in other major southern cities such as Charleston, South Carolina. The *gens de colour libres* tended to hold skilled jobs, property, and position in New Orleans and became, after the war, a readymade wealthy class among people of color—a class-based issue that black communities in larger southern cities encountered.[38] In terms of gender, southern cities faced the impact of war and occupation. Despite the particularly repressive tactics used in New Orleans by General Benjamin Butler, Richmond and Mobile, for instance, also faced shifting perceptions related to gender because of the war and occupation. Moreover, Louisiana's legal system—long argued as an incompatible anomaly in the South because of its Civil Code—holds more in common with other states than often recognized especially in the postbellum period, as Mark Fernandez argues in *From Chaos to Continuity: The Evolution of Louisiana's Judicial System, 1712–1862*. Most importantly, in the late nineteenth century, Louisiana was neither as aggressive in punishing wife beating as Georgia or West Virginia, nor as lax in its policies as states such as Arkansas or Florida.[39] Louisiana then represents more of the legal median of the southern states, and New Orleans, as the largest city in the state, presents the densest population study. This work is necessarily an in-depth analysis of the Crescent City, but for the reasons mentioned above, it still offers some limited insight into other southern cities in the postbellum era.

Sources

Understanding nineteenth-century masculinity, femininity, race, and case law is integral to interpreting intimate partner violence and female agency in the United States. Newspapers, manuscript collections, and court cases form the backbone of the research. Newspapers give important insight to social attitudes. I used no fewer than 440 southern newspaper articles, primarily from the New Orleans *Daily Picayune*. Manuscript collections, such as the Micajah Wilkinson Papers and James Knapp Papers, contain journals and private correspondence that support statements made in the newspapers, further enabling the reconstruction of the public's attitude on intimate partner violence.

Court cases—mainly criminal, although some divorce cases are integrated—provide another look at the social but also the legal response during the period. US Supreme Court and southern state-level supreme court cases provide important references and trends, but my focus centers on Orleans Parish court cases. (A brief list of landmark cases is included in the appendix.) As no index exists for the First Judicial District Court of Orleans Parish (as well as Jefferson, Plaquemines, St. Bernard, St. Charles, and St. John the Baptist Parishes), I examined 15,950 various types of cases from the 1840–1865 period and found 28 that dealt specifically with some form of intimate partner violence. From the 1880–1900 period, I sifted through 10,081 assault and battery cases from the Criminal District Court of Orleans Parish and found 393 cases that involved intimate partner violence. While intimate partner violence is addressed during the Reconstruction period these cases are not used in the statistical analysis because the South was under Union occupation and thus the judges, the organization of the courts, and the rulings are less reflective of the local population's views on gender and intimate partner violence. Only with the 1879 Constitution (effective in 1880) did the state of Louisiana reorganize the court system and the appointment of judges under "local self rule."[40] This judicial system remained intact for the rest of the nineteenth and early twentieth centuries.

Local courts, such as the Orleans Parish First Judicial District Court and Criminal District Court, provide important insight. They offer a glimpse into the day-to-day responses and typical rulings in intimate partner violence compared to federal Supreme Court cases or even state supreme court cases. Moreover, the local cases preserved the testimony of women who went before their magistrates in recorder courts. These recorder courts were often the first place where a justice of the peace or government official heard the complaints and decided which cases should go on to trial in the First Judicial District Court (during the antebellum era) or the Criminal District Court (after military occupation ended). Recorders often held relatively informal proceedings that generated blunt discussions of the incident in question. Women's testimony and that of the plaintiffs and witnesses provide critical insight into gender expectations and the right to be free from violence—different from the coaxed performance often enacted at the level of state supreme courts. Aside from those cases sent on for trial in the First Judicial District Court or Criminal District Court, all other records from Orleans Parish recorder courts have been lost, which makes the First Judicial District Court and Criminal District Court cases even more valuable. These local cases, a few landmark federal court cases, and some heavily cited southern state supreme court cases are a substantial component of this book and work collectively to demonstrate legal and social understandings in New Orleans and Louisiana as well as—to some degree—in the South.

As with any sources and data sets, however, limitations exist. Race for all of the court cases proved difficult to ascertain, namely after the Civil War, as court records stopped labeling the race of the plaintiffs and defendants. City directories, neighborhood maps, census records, and marriage licenses were all consulted, but again, the court cases gave few identifiers—only the names and addresses, not even birth dates. Many people moved around, and census takers often made mistakes. As a result, unfortunately not all those involved in the cases could be traced. Race could only be reasonably determined in 47 percent of 1880s cases and 31 percent of 1890s cases, compared to 100 percent of the antebellum cases. These numbers, however, are substantial enough to be useful, and, despite the limitations of the data set, they demonstrate the arguments made, particularly when compared to the percentages of people of color living in Orleans Parish.

To examine the dynamics of gender and reform, this work focuses on violence against women. The choice is deliberate but not meant to be dismissive of male victims or to privilege heterosexual relationships. Because intimate partner violence was largely defined as "wife beating" at the turn of the twentieth century and male abusers made up the overwhelming majority of assailants in intimate partner violence cases, female victims will be the focus of this book. While some historians have uncovered cases of cruelty involving the wife as the abuser, I only found two Orleans Parish criminal court cases from 1840 to 1900 that mentioned "husband beating," in which the husband was the victim. Contemporary gender expectations, including the idea that "real" men cannot be beaten by women, guided understandings and prosecutions of abuse. Men can be and are victims of intimate partner violence, but given the lack of New Orleans cases during the period that identify women as primary aggressors, the subject is beyond the scope of this work.

Likewise, same-sex intimate partner violence has drawn more attention in recent years and does warrant attention, but again, while power and control are crucial, the dynamics vary somewhat from heterosexual intimate partner violence during the period. Moreover, finding information on same-sex intimate partner violence in the nineteenth century is challenging given that homosexuality had become increasingly stigmatized by that time.[41] None of the court cases I examined addressed assault and battery between two men or two women living together openly or discreetly in a same-sex relationship. Turn-of-the-twentieth-century studies on gay and lesbian relationships have been explored in notable works such as Lisa Duggan's *Sapphic Slashers: Sex, Violence, and American Modernity* and George Chauncey's *Gay New York: Gender, Urban Culture, and the Making of the Gay Male World, 1890–1940.* Such issues are important, but this book focuses on violence against women, making the dynamic of same-sex intimate partner violence beyond the scope of this project.

Organization of the Book

Organized both chronologically and topically, this book is structured to examine each level of intervention and demonstrate changes over time. Chapter 1 focuses on the antebellum period. Manhood during the first half of the nineteenth century required the submission of dependents, and womanhood required obedience. Attacks on the brutality of slave society by northerners pointed to the prevalence of wife beating in the South as proof of slavery's destructive influence upon the most basic unit of society—the intimate relationship. Louisiana (as well as other southern states) started to address flagrant abuse that bled into the public realm, but overall, any social or legal challenge to the male privilege of chastisement was stalled.[42]

Chapter 2 examines the shifting gender expectations and the impact they had on intimate relationships in New Orleans. Facing occupation by Union soldiers, many women lived a reality that required action in the public realm. Men could not always be at their side or protect them from the impact of war. Essentially, the Civil War upended the "separate spheres" ideal, and even after 1865 resurrecting antebellum gender expectations appeared impractical at best. Demanding more reciprocity, women expected the right to be free from violence and sought help from the courts to enforce this right, which they overwhelmingly did during the 1870s and 1880s.

Chapters 3, 4, and 5 then analyze intimate partner violence during the postbellum era in New Orleans through the levels of intervention from the bottom up. Chapter 3 examines women's voices with regard to intimate partner violence and demonstrates their desire to be free from violence. Chapters 4 and 5 look at similar views in the community and the legal system, respectively.

Chapter 6 looks at the 1890s and the rise of an oppressive racial order in the South. Politicians throughout the region soon used misdemeanor assault and battery charges against a spouse as a "color-blind" method to disenfranchise African American men. As society focused on the issue of race, white women and black women lost rights, too. Without much legal recourse, women could not challenge the male privilege of chastisement, and major social and legal reform for intimate partner violence ended.

Analyzing intimate partner violence enables an in-depth look at the social and legal ties in addressing abuse in the United States from 1840 to 1900.

In the wake of changing gender expectations, courts reinterpreted the law to allow for female agency as well as state and social intervention in helping abused women. New understandings of manhood and womanhood promised to protect women from uncivilized, brutish men, and women could and did seek legal redress for abuse during the late nineteenth century. This book aims to make needed connections between changing gender roles and intimate partner violence. How these connections began and ended reform has massive implications for public policy, even now. Understanding this period also helps to uncover how gender expectations and racial ideologies can facilitate and hinder responses to intimate partner violence, and these social links to public policy are crucial to devising effective solutions to the complex issue.

Chapter One

"Husbands Are Men, Not Angels"

Gender and Intimate Partner Violence in Antebellum New Orleans

We have no means of ascertaining the origin of this domestic broil.
If the presumption in favor of the weak against the strong, operates
favorably to the wife as against her husband, the account given of
the defendant, in the evidence offered by the plaintiff, balances it.
Her subsequent conduct creates some suspicion, that she provoked
the defendant to the quarrel. Husbands are men and not angels.
—**Judge Justice Martin,** *Fleytas v. Pigneguy,* 1836

For much of the South's past, courts shied away from addressing the problem of intimate partner violence. Manhood depended in part on power over others, including slaves, wives, and children. Judge Justice Martin, in the frequently cited 1836 Louisiana Supreme Court civil case *Fleytas v. Pigneguy,* gives a glimpse into the intact right of chastisement that men held over their female partners. After fourteen years of marriage, Mrs. Pigneguy sued for separation of room and board, claiming that her husband had violently mistreated her on the night of May 13, 1835, and caused her subsequent miscarriage. Court records show that she asserted her behavior to have been that of "a good and affectionate wife" and her husband to have been disposed to being "brutal, abusive, and outrageous."[1] Upholding the ideal expectations for white womanhood, she believed that she was entitled to a separation, especially since she had afterward sought to "preserve the peace" in the marriage.[2]

The lower courts agreed and granted a separation on the grounds of habitual and grotesque mistreatment, given the history of the marriage and severe suffering with the loss of a pregnancy, but Judge Martin disagreed. He reversed the decision on the basis that the abuse was but one incident

19

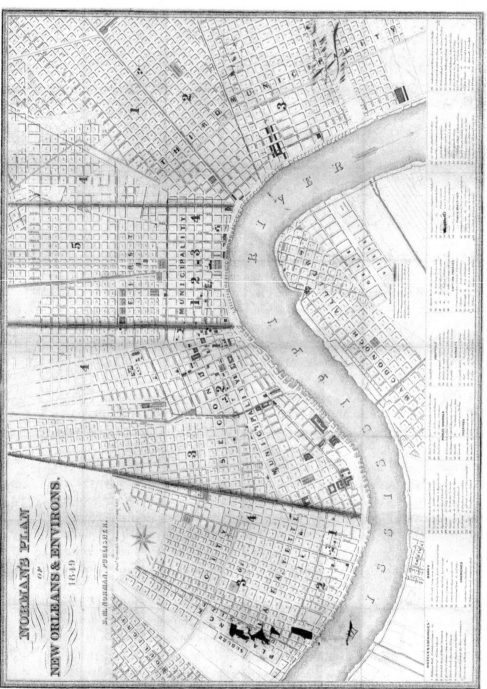

Norman's Plan of New Orleans and Environs, 1849. Louisiana Division/City Archives, New Orleans Public Library.

supposedly provoked by the wife. Mrs. Pigneguy, he claimed, was prone to "a degree of aggravation, from the circumstance of . . . being in an advanced state of pregnancy." Mr. Pigneguy's violence did not cause the fight or the miscarriage, then, but rather Mrs. Pigneguy had been the instigator. She had lost her pregnancy because of "her over-excitement" and "nervous sensibility."[3] The lesson gleaned here is that a white woman could pursue some civil action in Louisiana courts *if* she behaved in a manner upholding expectations of white womanhood, *if* the abuse was extreme, and *if* the abuse was regular. Otherwise, she had no right in the courts to demand freedom from violence. Men, on the other hand, could expect rights over their wives to include at least some physical measures taken to maintain submission. Antebellum courts clearly relied on gender expectations to decide on cases involving intimate partner violence.

Manhood in Antebellum New Orleans

White manliness in the Old South rested on a racialized patriarchy—mastery over women, children, and people of color.[4] White men found identity in upholding their responsibility to provide for their dependents while simultaneously exercising power over them, including the right of chastisement to secure sexual fidelity and submission of their wives. As Bertram Wyatt-Brown discusses, any white male could hold this "primal honor," not just white men of wealth.[5] The family, then, was central to an understanding of all white southern men's identity, but it relied on a public, performative aspect. In many ways, men sought to uphold their identity and reputation, but the public display of manliness required adherence to a preconceived set of behavioral expectations. As such, manliness in the antebellum era was strained, requiring constant, public validation.

Manhood, particularly wealthy white manhood, also emphasized family lineage, piety, hospitality, education, and sociability. Being continually contested and in tension meant, however, that these descriptors of manliness often came with qualifiers. For instance, the anti-intellectual streak in the South meant that a man had to be educated but not to the degree that it divorced him from the rest of society and hindered his interaction with others. *De Bow's Monthly Review* commented: "It is true that persons are not taught at such places [in the South] to read and write, but they are taught to think and converse . . . to perform the duties, to enjoy the pleasures of such intercourse, to please, to shine and to captivate."[6] Education meant the ability to exchange opinions with company and amuse them rather than a means of becoming part of the academic elite. This in part was due to the emphasis placed on hospitality. White manhood involved continual performance, but the expectations were far from simple.

These different views of manhood sent somewhat conflicting messages. If a man refrained from sexual indulgence, for example, he was laudably moderating his sexual appetite, but repressing desires also could supposedly lead to poor health or being labeled unmanly. If he engaged in a public extramarital or interracial relationship, he risked losing respectability, but if he acted discretely, he could indeed engage in such behavior—at least in Louisiana. Louisiana's Civil Code before the Civil War entitled a man to commit what for wives would have been considered adultery, provided it was not public and the mistress did not live in the man's home.[7] Despite the growing fear of "amalgamation of the races," Louisiana's Civil Code also permitted white men to take up with black mistresses, even providing financially for them, as long as the relationship was not flouted and men limited financial gifts to less than 10 percent of the man's moveable property. The state essentially protected, to a degree, sexual relationships that other southern states found typically beyond the bounds of respectability. What constituted a "public display" of an extramarital or interracial affair was of course a subjective judgment, and white men needed approval from their community. A nebulous line lay between what was acceptable and what was not. Society, not the individual man, determined what constituted manhood.

In keeping with the complex understanding of manliness among wealthier white men, "restrained manhood" allowed for actions that originated from emotion rather than factual, calculated logic.[8] Men could drink, gamble, and hunt. Such actions were also permissible as manifestations of a more aggressive manhood, particularly among less-wealthy white men, but wealthier white men could also engage in them provided they did not appear to lose control or allow a situation to get out of hand. Under "restrained manhood," southern men were expected to act in a dignified manner but not completely stoically in the face of a situation that excited their passions—they could not be sentimental, but also not barbaric. The line here again required a lifetime of learning from family and the larger community.

The community required that a man guard against slights to his reputation vigilantly. Being dishonored or insulted by a detractor of equivalent standing compelled white, well-off men to demand public satisfaction through the regimented ritual of dueling. The rules of duels ostensibly checked against unrestrained passions and barbarity, which lent respectability to the act. Dueling, like much in white manhood, was a public performance in which seconds and sometimes observers watched as the two principles exchanged volleys. In New Orleans, the infamous "dueling oaks" on Bayou Road in Lower City Park served as a prime location for such affairs, and the practice became so widespread that schools for dueling were advertised in the *Daily Picayune*. Despite the potential for a fatality, not all duels ended in bloodshed. One wife reportedly dissuaded her husband, after many arguments and pleas, by saying: "Well, I suppose you will have your seconds, but remember I shall have my thirds." Her reference to gaining ownership of a portion of his property persuaded him to decline "the honor of the duel."[9] Personal interest in this case at least kept blood from being spilled. Duels could be avoided with outside intervention or an apology, but men risked losing their honor if they shunned confrontation entirely. In the end, satisfaction and the demonstration of honor as well as shooting prowess were what mattered.

Those partaking in a duel sometimes faced legal prosecution with the passage of a Louisiana law criminalizing the activity in 1818.[10] In *State v. Thourett* (1840), Thourett stood trial for the crime of murdering another man in a duel. His defense attorney cited public opinion as "always more potent than the language of statute."[11] If public opinion approved, then dueling must be acceptable. Moreover, both men had consented to the guidelines of the duel, and, the attorney argued, Thourett acted in self-defense when he shot his opponent. The lawyer must have understood social attitudes better than the judge of the case (who sought to uphold the letter of the law) because the *Daily Picayune* declared the defense's speech "a masterpiece" and "brilliant." The public approved of duels, because they provided a codified means of performance in which respectable men could reclaim and validate their honor, which explains in part the absence of any prosecution of duels in the two decades between their criminalization and *State v. Thourett*. Violent and yet supposedly refined at the same time, white men in the South strove for a manliness in which the public could determine their respectability. Family and honor through violence was integral to white manhood.[12]

Outside the bounds of wealthy white manhood, black manhood in the Old South, as Darlene Clark Hine and Earnestine Jenkins state, is best described as "resistant masculinity."[13] Slaves resisted white-imposed ideas of black manhood by creating their own culture, refusing to work, feigning illness, and sometimes physically fighting back.[14] Rather than being internalized as an established hierarchy demanding slaves' submission and obedience to white owners, religion provided slaves with hope in the afterlife. Those enslaved believed that, in the next world, people would be equals regardless of race and be able to exist without misery; this religious interpretation marked a subtle but definite form of resistance and self-identification.

Trickster tales, such as the well-known Bre'r Rabbit story, illustrated ways in which enslaved African Americans could navigate within a slave society. In the Talking Turtle story, a young slave named John comes upon a talking turtle as he walks to the bayou to fill buckets with water. Eager to please his master, he tells him what he has found, and after much insistence, the white man follows, only to see a turtle behaving as turtles do—not talking. For wasting time, the master beats John and leaves. The turtle then turns to the child and says, "Black man, didn't I tell you you talk too much?" The lesson here was to be careful and cautious around whites, choosing to tell them only what was necessary or else face continual exploitation. White people's sometimes whimsical and often brutal power encouraged black resistance through clever half-truths or omissions.[15] Whatever the method, manhood (and womanhood for that matter) of those enslaved focused on surviving and navigating slave society, finding meaning and a measure of freedom on their own rather than through imposed white racial values.

For free men of color, black manhood in some ways mimicked white manhood, but because these men still faced racial discrimination, free black men resisted by securing a family and striving for economic success, particularly in New Orleans. The *gens de colour libres* saw marriage as a status marker of black manhood, and these men largely expected to hold the position of head of family and breadwinner. In providing for his family, a free man of color sought to earn enough to enable his wife to stay in the home, fulfilling white gender expectations of respectability. A sizeable number of them were able to do so. By 1850, almost ten thousand free people of color resided in New Orleans, and they largely worked as skilled laborers and owned a decent amount of property.[16] By upholding the "separate spheres" ideal, these men held some measure of influence in New Orleans.

Even those who did not come from families of substantial wealth aspired to become property owners, because property in part defined manhood. Poor white men also desired to become landowners. Michael Kimmel argues that, along with restrained and resistant manhood, another version of manhood existed—the "self-made man."[17] This type of manhood was predicated on both economic and political freedom. The freedom of a man to create his own identity through hard work and talent appealed particularly to black men, but as complicated as manhood often is and was, even the self-made-man version had qualifications. Whiteness and manhood had long been defined by what they were not, and in the antebellum period, race served as a barrier to attaining the status of a self-made man. Free men of color often faced discrimination in certain jobs or when seeking education, which limited their access to this version of manliness. Still, by holding slaves (at least 753 free people of color in New Orleans did by 1830) or by emphasizing their lighter skin color, some free men of color did achieve identification as self-made men. Others could look to them and aspire to a level of financial stability if not relative wealth.[18] Black men in the antebellum era, then, resisted the limitations placed on them by white men in power, and this resistance had implications for womanhood.

Womanhood in Antebellum New Orleans

Sanctioned supposedly by God and nature, "true" women were not only domestic but also chaste, religious, and, most importantly, submissive.[19] This ideal created expectations for men and women, although not quite a lived reality. Considered so substantially different, the sexes needed to be confined to separate realms. The domestic "sphere" in which women lived and worked incorporated the belief that women, as "angels of the house," were more moral and nurturing than men.[20] There, they tended to household chores, took care of children, and provided a buffer against the harsh public world in which their husbands lived.[21] To have meaning and status in society meant to marry and have children—all things domestic. As one New Orleanian wrote, "an unerring sign of innate vulgarity . . . [is when] ladies take particular pains to impress us with the idea of their ignorance of domestic matters." To catch a husband, they should, the writer argued, learn to become accomplished in ways "which make a good wife."[22] If a woman could not comfort her husband, he intimated, she would live a lonely life without status or fulfillment. Ideally, women remained solely in the domestic "sphere," but in reality, the "spheres" were more fluid. As morally superior beings, women engaged in charities and joined associations to improve society, such as temperance organizations. Some women by the 1840s promoted the recognition of women's legal personhood, including property rights, but the overall antebellum women's movement remained, for the most part, more influential in the North than the South.[23]

While many similarities existed between the North and South in terms of gender expectations, slavery created an important pillar of "true" white southern womanhood.[24] Assumed to be physically weaker but morally superior to men, white women represented a benevolent force in southern society and helped to argue for the South's superiority in the wake of criticism from antislavery groups. Race also buttressed white women's position by providing power to individuals who were legally and culturally deprived of many rights. Despite living in a patriarchal society, white women could maintain a level of influence, but only if they upheld the gendered and racial status quo. Their duties included tending to the moral and physical welfare of all dependents, including slaves.

While any woman could be submissive to God and to the man in her life, women of poorer socioeconomic classes and many African American women found themselves outside the dominant view of respectable womanhood created by those in power. Any women working outside the domestic sphere posed a threat to men's self-image and their potential to make an income. Society considered such working women "unnatural."[25] Free women of color usually worked in white homes as domestic laborers, and enslaved women were economically dependent on their owner. Sometimes, however, enslaved women worked in more complex roles as mammies. A mammy functioned as an asexual surrogate mother to white children, a nurse, and a domestic worker. She epitomized the white ideal of enslaved women because her roles and submissiveness to the master kept with the maternal ideal of the time, but her position as a mammy still did not grant her the status of womanhood.[26] Her fundamental classification as a slave supposedly undermined any virtue she may have possessed. African American women were additionally excluded from respectability because of their characterization as jezebels.[27] According to European ethnocentric interpretations of African dress and sexuality, women of African descent were deemed sexual, immoral, and vulgar.[28] The imagined lustfulness of black women supposedly tempted and corrupted white men. Still, enslaved black women found meaning and value, as enslaved men did, through their families and by creating their own culture and their own views of religion.

New Orleans's complex history with race, however, added different dimensions to womanhood for African American women. Some women of color in New Orleans maintained a level of respectability despite the race-based social expectations for womanhood in the South. For most of the nineteenth century, the people of New Orleans differentiated blackness not only by enslaved or free but also by skin tone. During French and Spanish rule of Louisiana, the small number of white women led white men to turn to women of color—both those enslaved and those free—for a significant other, resulting in children who often held status and rights within the colony. Colonial slave codes, moreover, permitted slaveholders to manumit their slaves and allowed those enslaved to petition for their freedom—rights that were not completely abolished until 1856.[29] This led to a sizeable free black population. Moreover, the Haitian Revolution and the French invasion of Cuba increased the free black population in Louisiana by several thousand.[30] In total, three-fifths of the state's nearly ten thousand free people of color were women, who married and upheld common values for woman-hood with white women.[31]

Domesticity, modesty, refinement, and piety mattered to these women. Although some historians point to concubinage as an arrangement in which free black women acquired a form of economic security, other scholars disagree about the frequency of such relationships. As Emily Clark argues, "weddings . . . announced the capacity of black women and men to match the moral and social standards claimed exclusively by the whites around them," and therefore "marriage, not concubinage, was the tradition New Orleans free people of color established and perpetuated."[32] Staging formal weddings and wearing fine clothing were performances that wealthy free women of color adopted to claim status. Those free women of color whose families needed them to work outside the home typically did so as laundresses and cooks—employment almost exclusively held by black women.

Regardless of whether an African American woman worked or not, she could find status in the church. Through attendance and participation in church functions, free women of color demonstrated their commitment to piety and community. They carried this into the home and provided moral instruction. Being a devout Christian enabled a free woman of color to claim a "good" character and the status of black womanhood. While their options became increasingly limited because of their race particularly by the mid-1850s, wealthy women of color in New Orleans could and did hold a degree of respectability in the city, even if denied the complete white ideal of womanhood.

Expectations for womanhood varied somewhat based on socioeconomic class, race, and region, but the ideal of womanhood shaped women's experiences. Many upheld the status quo because they could find an honorable identity within the white, male-dominated social structure of the period. White women especially benefited from the gender expectations, but given New Orleans's fluid racial dynamics, some free women of color could obtain a measure of respectability within white society by adopting white norms. Ultimately, however, expectations of womanhood in antebellum New Orleans empowered men and left minimal recourse for victims of abuse.

The Legal System in Antebellum Louisiana

While southern states were similar in their legal treatment of men and women, Louisiana developed some variations. Borrowing laws and legal precedents from elsewhere is not unique to Louisiana, and Louisiana's legal history contains an interesting mixture of Roman, Spanish, and French influences.[33] The most distinctive difference in Louisiana's legal system compared to that of other states is the civil law system under which it operates, parts of which were adopted as early as 1804 despite initial reservations from Governor William C. C. Claiborne. By 1808, the legislature of the Territory of Orleans officially adopted the *Digest of the Civil Laws Now in Force in the Territory of Orleans* (more commonly referred to as the *Digest* of 1808).[34] Influential Spanish sources included the *Partidas*, the *Fuero Real*, and the *Leyes de Toro*, and the *Digest* of Justinian was also consulted, but the *Digest* of 1808 contained material from French works as well, notably the *Code Napoléon*.[35] Collectively, these earlier codes helped to create a civil law system in the territory.

By 1823, attempts to redraft the *Digest* of 1808 to adopt common law principles from other states and to account for Louisiana's newly acquired statehood were underway. The committee assigned to rewrite the *Digest* relied heavily on the territorial code but also continued borrowing legal precedents from other countries, including the Justinian Code and the Napoleonic Code as well as British legal treatises such as William Blackstone's *Commentaries on the Laws of England*. The final document—the 1825 Civil Code—contained hundreds of revisions and almost 1,800 new additions largely based on common law.[36] The 1825 Civil Code was still ultimately grounded in civil law but was adjusted to its surrounding legal systems by also utilizing legal precedent, which was the practice in most states. Simultaneously, other southern states adopted some elements of civil law, such as considering mental or verbal cruelty as grounds for divorce, aligning Louisiana more closely with those states. The 1825 Civil Code remained intact until revisions were again undertaken in 1870.

Most states created laws clarifying marriage ceremonies, issues with property, and rights of husbands and wives. Louisiana's 1825 Civil Code went so far as to specify the duties of spouses. According to the code, husbands and wives owed "to each other mutually, fidelity, support, and assistance."[37] The husband's duties also included an obligation "to receive" his wife and provide for her "in proportion to his means and conditions."[38] The wife's responsibilities included an obligation to live and move with the husband as he saw fit as well as the restriction that she could not testify in court or use the court system without the consent of her husband or the approval of a judge. Although Louisiana's Civil Code enabled a married woman to own property, she could not sell or mortgage whatever property she legally possessed without written authorization from her husband (barring a decree of separate room and board addressing the division of the estate). Coverture, then, remained fairly intact even in a state that recognized a woman's ability to own property separately from her spouse.

Criminal law in Louisiana developed differently from the Civil Code. Rather than being immediately codified, criminal statutes developed continually throughout the territorial and antebellum periods. An early attempt to legislate crime came with the Crimes Act of 1805, which embodied the common law of crime found in many other states.[39] Particular crimes were listed within the Crimes Act, but almost every legislative session led to amendments or additions defining and punishing violations. Often, this led to contradictions in statutes and problems with jurisdiction. The First Judicial District Court, for instance, held full jurisdiction for criminal offenses in Orleans, Jefferson, Plaquemines, St. Bernard, St. Charles, and St. John the Baptist Parishes. Plaintiffs and defendants moreover lacked the ability to appeal to a higher court under the 1812 Louisiana Constitution. The Louisiana Supreme Court could only rule on civil cases that involved $300 or more in funds or property. Any civil cases dealing with lesser sums were resolved exclusively in the lower courts without any ability to appeal. These issues were not resolved until the 1845 Constitution, which permitted the state Supreme Court to hear criminal cases involving imprisonment with hard labor or the death sentence.[40]

Aside from jurisdictional changes in the 1845 Constitution, Louisiana criminal law remained uncodified. (In fact, a modern criminal code was not adopted until 1942.[41]) Keeping track of annual changes meant closer monitoring of legislative sessions, and individual criminal statutes and their amendments were published and updated in various compilations. Consequently, the basis for early Louisiana criminal law focused on the Crimes Act of 1805 and publications on legislation recently passed, but the Crimes Act only applied to whites and free people of color. The 1806 Black Code applied to slaves accused of capital crimes and allowed for tribunals comprising a judge and a few slave owners rather than trials within the courts to decide slaves' fate.[42] Whether a defendant was white, free, or enslaved, however, criminal law in the territory and later state of Louisiana was based on English common law principles, unlike the *Digest* of 1808 or the 1825 Civil Code. Even though a civil law system, Louisiana's criminal statutes more closely resonated with those of other southern states.

Before 1840, most states relied on localized law. Individuals, including free people of color and women, could utilize the court system, but their use did not translate into recognition of rights, as an individual's access was predicated on his or her relationship within a patriarchal family and community. Under such a system, southern law created an odd dynamic or "double character" that recognized those who were enslaved as both property and persons.[43] Overwhelmingly, the legal system operated for and benefited primarily white men. Southern courts in the antebellum period recognized women as dependents and ultimately upheld white male power. The judicial system privileged male voices and refused to allow women the right to testify, especially against their husbands. Ultimately, courts vigorously asserted the rights of white men over women, slaves, and free people of color.[44]

Within such a legal system, white men could, however, face a court that ruled against them if they transgressed social expectations of manliness. Honor relied on behaving within the bounds of social expectations. Extreme violence against dependents violated those expectations and would not be tolerated if they were habitual and if neighbors took notice. Once their behavior spilled into the streets, men's reputations suffered as people gossiped about what had previously been a "family matter." Men who acted with wanton cruelty and who frequently and severely beat women such that the public learned of it could find themselves without their neighbors' respect, forfeiting their right to privacy. In both civil and criminal courts, petitions or formal charges often focused on the man's actions as being against the peace and dignity of the state. As families represented a linchpin of society, dysfunctional families whose discord affected public spaces or public discourse threatened the stability of the community and the state. For the larger good, men who violated these expectations could face consequences, but ultimately, keeping the peace and not upholding individual rights drove much of police and court intervention in intimate partner violence.[45]

The Legal System and Intimate Partner Violence

During the antebellum period, states began to question the male privilege of chastisement, as reformers criticized violence in slavery and corporal punishment in the penal system. Still, courts upheld a man's right to beat his significant other, just not when it violated expectations of manhood. Reva Siegel, in her study of rulings on intimate partner violence, points out that a few rulings in states such as Connecticut limited the right of a man to abuse his wife, but, she contends, US courts in general and mid-Atlantic and southern courts in particular reaffirmed the male right of chastisement.[46] Laura Edwards similarly argues: "The South as a whole was clear on the subordination of wives to their husbands.... [The law] also gave them [husbands] sweeping authority over every aspect of their wives' lives."[47] In Mississippi, for example, the 1824 case of *Bradley v. State* set limits to a man's ability to discipline his wife but ultimately affirmed a husband's privilege to "correct" her. The state Supreme Court expressed disgust with the practice of wife beating by prefacing the ruling with the disclaimer: "However abhorrent to the feelings of every member of the bench . . ."[48] The justices ended by advising the use only of "moderate chastisement, in cases of great emergency."[49] In 1852, the North Carolina case *State v. Hussey* similarly affirmed the male prerogative, stating:

> We know that a slap on the cheek, let it be as light as it may, indeed any touching of the person of another in a rude or angry manner—is in law an assault and battery. In the nature of things it cannot apply to persons in the marriage state, it would break down the great principle of mutual confidence and dependence; throw open the bedroom to the gaze of the public; and spread discord and misery, contention and strife, where peace and concord ought to reign. It must be remembered that rules of law are intended to act in all classes of society.[50]

Like other cases of the time, *State v. Hussey* did set limits. If the beating caused permanent injury or serious physical damage, the husband could be held legally accountable. Although Georgia and Tennessee passed legislation criminalizing intimate partner violence in the 1850s, clearly most southern states were not prepared to intervene regularly in family matters and thereby "spread discord and misery."[51]

Louisiana's civil courts permitted a full divorce (*a vincula matrimonii*) for adultery, desertion, gross ill treatment, and conviction for a serious crime, but judges infrequently granted full divorces. Slightly more easily obtained, Louisiana's Civil Code granted separation of room and board (divorce *a mensa et thoro*) in cases of public defamation, chronic drunkenness, and "cruel treatment, or outrages . . . that rendered living together insupportable" in addition to the previously listed reasons for full divorces.[52] While the grounds seem fairly extensive, separation of room and board or a full divorce for adultery could only be granted if the husband brought his mistress to live in the same home with his wife "or open and publicly in another."[53] Because the state recognized "open concubinage," adultery by the husband required more evidence than one act of extramarital sex, even if the concubine was a free woman of color.[54] Unfaithful wives on the other hand need only have been found guilty of illicit sex once, since coverture entitled a husband to ownership of his wife, including to some degree of her body. Gross ill treatment as grounds for divorce also proved less than clear. As in the case of *Fleytas v. Pigneguy* at the beginning of this chapter, evidence of physical abuse did not always appear severe enough to judges. Women seeking divorce or separation of room and board, while increasingly successful as the nineteenth century wore on, required substantial evidence pointing to extremely obvious breaches of the duties of manhood, as well as sufficient funds to hire persuasive legal advocates.

Because antebellum courts were considered a public (ergo male) domain, women who employed a lawyer could obtain a successful ruling in a civil court more often than those who did not. Subjectivity played into verdicts rendered, a fact that lawyers took into account when strategizing their cases in order to improve their chances of winning and increase their clientele. When drafting a petition for divorce, counsel used phrases such as "most violent," "maliciously," "barbarously beaten," "abused, assaulted, and beaten in a shameful manner," "willfully [and] feloniously," "bodily fear," "calling her the most opprobrious names," and so on.[55] Saying only "struck" or "attacked" simply would not do. Actions needed modifiers to emphasize the severity and unmanliness of the crime; otherwise, the public and the court might believe that the behavior was not illegal and fell within the domain of a husband's right to chastise his dependents. Lawyers then sought to prove the vicious and uncivilized nature of the attacks to illustrate these abusers as violators of the expectations of manhood and as barbaric and undeserving of the backing of the public and courts.

Lawyers, moreover, knew that while discussion of a violent beating or choking would win sympathy from a judge, evidence was critical to proving a woman's claim. They sought witnesses who would testify to the nature of the abuse and the dispositions of the husband and wife. Neighbors often provided testimony about the couple's day-to-day relationship. If either party frequently drank, swore, yelled, broke furniture, or hit the other, neighbors told the judge. Those summoned could also give credence to the plaintiff's or defendant's character.

As in *Fleytas v. Pigneguy*, witnesses could and did provide damning portrayals of the wives based on expectations of womanhood. In a similar Louisiana case involving a white couple, Jane Rowley sought a separation of room and board from her husband Charles and listed a few reasons in her petition—one of which involved "injustice and oppression . . . [and] repeated acts of cruel treatment and outrage."[56] She charged that, in seven years of marriage, she had upheld her duties as a wife but could no longer live with her husband, given his temperament. She claimed that he did not support their family, particularly her daughter from a previous marriage, and that his "unnatural conduct" caused her much grief. Charles Rowley counterclaimed the reverse to be true: that he behaved affectionately and kindly toward his wife, who was prone to "frequent paroxysms of her unforgiveable passions." He testified that she had behaved this way periodically throughout the marriage and that without cause she would fly into a rage without any sense and disabuse him. He further said that he frequently employed calming techniques, but they did not work. Witnesses supported Charles's story and painted Jane as a hysterical woman who would throw "a silver slop bowl" when enraged.[57]

The charge of cruelty meant more than whether a separation could be granted. A good portion of the maneuvering by both lawyers focused on the large amount of property involved and which party deserved what amount. Louisiana judges as well as many other southern judges recognized the need for effective management of a couple's land and protected property rights, even a woman's right to property, at least to a degree. After all, much legislation on divorce in Louisiana revolved around property. A husband could and did use, develop, and administer his wife's property, but he could not sell it without her consent. Louisiana courts, moreover, recognized a wife's ability to reclaim paraphernal property, as it was property separately owned by the wife prior to marriage and not part of the dowry. Half of the property that a husband and wife acquired together during the course of a marriage (commonly referred to as community property) could also be claimed by women in Louisiana and later in Texas.[58] Jane Rowley owned one-third of a plantation in Concordia Parish prior to her marriage valued at over $43,000, and she was therefore was a wealthy woman in her own right. She sought to gain control of her paraphernal property, half the community property acquired during the marriage, and $200 a month in alimony.[59]

The court ended up giving a mixed ruling. The judges believed the witnesses' damning portrayal of Jane and cited the *Fleytas v. Pigneguy* case, declaring that Jane deserved any ill treatment she received because she had provoked him. After all, the judges argued, "husbands are men, not angels," and they used the common law principle of legal precedent to buttress their opinion. As such, she had not proven the grounds necessary for separation of room and board. In terms of the property, however, Jane Rowley fared better. The court restored her legal right to her property owned before the marriage, including all interest owed to her from her husband mortgaging the plantation. The civil law system in Louisiana did protect property rights, even those of a married woman, somewhat protecting Jane from the whims of her husband. Still, the judges relied on witnesses rather than allowing themselves to be swayed by the descriptive phrases used by Jane Rowley's lawyers, and the witnesses failed to provide a solid case for abuse, as that depended on a wife upholding gender expectations.

Sometimes, witness testimony in favor of the wife proved insufficient, as a supposedly recalcitrant husband could thwart his wife's suit for divorce. In *Bienvenu v. Buisson*, another Louisiana case involving a white couple, Jules Buisson cursed his wife, threatened the lives of her children from a previous marriage, and admitted to being prone to anger. In Judge J. Buchanan's opinion, the young couple was "of hasty temper."[60] That Estelle Bienvenu moved out of her husband's house after the quarrels and insults, Buchanan claimed, "was natural enough in a lady of refined manners and education."[61] But, as the judge made sure to mention, she promptly forgave him when he asked for forgiveness, which negated any claim she could have made for a separation. A lady with a supposedly delicate constitution might certainly remove herself from a place where the foulest words in the French language were spoken, the judge claimed, but as the moral center of the home she was also obligated to forgive her husband when he promised to change and resume their marriage. Her duties as a woman and wife demanded it. Only by leaving and not returning under any circumstances could a wife demonstrate that the extreme violence in her household fell far beyond the range of acceptable "chastisement." The expectations and legal duties of white womanhood purposefully kept many incidents out of the courts, since a woman needed to flee her home and remain separated to prove that she had sufficient grounds for divorce.

Between 1840 and 1861, the Louisiana Supreme Court heard seven cases involving some form of domestic abuse—"cruelty" as it was then called (see table A.2 in the appendix for a list of these cases). Four of the seven (57 percent) failed to acquire even separation of room and board, but a growing concern about abuse definitely existed, to which the 43 percent success rate at the highest court in the state of Louisiana attests. Still, the courts exhibited some hesitancy to dissolve marriages. As one Louisiana justice wrote in 1857, "greater forbearance in undergoing the petty annoyances of domestic life" and "a general suppression of such scandalous scenes as it has been our painful duty to review" were needed.[62]

Moreover, separation of room and board or divorce was available typically to wealthier white women, not working women or women of color. Given the need to prove an overwhelming fear of their husbands by fleeing the home, many women could not meet the divorce requirements for a judge. Leaving their residence meant having the resources or a support network to provide shelter, food, and other necessities of living until the case could be concluded. At the very least, women needed the funds to hire competent lawyers to be their advocate in the male arena of the courtroom. Many women simply lacked such financial means. In the civil courts, then, Louisiana women seeking a divorce made multiple claims about their husband's cruelty but often included his inability to fulfill his duties, namely his mismanagement of her paraphernal property and its subsequent loss of value.[63] Judges often saw the squandering of land and fortunes by irresponsible husbands as cause enough to separate property if not grant a woman's request for a legal separation or divorce.

Despite the restrictions and obstacles to ending an abusive marriage in the antebellum period, white women could and did win some form of divorce from their violent husbands. After all, 43 percent of Louisiana Supreme Court cases did find in favor of the abused wife. Usually, however, the judgments were limited to separation of room and board without the ability to remarry. Other historians have examined divorce in the Old South and found that for those cases that judges heard, female petitioners won more often than not. Loren Schweninger's study of over four hundred families in the antebellum South found that wives won divorce suits for abuse in 78 percent of the cases, but Schweninger similarly concluded that these women typically ended up being wives to slave owners.[64] The issue of finances and property, both moveable and immoveable, factored into the decision, making divorce or legal separation for abuse overwhelmingly a recourse limited to white women with means.

The criminal courts offered another avenue by which women could seek redress for intimate partner violence, but southern antebellum criminal courts in general and antebellum New Orleans criminal courts in particular provided even more limited assistance to the problem of intimate partner violence than civil courts. Part of the issue lay in the fact that prosecution for the crime of assault and battery would recognize additional legal rights of women outside of property and limit the right of chastisement of the husband. To justify the prosecution of a man for beating his wife, courts fell back on the guiding foundation of the courts and expectations of gender. Criminal prosecutors typically depicted men guilty of intimate partner violence as outside the bounds of manhood. Part of the duty of husbands, as stated in Article 121 of the Louisiana Civil Code, included providing "fidelity, support, and assistance."[65] Direct attacks on a wife's life necessitated her seeking outside assistance. If a wife had to enlist outside help to maintain the peace of her family, then a husband no longer fulfilled those duties, and consequently he was seen to neglect the expectations of manhood. These criminal charges often listed assault and battery with the intent to murder. The attempt to kill warranted obvious intervention by the state, given the severity of the charge.

Outside of attempted murder, legal intervention typically occurred in extreme situations in which violence spilled out into the streets. Police, family members, and wives could have a husband arrested for disturbing the peace. In April 1850, Mrs. Elizabeth Houston notified the New Orleans police about a ruckus on Prytania Street. She insisted that James Tenney, a white man, was drunk and causing issues for his neighbors. He had, as it turned out, been arguing with his wife on the street and started to beat her there. Charged with disturbing the peace, Tenney faced the local Recorder's Court for his crime.[66]

Of special note, it was a bystander and not the victim of abuse who sought legal help, and Tenney's violation came from disrupting public order rather than beating his wife.

This charge, however, disproportionately affected those who were not particularly wealthy and could end badly for the abused wife as well. In March 1840, the New Orleans police arrested Mr. and Mrs. Tom Kelly, an Irish couple, for disturbing the peace. Tom Kelly had been beating his wife, but because the charge was disturbing the peace and not assault and battery, both husband and wife were brought into the station.[67] Not much information is given on the exact location of the incident, but likely the abuse started in a public setting or was loud enough for neighbors to notify the local officer on watch. The husband, then, had not broken the law by beating his wife but rather for having it spill into the public sphere. His wife, moreover, faced prison time for being involved rather than being treated as a victim of abuse. In another instance, Henry Graham, a white man, faced arrest for "disturbing the peace of the neighborhood" after beating his wife. Graham attacked his wife in their New Orleans home, but the neighbors overheard and made a complaint, and the police found that the wife was deathly ill and lying in bed, a circumstance a reporter declared as "inhuman."[68] Graham's actions landed him in jail because others overheard the act, and his behavior transgressed boundaries by injuring a bedridden dependent. In these arrests, the right to privacy remained intact, since the law only intervened when the transgression affected the larger community.

People could also swear out peace warrants. Usually, this was testimony taken under oath about what had occurred. The accused was brought before the local magistrate and either bonded out or detained in jail. In New Orleans, many offenders would be placed under a peace bond as an incentive to behave and avoid creating any further public disturbance. John McCaffrey, for example, beat his wife in September 1859. When brought before the local Recorder's Court, he only had to post a $250 bond to keep the peace for six months. He did not serve jail time or face further prosecution unless he disturbed the peace before March 1860. No one was reported as having been committed to trial in the First District Court or having lost their bond for committing the same offense within the prescribed time period, however. Victoria Bynum found similar results in her examination of the Piedmont area in North Carolina in *Unruly Women*. She located thirty-nine women who swore out peace warrants against their abusive husbands in three counties from 1850 to 1860.[69] Despite dealing with abuse in some form, criminal courts initially tried to avoid addressing intimate partner violence directly or challenging the veil of privacy that protected marriages from outside or formal intervention.

Only in the decade before the Civil War did southern criminal courts start to respond to intimate partner violence, but only as part of a larger attempt to defend the South. Many southerners in the 1850s sought to justify the South's way of life, particularly slavery, in the face of mounting critiques from northern antislavery groups. The famous southern apologist and social theorist George Fitzhugh wrote on the subject, stating that "a man's wife and children are his slaves," and yet "public opinion unites with self-interest, domestic affection, and municipal law to protect the slave. The man who maltreats the weak and dependent, who abuses his authority over wife, children, or slaves, is universally detested."[70] Fitzhugh and other southerners did not place women on the same level as slaves per se but rather saw them all as subservient to the white, male head of household. The metaphor, however, illustrates the patriarchal structure and gender expectations of the South. Men expected compliance because it was (ostensibly) the law of nature and God that dictated such a hierarchy. Fitzhugh did soften this division by stating that a man owed his dependents—wife, child, or slave—a basic standard of living, as it was his duty to care for those who supposedly relied upon him for their survival.

Fitzhugh went on to make an even more direct connection between marriage and slavery in his defense of the South. He stated: "[S]lavery here . . . governs him [the enslaved] far better than free laborers at the North. . . . There, wife-murder has become a mere holiday pastime; and where so many wives are murdered, almost all must be brutally treated."[71] The South, he claimed, was better than the North *because* of slavery, and this conclusion was supposedly evident in men's treatment of their wives. He believed himself correct in this assessment, stating that wives must be treated horribly in the North, "Nay more: Men who kill their wives or treat them brutally, must be ready for all kinds of crime, and the calendar of crime at the North proves the inference to be correct."[72] Fitzhugh and many southerners believed that this paternalism extended into every aspect of their lives, and their duty to take care of dependents made southern men less violent. Northerners did not have slaves, so a comparison there could not be made. But northern men did have another type of dependent—wives. This contrast directly linked the slave society of the South to intimate partner violence. To maintain the region's superiority, men needed to soften their violent southern male image and take care of their dependents. Gross violations of the right of chastisement consequently came under new scrutiny. After all, the integrity of manhood and of the South itself now rested upon shunning intimate partner violence while simultaneously upholding a man's power over his wife and other dependents.

The temperance movement also drew attention to the problem of intimate partner violence, if indirectly. Fighting the demon whiskey (a favored drink in antebellum New Orleans), the temperance movement took on the city with zeal in the 1840s. According to a speech given by temperance advocates, New Orleans had more than 833 establishments that served liquor.[73] Alcohol abuse, they claimed, cost the city upward of $1.5 million annually, resulted in four-fifths of all deaths at the local Charity Hospital, led to the arrest of more than nine thousand people a year in the city, and created untold strife and heartache for families, notably "that lovely wife . . . [of an] intoxicated husband" who was "butchered" because "his brain phrenzied [sic] by the use of rum."[74] Violence against wives, they argued, led to the degeneration of society because, like a plague, it would spread from family to family and not stop until every person in the city suffered from the ills of drinking.

Combined, northern criticism of a violent southern culture and the temperance movement brought some attention to the issue of intimate partner violence. Courts started to take the issue of "wife beating," as the newspapers then called it, more seriously, and criminal prosecution for assault and battery occasionally landed some abusers in the New Orleans local courts. In the First District Court of New Orleans, the number of criminal cases involving intimate partner violence remained relatively small. Out of roughly fifteen thousand cases before the outbreak of the war, only twenty-five intimate partner violence cases made it to the First District Court. Intimate partner violence cases, then, only accounted for 0.16 percent of the cases decided in the First District Court from 1846 to 1860. All of these cases, however, were heard in the 1850s; not a single one occurred in the 1846–1849 period.

Table 1.1. Intimate Partner Violence Criminal Cases in the First District Court of New Orleans, 1850–1860		
Year	Number of IPV Cases	Convictions
1850	3	1
1851	0	0
1852	1	0
1853	1	0
1854	2	0
1855	4	0
1856	1	0
1857	0	0
1858	1	0
1859	6	1
1860	6	5

As shown in table 1.1, three cases of criminal assault and battery for intimate partner violence occurred in 1850, increasing to four by 1855, and then going up to six in both 1859 and 1860. New Orleans courts started prosecuting some (albeit not many) cases in the 1850s with an uptick in the second half of the decade. The fact that such cases exist at all shows some emerging concern for the social problem of intimate partner violence, but the limited numbers speak to the legal and social belief that the abuse of a wife was not a crime.

All of these antebellum criminal court cases sought to prosecute white abusers. None involved a free person of color or an enslaved man or woman. The prosecution of intimate partner violence—as infrequent as it was—focused on such abuse as a crime of white men. White men upheld southern respectability and needed to maintain their duty and to show restraint, particularly in the face of northern attacks on southern society and slavery. On October 11, 1854, the *Daily Picayune* remarked on the racial dynamic of intimate partner violence, saying: "Even the negroes in the Third District are catching the contagion of wife beating."[75] Overwhelmingly, intimate partner violence seemed to be a problem among whites, but it was seen to be emerging in the black community by the mid-1850s, at least according to the *Daily Picayune*'s reporter.

Most Orleans Parish criminal cases addressing intimate partner violence sought to show the severity of the violence, usually through the husband's use of a weapon of some sort. In fourteen of the prewar cases (56 percent), the defendant used an object to attack his wife. The weapons included knives, trowels, slingshots, shoes, hand irons, bottles, clubs, sticks, and axes. The lethal potential of a knife or ax is readily apparent, but the use of a trowel, stick, or hand iron gives insight into the incidents. In these cases, men grabbed whatever lay nearby and attacked their wives in the home. In fact, most of the incidents took place in some room of the house, usually a more intimate and less formal room such as the bedroom or kitchen; only three cases (12 percent) took place outside the couple's residence. Given the location, the weapons of choice speak to violent tempers, again displaying the lack of control and respectability of the husband. The use of a weapon gave credence to the potential for murder, which more clearly warranted outside intervention by the community and courts.

The case of Xavier Simeon is one example in which the district attorney sought to show that the transgression was beyond the bounds of chastisement because deadly force was used. On June 7, 1860, Simeon struck his wife, Mary, "without cause or provocation," threatened her life, and called her "the most opprobrious names."[76] The two had been married seven years, but frequently during the period neighbors complained of hearing violent quarrels in the couple's home. On this occasion, Xavier hit Mary with his shoe, calling her a "bitch and a whore," and accused her of adultery. When she protested, he threatened her life, and she was forced to flee with their infant to her mother's home. Several witnesses testified about the character of both the husband and the wife, and the judge ultimately decided against Xavier, fining him $20 (roughly the equivalent of over $500 in 2015 currency).[77] The guilty verdict and hefty fine spoke to the unmanly transgression Xavier Simeon had committed. Xavier had consistently beaten his wife. He threatened her life. Witnesses provided evidence against the defendant and his violation of manhood, and Mary acted within the bounds of respectability for women by remaining submissive, faithful, and nonviolent. She also showed fear for her life by leaving the marital home and not returning. If any of those factors had not been fulfilled, the prosecution would have lacked a strong case and an acquittal would have resulted.

Despite the twenty-five cases of intimate partner violence that made it to the First District Court in New Orleans and the increasing awareness of the problem, people still believed in the male right of chastisement. The failure to prosecute testifies to the belief that intimate partner violence was almost a relative nonissue in the antebellum period. Of the twenty-five antebellum cases, only seven cases (28 percent) resulted in a guilty verdict. The rest were nolle prosequi—cases dropped or withdrawn for whatever reason. The abused wives often displayed some internalization of the conservative gender expectations in the nolle prosequi cases. For example, on September 3, 1854, Josephine Mayers swore in court that her husband, John, had beaten her so badly that she feared that "unless restrained by law" he would continue to harm her, and the recorder sent the case on to be prosecuted in the First District Court. Not long after, however, Josephine submitted a note asking for the case to be dropped, as she did "not wish to appear against ... [her] husband."[78] Anything could have changed her mind, from the economic need for her husband to continue to work to the fear of what he might do if charges were not dropped, but ultimately Josephine refused to stand against her husband in the courts and indirectly upheld his legal right to "discipline" her.

Newspapers covered some similar instances of women not wishing to press charges against their husbands. On August 12, 1859, the *Daily Picayune* reported that Patrick O'Flaherty, an Irish immigrant, had been brought before the local Recorder's Court for abusing his wife, Bridget. She supposedly spoke to her husband in the courtroom and cried that she was not responsible by saying, "O, Patrick, Patrick dear! It's not my fault. I didn't do it."[79] Then, turning to the judge with her baby cradled to her chest, Bridget O'Flaherty begged for her husband's release, claiming: "He won't do it anymore, your Honor; it was an accident. . . . I can't swear against my husband."[80] On exiting the court, the *Daily Picayune*'s reporter described the wife as embarrassed and trying to make her husband feel better. The arrest gives further insight into wives who did not wish to testify. In Bridget O'Flaherty's situation at least, she had not sought prosecution; rather, a policeman had. This willingness on the part of a law officer to intervene in a marriage despite the protests of both partners could well be due to prejudice against Irish immigrants, but still, the wife herself did not think that the violence warranted legal intervention. She felt ashamed about the arrest, and in addition to claiming that the abuse had been accidental, she soothed her husband. Whatever her emotional or physical distress from the assault, his emotions ranked above her own. From the plaintiff's and judge's standpoint, intimate partner violence largely resided outside the domain of the legal system. Only in cases of extreme and habitual abuse did husbands overextend their rights as men.

◆ ◆ ◆

Overall, intimate partner violence fell outside the bounds of New Orleans's criminal courts and to a degree its civil courts before the Civil War. Gender expectations facilitated this by providing men with power over their wives and the privilege of chastisement. Women who did not act submissively could not expect assistance, and their voices remained silenced. Even with rising regional antagonisms and reform movements, social and legal views on intimate partner violence shifted only incrementally. Only if the abuse was extreme and frequent and spilled into the public gaze did a man act outside of the idealized view of manliness, warranting intervention into his family.

Hardee Map of New Orleans, 1878. The Historic New Orleans Collection, acct. no. 00.34 a, b.

Chapter Two

"We Are All Men"

Transforming Gender Expectations in New Orleans during the Civil War and Reconstruction

> This is a dreadful war, to make even the hearts of women so bitter! . . . For
> what else do I wear a pistol and carving-knife? I am afraid I will try them on
> the first one who says an insolent word to me. . . . O! if I was only a man! Then
> I could don the breeches, and slay them with a will! If some few Southern
> women were in the ranks, they could set the men an example they would not
> blush to follow. Pshaw! there are no women here! We are all men!
> —**Sarah Fowler Morgan**, *A Confederate Girl's Diary*, May 9, 1862

Sarah Fowler Morgan was born in New Orleans but, from 1850 to 1862, lived
roughly eighty miles away in Baton Rouge, until the war forced her and her
remaining family members to flee to various locations and eventually back
to occupied New Orleans.[1] War created a disruption in all that Morgan had
known. As with Morgan, war upended everyone's lives and altered gender
expectations. Many southern white women and women of color lived on the
battlefront, and they experienced the war firsthand. For instance, Lisa Tendrich Frank demonstrates in *The Civilian War* that wealthy women in Georgia and the Carolinas suffered at the hands of General William Tecumseh
Sherman's troops, even having their most private spaces—their bedrooms—
looted, their underwear ripped up to serve as handkerchiefs, and, in some
cases, their clothes forcibly removed.[2] The loss of life, displacement, and food
shortages all impinged on the private, domestic realm of women. In her diary,
twenty-year-old Sarah Morgan wrote of her reaction to the Civil War and
commented on the gendered impact of the war, finding that it forced women
into masculine roles. This shift in white and black manhood and womanhood

meant that relationships would feel the effect of the war as well, especially in regard to intimate partner violence.

The War and Southern Manhood

Antebellum views of manhood glorified men's service as soldiers. Fighting for God, country, and home, these military men fulfilled their ultimate role as protectors. Newspapers and condolence letters spoke of men who died proudly, accepting their death as vital for the cause and believing that they would be reunited in heaven with God and lost loved ones.[3] Men internalized this message, with nearly three-fourths of southern white men of fighting age serving in the war.[4] As early as 1861, however, the patriotic fervor that induced many men to enlist in the Confederate military had already started to wane, especially as reports came back about men's experiences on the battlefield. Joseph D. Hunstock of the First Louisiana Cavalry wrote home and alluded to some of the horrors by stating: "By the time we meet again, I doubt whether you would know me for my head is getting quite white from the troubles of this cruel war."[5] He then spoke of the difficulty of keeping soldiers in the ranks: "You ask if I like soldering in my home state, I do not.... [Soldiers] will not do as told to, they are too fond of returning home."[6] If fighting and dying in the war was not a "Good Death," then what was the meaning of the war? And, more importantly, how manly were these men? Competing images of manliness in the South coexisted uneasily during the antebellum period. The Civil War, however, exacerbated these tensions.

In 1864, the Union's General Sherman wrote: "War is cruelty, and you cannot refine it; and those who brought war into our country deserve all the curses and maledictions a people can pour out."[7] He described war in the starkest of terms: "War is cruelty."[8] Even before Sherman's transition to waging hard war with the destruction of civilian property and the emancipation of slaves, soldiers recognized that war indeed was hell.[9] Deaths alone could testify to such a statement, and deaths occurred in numbers that surpass American deaths in all other wars combined. Some scholars, such as J. David Hacker, estimate that the death toll actually reached as high as 851,000.[10] Regardless of the precise number, soldiers witnessed an unprecedented slaughter, and this impacted their views on manhood.

The reactions to such large numbers of casualties caused some to betray their ideals of manliness and the "Good Death." In losing close brothers, whether blood relations or brotherhoods formed through shared war experiences, men sometimes wondered about the meaning of the war, as demonstrated in the popular song "My God! What Is All This For?"[11] Some, such as Louisiana Confederate soldier John P. Nugent, wrote home about the depressing realities of war:

> [M]y shoes gave out and I had to travel about five hundred miles barefoot. My feet were so sore I could hardly walk. One of them had thirteen blisters under the bottom.... You can hardly think how the poor men looked marching twenty-five miles a day barefoot and hardly clothed enough to cover their nakedness. I am not in good health. I have had diarhea [sic] for more than two months and have it yet the very worst kind. I would very much like to come home and see you.[12]

Nugent graphically expressed just a fraction of what soldiers suffered. The low supplies, rampant disease, primitive hospitals, and incompetent surgeons all were part of the military experience.[13] Nugent could only describe the war as a kind of hell, not as a worthwhile endeavor in which he and his fellow soldiers took part.

Some could not buy into the notion of a "Good Death." To them, the establishment of the Confederate States of America was not worth the hundreds of thousands of deaths, and these men's experiences led them to question the larger issue of humanity. A number of soldiers, fueled with the desire to avenge their friends' deaths, sought to kill as many as their enemies as possible. In *This Republic of Suffering*, historian Drew Gilpin Faust argues that men in the war had begun to "delight in killing."[14] Some became "quite another being," possessed with "almost maniac wildness" as they fought and viewed the fields of dead.[15] Even when not fighting on the battlefield, soldiers acted at times without restraint. Military occupation brought out the worst in others, with reports of stealing and sexual assault reaching commanders. As men fought, raped women, stole supplies, and butchered their enemies, what had become of the humanity of the soldiers?[16] To what degree were these soldiers really men if they harmed women and "delighted in killing"?[17]

Between 1861 and 1865, service as a soldier remained a mark of manhood even as it began to be questioned, but after the war, Americans started to shun veterans who had been physically disfigured by war. Amputations were performed "around the clock" in military hospitals, and body parts piled up outside the entrances to be seen by weary soldiers and army nurses.[18] Newspapers reported on the arrivals of trains with injured soldiers, and people came "to watch the spectacle of soldiers being unloaded and carried onto stretchers."[19] Whether out of morbid curiosity or honor for those who had served in the war, people gawked and stared at the amputees. At home, these men attempted to acclimate to domestic life with their injuries. Many, however, could not make a successful transition. Those without an extensive support network found it difficult to continue as breadwinners and protectors for their families. Even if their disfigurements could be seen as physical scars of manliness and sacrifice, amputees were confronted by internal conflict, and many disabled veterans faced a postwar life that challenged their conception of manhood.

Some men came home with debilitating emotional scars despite their bodies surviving the war unscathed. The pressures of the war and threat of death left an impact with which not all men could come to terms. The fear of snipers and the loud shelling had made many men panic. One soldier wrote: "One second you are filled with anxiety; the next with fear; one second you want to, and the next second you don't."[20] Sometimes the pressure led men to act "with demoniacal fury and shouting and laughing hysterically."[21] When they returned home, the war was not always left behind. A number of men continued to struggle with the memories and anxiety. During the later part of the nineteenth century, Dr. Silas Weir Mitchell studied the phenomenon and labeled it "shell shock."[22] Mitchell wrote that "soldiers who had ridden boldly with Sheridan or fought gallantly with Grant become . . . as irritable and hysterically emotional as the veriest girl."[23] He argued to the medical community that the war had tested even the healthiest of males, and self-control or the lack of it did not explain the serious mental injury some men had sustained.

Fearful of what an epidemic of shell-shocked men could mean for the war and manhood, mental hospitals throughout the country created reports during the war arguing that "the aggregate population of citizens and soldiers has probably not furnished during the war a larger number of insane than would have occurred independently of the war."[24] Eric T. Dean Jr. has identified nearly three hundred men who suffered from mental disorders caused by their war experiences.[25] Some had to be institutionalized, such as Lieutenant Allen Wiley, who suffered from insomnia and lapses during which he relived the war by demonstrating panic, anxiety, and rage. After beating his wife several times, she filed for divorce and left him. He was finally institutionalized in Indianapolis in 1870.[26] Men were supposed to have enough self-control and strength to endure the hardships of the war, but clearly some fell short of this expectation. Were these men who suffered from the anguish of war not sufficiently masculine? Was the South's idea of manliness somehow flawed if some veterans returned unable to function in peacetime?

Black men also served in the war, making up 10 percent of the Union army and 25 percent of the Union navy, and this service heightened expectations for black manhood. Although the Fifty-Fourth Massachusetts Infantry Regiment is well known for its heraldry (in part from Edward Zwick's 1989 film

Glory), New Orleans also had active troops serving the war, including thousands of men of color. Among the first military groups to be organized were the militias, including the Plauche Guards and the First Louisiana Native Guard, a Confederate militia serving in "defence [*sic*] of their homes . . . against any enemy who may come and disturb [their] tranquility."[27] Exclusively free men of color except for a few white officers, these militiamen in the Plauche Guards and First Louisiana Native Guard often held positions of some influence in the city as well as property, including slaves.[28] Their enlistment with the Confederacy served many purposes, not the least of which was preserving and defining their status as not fully black. Historian James Hollandsworth closely examines the Louisiana Native Guard and argues that the reasons for enlistment ranged from fear to the desire to protect shops, homes, and identity.[29] Serving with white secessionists, then, appeared logical. By January 1862, however, Louisiana's legislature limited military service to white men and voided the prior legitimacy of the Louisiana Native Guard.[30] These men ceased activity until the Battle of New Orleans that April, when, briefly, the militia served before Union occupation.

General Benjamin Butler initially refused to create black Union regiments in the city, but the lack of reinforcements and continued Confederate efforts in the state forced reconsideration. Butler turned to the enslaved men who had flocked to his lines as well as free men of color in New Orleans, but the Union's First Louisiana Native Guard built upon the former Confederate militia in more than name.[31] Some from the Confederate Louisiana Native Guard joined the Union's First Louisiana Native Guard. As with the Confederate militia unit, officers in the First Native Guard were both white and black. The duties of the Native Guard, however, reflected racial stereotypes, even as perpetuated by white northerners.[32] Butler relegated black troops to menial tasks and difficult labor, as he had done previously with runaway slaves as "contrabands" of war. They dug ditches, harvested crops, and guarded important avenues of transportation.

Only under Butler's replacement, General Nathaniel P. Banks, did the Native Guard see battle—first in a small skirmish in Pascagoula, Mississippi, and then more famously in the Siege of Port Hudson, Louisiana. Their valor in holding the area before being forced to retreat made northern newspaper headlines that celebrated the troops' courage.[33] By 1863, however, the First Louisiana Native Guard was reorganized again into the Corps d'Afrique and again in 1864, becoming the Seventy-Third and Seventy-Fourth Regiments of US Colored Troops. While the men saw some activity in the Red River Campaign, most of the soldiers spent their time on garrison duty and dealt with racial inequality in both pay and treatment.[34]

Regardless, service in the military meant a great deal to African American men. The defense of one's family and military service for one's country helped to define black manhood, but even while demonstrating this most basic role of male citizenship, men in the First Louisiana Native Guard faced poor pay, lack of supplies, and resistance from white officers and civilians. When black veterans returned home, they also faced intense backlash from whites. During an 1866 attempt to gain public support for black men's right to vote, a parade—including members of the Native Guard—met with white hostility. A race riot broke out resulting in thirty-eight deaths, mostly black.[35] Many local New Orleans men of color joined the Equal Rights League to achieve legal personhood—a critical aspect of postwar freedom and manhood—but experience showed that goal to be a harder battle than the war itself.

The Civil War impacted a whole generation of men. The majority of young white men and many African American men in the South served in the war, and their struggles in the postbellum period created a crisis in manhood. Southerners wondered if aggressiveness, physicality, honor, and duty really defined the ideal man. As southerners tried to make sense of what it meant to be a man in the postwar years, they were not alone in reflecting on their identity. Women, too, threw off the rigid expectations of antebellum womanhood in large part due to their Civil War experiences.

The War and Southern Womanhood

On the home front in the war-torn areas of the South, women's experiences not only taught but also necessitated a shift in gender relations. With many men gone and serving in the war, women often had to take on what had previously been considered male duties. Women also faced hardships they alone had to address. Confronted with such situations, women quickly learned that they could not wholly confine themselves to the domestic sphere without repercussions. This awareness led to more fluid gender expectations in the postbellum period.

Women encountered severe hardship during the Civil War. Some participated directly in the war effort as soldiers or spies, such as Belle Boyd. A still larger group of women served as nurses in the military. Approximately thirteen thousand women in the Union and Confederacy worked as military nurses, while thousands more were volunteers.[36] As nurses, they witnessed some of the grotesque realities of the war. Emily Bliss Thacher Souder commented in a letter after the Battle of Gettysburg: "The amputation-table is plainly in view from our tents. I never trust myself to look toward it."[37] Female nurses witnessed the bloody scenes of field hospitals and the agony men faced. Souder commented, "dying [is] all around us and there is no time to say more than a friendly word."[38] The heavy demands after a battle stopped women from even offering solace to the dying and those who recently had undergone surgery. As Souder recognized, the war resulted in an unprecedented number of deaths, and not all women stoically endured the graphic scenes of death, disease, and misery.

Some nurses tried to comfort themselves with the idea that these men at least had died a "Good Death," quietly accepting their fate as soldiers in a righteous war, but by the end of the war, nurses often spoke differently. Confederate nurse Kate Cumming wrote in her journal: "That morning was the gloomiest I ever passed. . . . Hundreds of wounded men, dirty, bloody, weary, were all around us. And when I thought of the many more which were expected, I was filled with despair and felt like humbling myself in the dust and prayed that God would send us peace."[39] The "Good Death" had given way to fear and anxiety, even as Confederate general Robert E. Lee surrendered. What was the purpose of the war, what protection did men afford if they did not fulfill the gendered expectation of resigning them-selves to their death?

While the battlefield and camp hospitals affected some women, others keenly felt the cost of war on the home front. Women mobilized wartime patriotism through benevolent societies, fund-raising, tableaux vivants, and other displays of pride in the Confederacy. Civilians dealt with shortages in supplies and food, inflation, displacement, disease, poverty, and violence such as rape and theft in the occupied South.[40] This surely taught the lesson that men could not be relied upon to protect women all of the time. Living through such hardships, women took part in the infamous draft riots and bread riots. In doing so, they engaged in aggressive public action, voicing an opinion they could not express through the franchise.

The hardships of the war were intense. Because the South had a smaller population than the North, a higher percentage of southern men fought in the war, and consequently a greater number of southern families were affected by absent husbands, brothers, and fathers. Many southern white women, like Mary Pugh of Louisiana and Hattie Motley of Alabama, took over manage-ment of their household or plantation. These women engaged in economic practices as "deputy husbands," acting in place of their spouses. Their partak-ing in "masculine" roles extended to employing more violence when disci-plining slaves than their male counterparts did.[41] Their expected participation in the public sphere constituted a temporary but necessary wartime mea-sure, but their use of physical discipline—a male privilege—bordered on a violation of gender expectations. Engaging in what was considered a male pursuit shook views of manhood and womanhood in the South.

As Civil War experiences created a space in which gender roles were challenged, some southern women in occupied areas began to assert themselves more than previously, including women in Louisiana. Union troops captured New Orleans fairly early in the war (1862), and under Union general Benjamin "Beast" Butler, the residents of the city experienced strict marital law. This combination led to increased resentment among the residents. In defiance of Butler's order that "[a]ll devices, signs, and flags of the Confederacy shall be suppressed," women such as Sarah Morgan vowed, "I devote all my red, white, and blue silk to the manufacture of Confederate flags. As soon as one is confiscated, I make another, until my ribbon is exhausted."[42] Refusing to accede to the laws, women acted publicly to demonstrate political views. These white women faced arrest and possibly jail time or a fine, and yet they continued. Mrs. James Skellet of New Orleans, for instance, was arrested in March 1863 with her husband, an injured Confederate veteran. Both had been singing "Bonnie Blue Flag" and "insulting a policeman."[43] They were, however, discharged. On this subject, Morgan went on to say, "the man who says take it [a pin of the Confederate flag] off will have to pull it off for himself; the man who dares attempt it—well! a pistol in my pocket fills up the gap. I am capable too."[44] Sarah Morgan articulated a direct threat to Union troops and policemen, who were charged with the duty of enforcing "Picayune" Butler's orders.[45]

In February 1863, one of the most well-known incidents of women disobeying Union orders during General Nathaniel P. Banks's occupation of New Orleans was the aptly named Battle of the Handkerchiefs, an event that flouted Confederate patriotism. Confederate prisoners of war being held in New Orleans were to be transferred and exchanged for Union prisoners of war, but this meant moving them along the Mississippi River in full view of the local populace. White secessionists held revelries and dances in the days before the exchange to celebrate the freeing of Confederate troops. White women took to the banks of the Mississippi to show their patriotism. Waiving their handkerchiefs at a ship carrying Confederate prisoners of war, these ladies "were surly, and the guards at the head of the gangway heard many a caustic aside expressive of contempt for Yankees and devotion to the Confederates."[46] At one point, soldiers aimed at the crowd and ordered them to disperse, but the women only relocated. Some, however, were arrested. The *Daily Picayune* wrote that "several women" stood before Judge Peabody and were discharged "for waving handkerchiefs etc at the Confederate prisoners when they went on board the steamer *Empire Parish*."[47] Banks, like Butler before him, treated women's actions as political and held women accountable. These white women, however, kept defying Union orders, acting publicly even under marital law and the threat of legal consequences.

Women blatantly disrespected Union soldiers in occupied New Orleans. Some women verbally insulted Union soldiers, while other women dumped dirty chamber pots out the window on occupying troops passing along the street below. Butler found such incidents frequent enough to respond with his infamous Woman's Order and declared that rude females should be treated as prostitutes. Clearly, women—even women of status and wealth—did not strictly adhere to traditional ladylike behavior in the Civil War. Alecia Long, in *Occupied Women*, argues that, despite Butler's claim that Order No. 28 worked at shocking and silencing the defiant women of New Orleans, these white women continued to be brought before courts for disrespecting Union soldiers.[48] Even the threat of being jailed did not deter them. Antebellum white womanhood and its expectation of submissiveness and domesticity were no longer intact.

African American women also felt the effects the Civil War, and their ideals of black womanhood shifted. In both the North and the South, African Americans were denied full social and legal equality, but in the South, African Americans faced the most intense transition from slavery to free labor. For enslaved women, the proximity of Union troops created opportunities to claim their own freedom. Some women remained on the plantations with their children, but others seized their liberty by flocking to Union lines. Once there, however, they were often turned away in the early part of the war, or—after the Confiscation Acts—declared contraband of war. Usually, women performed odd jobs while camping with the troops. Conditions were abysmal even with the New Orleans Corps d'Afrique militia unit, and many died or contracted devastating illnesses such as fever or chronic diarrhea.[49] Others flocked to New Orleans for refuge, and by the middle of 1862 roughly ten thousand black men and women resided in New Orleans, searching for freedom and safety.[50] Their situation, however, did not mean that freedwomen resorted to any occupation. White widows complained about having to continue running their lands and homes, unable to find women of color to work for them. As Darlene Clark Hine and Kathleen Thompson argue, "black Americans had three goals—to find their family members and reestablish families; to make a living; and to live, as far as possible, lives that did not resemble slavery."[51]

Some attempted to follow northerners' advice, especially as given by the Freedman's Bureau, to adopt values of "true womanhood" that confined black women to the private, domestic sphere.[52] Still, even when black women incorporated white gender expectations into their value systems, they did not relinquish their sense of self or their goals. Many historians, such as Nancy Bercaw and Laura Edwards, have shown how black women both accepted and rejected these new white gender values to hold onto some autonomy. In a congressional inquiry about racial violence in Louisiana, Eliza Pinkston, an African American woman in New Orleans, demanded an investigation into the death of her common law husband. When asked if she was married, she replied "yes," demonstrating her view of marriage despite not having a legal marriage license. In her testimony, she described the murder and how she was also beaten in the attack. When asked if she had been hit, she confirmed it but was quick to add that it had not made her lose consciousness: "It would take a heap to knock dis here woman senseless."[53] She both demanded legal redress for the attack against her and her husband and asserted herself as a strong woman, denying racial, white gender, and marital expectations.

This sense of self carried over into work. Even when black women worked for white households, they did not lose sight of their primary aims. Many white women complained that they could not keep servants, including Anna McCall Watson, who wrote in her diary about this problem on Cross Keys Plantation in Louisiana. Along with remarks on the weather, illness, and visitors, Watson recorded each time the cook or laundry "girl" left without notice and how she had to "do the laundry again" or had "breakfast to get" by herself.[54] The high turnover rate showed that African Americans utilized their new freedom to move, locate family members, and find better employment. With the death of slavery, racial upheaval destabilized gender roles, particularly white middle-class ideals.

The war broke down rigid gender barriers. War required many women to take on "masculine" roles, placing the antebellum notion of white womanhood in serious jeopardy. Many continued to seek the ultimate goal of marriage by finding husbands among soldiers camped nearby.[55] Despite some attempts to cling to domesticity and ideal white womanhood, the fact cannot be dismissed that one effect of the Civil War was for women to act independently and not "celebrate helplessness."[56] Women emerged more aware of the drawbacks of antebellum gender expectations and sometimes more critical of the institution of marriage.

For women, the transformation in gender expectations was particularly dramatic, but men faced a shift as well and were forced to redefine manhood.[57] A white male–dominated society rested on privilege and required power over women and people of color. The Civil War disturbed all this. The emancipation of over four million slaves knocked out one pillar of southern white manhood, and the shifts in women's attitudes weakened another part of the foundation for white and black men.

Regionalism after the war exacerbated this anxiety. As historian Nina Silber discusses in *Divided Houses: Gender and the Civil War*, white southern masculinity and southern womanhood came under full attack as northerners sought to show how the southern way of life was inferior and even backward.[58] The capture of former Confederate president Jefferson Davis illustrates the intense criticism southern men faced. Davis supposedly wore female attire, including a dress and bonnet, in his attempt to avoid arrest. Northern newspapers and journals, such as *Harper's Weekly*, picked up on the story and added illustrations that mocked Davis for his cowardly behavior, but these journalists went further than just Davis. The drawing in *Harper's Weekly* included the letters "C.S." on the hatbox Davis carried, intimating that the entire former Confederate states were feminine as well.[59] Loss of the war, by itself, impugned white southern manhood. How could martial valor or southern honor exist if the Confederacy was defeated? Historian Gaines Foster states that the infamous capture of Davis in women's clothing "certainly suggested that on some level people perceived surrender as a form of emasculation."[60] The North constantly reminded the South of its loss, particularly with the start of Radical Reconstruction and the 1867 Military Reconstruction Act. Occupation humiliated many white southerners, particularly men who could not resume the political roles they had held previously. By denying many white southern men the right to vote or hold office, northerners challenged southern men's masculinity. In rebuilding itself, the South faced the need to claim respect somehow. This required, in part, redefining white southern manhood and womanhood. The redefined gender roles enabled legal reform for women, such as by criminalizing intimate partner violence.

Despite its regional distinctiveness, southern masculinity was predicated on northern respect. Reconciliation and the South's reentry into the Union required the reduction of animosity between the two parts of the nation and northern admission of the worth and honor of the South's efforts, even if it had lost its gamble to secede. Examining northern travelers in the postbellum South, Gaines Foster finds that southerners were often defensive and quick to "put the Yankee in his or her place," but "if the traveler met the southerner properly, in other words if he or she thereby acknowledged southern honor, the southerner reciprocated with a kind welcome and considerate behavior."[61] This, Foster argues, shows that indeed southerners "valued northern respect."[62] In an attempt to "prove" themselves, southerners increasingly focused on being civilized.[63]

To be civilized meant that white southern men should shrug off the label of "backward" and "brutal"—phrases that the North had used to define southern society and its reliance on slavery during the antebellum period. The

South could reestablish its honor, its pride, and consequently its masculinity by proving itself "civilized." The term became a buzzword in southern news-papers, as did its opposite—"brutal." The South contended that its superiority lay in its combination of old and new.[64] It held onto chivalry, neighborli-ness, and honor while modernizing by accepting some ideas of progress. The South's industrial advancement, for instance, helped to make the region more "civilized." Henry Grady, editor of Atlanta's *Constitution*, gave a speech in 1886 to the New England Society of New York in which he spoke of the South as embracing industrialization in farming and transportation. Grady also praised the South for holding onto some of its older regional expectations. Historian Edward Ayers describes Grady's speech as "a rationale that allowed the South to have it both ways, to be proudly southern and yet partake in the new industrial bounty."[65] The tension between the old and new remained as the South sought to prove itself. In order to obtain a civilized status, however, the South also had to condemn behaviors of southerners that did not live up to the ideal. Before the 1890s, these terms were applied to those of any race or ethnicity, since southerners could not condone uncivilized behavior. Men who abused their wives, for instance, were slurred as "brutes," "monstrous fiends," "inhumane," and "unmanly."[66]

The War's Impact on Relationships

The Civil War created what historian LeeAnn Whites aptly calls "a crisis in gender relations."[67] Following the war, women faced challenges that hindered a return to rigid gender expectations. The Civil War had taken its toll in human lives with hundreds of thousands of deaths, impacted an entire gen-eration, and resulted in many changes to gender roles.

White women after the war found a lack of available men to marry, and as a result many were potentially without the ability to uphold the white upper-class ideal of womanhood. In a letter to her grandmother in November 1878, nineteen-year-old Thelia Bush from Louisiana wrote: "[T]hat old maid you spoke of marrying was old indeed but it is some encouragement to all the rest of us girls. It will make us think there is a chance for us whether there is or not."[68] Marriage remained important since it afforded women some advan-tages. Without marriage, "[o]ld maids" were considered "abominable," and they found in their declining years that they were "desolate and alone while the married woman ... [was] moved by the love and ties of the family circle."[69] Family offered women protection against loneliness, lack of social status and respect, and economic destitution. Between unmarried young women and war widows, the rate of women without husbands increased. Rising numbers of single and widowed women further proved that women's reliance upon men was not always possible, leading to a changing status of women in the postbellum years.

For many white women, antebellum womanhood could not be resurrected intact, especially female submission. A former Catholic nun, Désirée Martin, wrote about southern women's expectations of men. She said, "Men must be helpful and attentive to women. A society where no one would exercise restraint, where there would be no respect for one another would soon provide no enjoyment, and turn men into savages."[70] In her journal, which was to become a book of advice for her nieces and nephews, Martin expressed the expected benefit of a female's subordination—chivalry and protection.[71] If men did not place women on a pedestal, Martin claimed that it would "turn men into savages."[72] Here, she tied masculinity, with its protectiveness and "restraint," to being civilized. When men did not help keep women in comfort, society suffered and men became "savage." Martin (perhaps unintentionally) demonstrated that, in her opinion, the South, with its new gender roles, remained respectable and civilized.

Martin's writings illustrate more than this, however. She spoke of respect and seemed to suggest a sense of reciprocity between men and women. Men had to respect women by showing esteem in their behavior, such as being attentive. Even while submissive, women insisted on respect. Manhood was dependent on men's attitude and behavior toward women. Lack of restraint toward women and dereliction of duty to women meant that a man had failed to live up to the new gender expectations.

These new expectations for men were evident in marriage vows. Adelbert Ames, a Radical Republican who served as governor and US senator from Mississippi from 1868 to 1874, wrote to his fiancée, Blanche Butler, in 1870 about their upcoming wedding. In it, Ames discussed whether a wife should obey her husband.

> You say you are not going to promise to "obey." Well, Love, that does not frighten me. Do you think people love, honor and obey because they promise to do so at the altar? Do all who so promise keep their word? If one did not love and honor, how could one get married?—and be honor-able? If there be "love" and "honor" what need of the "obey"—with them there would be no need of it as promised at the marriage ceremony, no "obey" at any time. When a wife ceases to find her love strong enough to be a motive power, no promise will control her to the good and happiness of her husband. Suppose you give "obey" its full force. Obedience without love, obedience to the will of any master, soon will become unbearable—and

unless a man be very little he would find such orders and such obedience the saddest moments of his life. No, Blanche, I do not ask that you promise to obey me—I only ask that you love me—love me and all that can tend to make our home happy will flow from that—honor, for we could not love unless we honored each other.[73]

Blanche Butler in a previous letter had refused to say that she would obey her husband. Her refusal was an assertion of the new womanhood emerging during the period. In response, Ames responded by linking obedience to a master-servant relationship. This is not surprising, given his political leanings as a Radical Republican. With the end of slavery, some linked other relationships to the dynamics of slavery. Given that the enslavement of African Americans had largely been accepted, particularly in the North, as an evil vanquished, similar relationships that denied a person's autonomy fell under scrutiny, such as husbands' dominance over their wives. Ames stated that obedience was replaced by love and honor, because men, he implied, should not base their marriages on expressions of power and demands for wifely obedience. Instead, mutual affection and respect served as the basis of his relationship with his soon-to-be wife. New expectations of manhood and womanhood influenced intimate relationships between men and women, challenging the power dynamics between even husbands and wives.

Advertisements illustrated this emerging new manhood. In a promise to cure colic, ads for Dr. M. A. Simmons's liver medicine depict a tired father holding a crying infant. In the background, the mother sleeps undisturbed, and a crocheted piece on the wall has the words "Home Sweet Home." Underneath, the advertisement describes its product, saying: "Many midnight hours find a multitude of tired fathers walking the floor with screaming babies who are in agony with colic. . . . It is enough to tempt the father in the household similar to the one illustrated above to turn in the Home Sweet Home inscription."[74] Printed in a memorandum book sold largely to men, the ad portrayed the father as an involved parent—even more so than some had been before the Civil War.[75] The mother, on the other hand, seemingly deserved rest and a break from the demands of raising children. While it's unlikely that all men listened to this advice, the advertisement touched on some emerging views of fatherhood during the1800s, whether such views reflected lived experience or were merely aspirational. After all, if the advertisement did not reflect society or its ideal in some manner, then the company would have been terribly ineffective in its strategy to sell its product. Since Dr. M. A. Simmons's liver medicine remained a popular tonic until at least 1901, the message must have appealed to a broad audience.[76]

Despite expectations for changes in men, not all women were believed to deserve such respect from men. Désirée Martin, traveling on a train in Ohio, described a northern woman who was, she declared, "a pseudo-sophisticated lady," "one of those Always First type ladies, who seemed to believe the ship, the train, and the world were created exclusively for their own particular convenience."[77] A self-interested woman lived against the feminine ideal of selflessness. By nurturing and helping others, a woman supposedly fulfilled her duty, and the woman Martin described defied the expected norm. As a result, she forfeited the respect of men and the status of a "true" lady. Martin further articulated this sentiment when she reminded her nieces:

> However, if gentlemen are bound to be considerate and courteous toward women, remember too, my dear nieces, this is no excuse to take advantage of that kindness and courtesy.... it is only ostentatious and temperamental women who behave on the trip as the lady about whom we just spoke.[78]

Men and women did not automatically deserve certain treatment by the very nature of their sex. Instead, women were expected to show deference to men, provided men acted respectfully toward women. A sort of reciprocity existed between the sexes that enforced adherence to gender expectations, which is important to note.

Despite the overall stress placed on female submissiveness, Désirée Martin, perhaps influenced by her experience during the war and the military occupation of Louisiana, conveyed another hint of female autonomy when she later asserted: "Respect is a barrier that protects big and small equally, and which makes it possible to look at each other face to face; and I repeat to you, the woman who respects herself always has, by an inalienable right, dignity and respect."[79] Her use of the phrase "inalienable right" resonates with the values of natural law—the concept that, as human beings, individuals are born with certain rights and not given those rights by any government—as expressed in the Declaration of Independence and the US Constitution. A woman is entitled to "dignity and respect" if she feels herself worthy, not if a man decides that she is worthy. This implies more than the Victorian adoration of the "angel in the house."[80] Women held value independent of men, which was a new component of womanhood and different from the antebellum feminine ideal. The new view might demand women to be dependent upon men, but it required more from men than previously.

Relationships also changed for black women, particularly freedwomen. Some rushed to have their marriages legally recognized after the war, and many martial contracts upheld this implementation of white gender values for black women. In Louisiana, an 1868 act combined with the 1870 Amendment to the Civil Code recognized marriages "of all persons of whatever race or color" for those who previously lived together in an unmarried state and granted legitimacy for children born from those relationships.[81] Essentially, marriages for freedmen and women could be retroactively legalized provided they immediately sought state recognition through licensure. These legal contracts gave African American women the "rights and protections" of a wife but also required submission to the husband.[82] With citizenship, black men sought to provide for their families, manage work contracts, and speak for their wives in any legal issues. No legal document that an African American woman signed without her husband's consent could be valid. Marriage, then, empowered black men to exercise control over their wives, specifically their paid and unpaid labor, and to have sexual access to their wives, but because black men lacked the power and rights of white men, it was impossible for them to establish a complete patriarchy. Black men keenly felt their inability to protect their wives from sexual assault by white men in a legal system that viewed African American women as hypersexual and incapable of being raped. Instead, legal marriage for blacks meant a male-headed household where black women exercised proportionately more influence than white women in white marriages. Other blacks refused to conform to white expectations for marriage and held onto informal living arrangements, such as sweethearting and taking up.[83] When these relationships ceased to function, the couple could "divorce" by quitting each other and moving out of a shared home. Still other women—white and black—could not afford the two-dollar charge for a marriage license and lived outside the state's recognition of marriage.[84]

Black relationships were still headed by men, but some challenged this view. In Savannah, an African American woman sent a letter to the editor stating:

> If God has designed woman as man's master, he would have taken her from his head; if as his slave, he would have taken her from his feet; but as he designed her for his companion and equal, he took her from his side. We comment the above to the dirty rascal who was beating that poor woman [his wife] on Tuesday last on Jefferson Street, and if he calls himself a man, let him reflect over it.[85]

Black women used the Bible to argue for women's rights in the late nineteenth century. Rather than being radical, these women's reinterpretation of the Bible served as an effective method for such an argument, especially since the church existed as "the most powerful institution of racial self-help in the

African American community."[86] One of the most widely used examples of women's equality was the creation story. Eve, taken from one of Adam's ribs and not his foot or head, was interpreted as his equal partner. Similar sentiments were voiced by black women of New Orleans. One black woman wrote in the *Louisianian*: "The day has past when subjection shall content the minds of women!"[87] In part because black families often relied on the woman's wage in addition to the man's, a complete patriarchy could not be achieved among most African Americans. Still, the desire for a male breadwinner and a male-headed household dominated many black relationships.

The Civil War provoked a transformation in gender relations and forced the redefinition of masculinity and femininity. In some ways, antebellum notions of gender remained intact. The country clung to past notions to create stability amid intense change, but still no one could completely resurrect the past. Too much had changed. Slavery ended, wiping out a crucial foundation of social organization in the South. The war forced women to face the drawbacks of relying completely on men. Overwhelmingly, women looked to the state to mediate the new relationship, since the war and its aftermath galvanized women, creating a heightened awareness of the inequality between the sexes. Throughout the South, many women recognized the problem of complete female dependence.

Intimate Partner Violence in New Orleans during the Civil War

The shifting gender expectations among southerners during the war started to affect the legal response to intimate partner violence. In the First District Court of Orleans Parish, only four cases from 1861 to 1865 involved intimate partner violence. Before Union occupation, recorders sent three cases on to the First District Court—*State v. Anthony Howe, State v. Sandberschwartz,* and *State v. John Mooney*. All the men charged were white. One case lacked record of the sentence, and the other two resulted in a nolle prosequi. The dropping of Howe's case occurred on April 15, 1861—just three days after the firing on Fort Sumter. In the Mooney case, Catherine pressed charges against her husband, Ernest, asking that he be dealt with according to the law, but dropped charges February 15, 1862—approximately two months before the Battle of New Orleans. Despite the handful of cases, the fact they even were recorded and charges pressed is remarkable.

During Union wartime occupation, intimate partner violence drew the attention of newspaper reporters and to a degree the courts. The *Daily Picayune* covered a story of "wife beating" involving John Silver on St. Philip Street, and commented that "domestic inflexity [*sic*]" was "becoming quite common of late."[88] Whatever the cause, the newspaper reporter claimed to have witnessed an increase in male violence against female partners and remarked on the change. Courts in occupied New Orleans continued to address intimate partner violence, but only one case came before the First District Court. This 1864 case illustrates gender shifts with intimate partner violence. Mary Miritare, a white woman, sought legal redress after her husband, James, attacked her. She refused to allow him into the home, and he pulled a gun and fired at her. Mary was wounded yet "wrestled with him to get the pistol."[89] The court found him guilty, although the sentence was not recorded in the files. The Miritare case is a departure from all the other antebellum intimate partner violence cases that had made it to the First District Court. Rather than upholding previously accepted behavior for women, Mary fought back and testified to the fact, and the case still ended in a conviction. Northern oversight in legal matters affected the courts, which partially explains the different ruling, but the case captured Mary's voice and determination to gain the right to be free from violence—through self-defense and the courts.

Black southern women seeking legal intervention during the war often turned to the Freedman's Bureau. Mary Farmer-Kaiser examines this in *Freedwomen and the Freedman's Bureau* and argues that federal intervention often came in the form of a lecture on the duties of husbands and wives.[90] The marriage of freedmen and women meant to whites in power that children produced from such unions would be legitimized and cared for and that family units would become "stable" for social order. Black women, however, viewed marriage differently and contested these goals by demanding the right to be free from violence. When the Freedman's Bureau did not intervene more directly, freedwomen would sometimes leave their husband and take up with another—a common relationship pattern outside the legal system's goal of state-sanctioned marriage. Reluctantly, the Freedman's Bureau recognized freedwomen as "worthy of equal protection under the law, bodily integrity, and voice."[91] Southern courts, then, began to recognize women's voices—both white and black—in the wake of the Civil War.

◆ ◆ ◆

Women knew that some burdens they would have to bear alone, that men could not always be relied upon for protection or even survival during the Civil War. Moreover, Union occupation led many southern women to act more publicly and with more "masculinity" than gender roles permitted in the antebellum period. The blow to southern manhood, with the loss of the war and the destruction of slavery, further upended the structure of southern society from its prewar framework. In the wake of such upheaval, southern society attempted to rebuild itself. Antebellum manhood, however, could not be wholly resurrected, in part because of shifting gender expectations.[92] This dynamic allowed for a new womanhood that provided avenues, albeit small and complicated, for the advancement of the "weaker sex," particularly on the issue of intimate partner violence.

Chapter Three

"Strike Me If You Dare"

Abused Women of New Orleans and the Right to Be Free from Violence

I asked my wife where my dinner was, and she [asked] where I had
been all day long. I said, "Give me my dinner." . . . I kicked the chair
in the street. . . . My wife said, "You shit, strike me if you dare."
—**Sylvester Conlon,** *State v. Sylvester Conlon,* 1884

In September 1884, Sarah Conlon of New Orleans demanded to know where
her husband Sylvester had been all day, and when he threatened to become
violent, she refused to back down. She challenged him, saying: "Strike me
if you dare."[1] After he struck her, a neighbor overheard Sarah promise that
"she would fix him for that," and she did.[2] Sylvester Conlon spent time in jail
and lost his family because Sarah vowed never to return to his household
with their child. The fluid gender expectations after the Civil War created an
opportunity for women to renegotiate relationships with men, as shown with
this white couple. The postbellum years prompted female agency to combat
the problem of intimate partner violence. While not all women were as bold
as Sarah Conlon, women generally saw abuse as a violation of men's duties,
and many demanded that their rights be upheld.

In contrast to claims made by some previous studies of the period, New
Orleans women in the postbellum period pushed for the right to be free from
violence. Linda Gordon, in *Heroes of Their Own Lives,* for instance, examines northern women in the same time period and argues that "many women
clients did not seem to believe they had a 'right' to freedom from violence"
even if they morally condemned abuse and fought against it.[3] In contrast,
while most New Orleans women did not verbally articulate a "right" to not
be abused, their actions insinuated such a mentality. The very act of pressing

charges suggests that they believed the abuse was wrong and that violence was an unacceptable behavioral choice. In 1881, Betty Williams stated in her testimony: "He hit me on Saturday night . . . and this is the reason I had him arrested."[4] Betty's statement seems so simple. Arguably, she wanted protection, but in going to court and pressing charges, Betty Williams asserted her belief that husbands cannot abuse their wives. She did not drop the charges, and her husband, George, stayed in jail for twenty-four hours for his attack. Although George might not have changed his ways, Betty's actions suggest a shift in social attitudes about intimate partner violence.

Power

Ultimately, intimate partner violence rested on the issues of power and dominance, which is why the renegotiation of gender roles emboldened women to attack the male privilege of chastisement. As Elizabeth Janeway perceptively states, although it is not the only method, "sex is the most intensely stressed physiological fact that has been used to distance a group from power by ranking its members low."[5] Abuse aimed at asserting or maintaining the dominance of those in power, who in the late nineteenth century were, in general, men. Since legally and socially the male sex held positions of authority in relationships with women, even men of color and poorer socioeconomic status who had relatively little power in society could exert influence in their own home.[6] Many Orleans Parish cases in the postbellum era demonstrate blatant male displays of power. In 1885, John Heir, a white male, told his wife, Elise, not to go outside, but she went to tend to her garden anyway. He responded by beating her. In her testimony, Elise stated:

> He said you go nowhere or I will kill you. . . . He come and cursed me for all
> the dirty names. . . . He held me by the throat . . . and then he slapped me in the
> face . . . [and] in the mouth with his hand, and then he pushed me down and come
> out with a stick of wood and hit me again in the side . . . and he kicked me too.[7]

She testified that he had had a hard day at work and was contentious upon his return home. John provided no reason why he did not want her to work in the garden, but when she disobeyed him, he flew into a rage and viciously beat her. Perhaps he felt that he had the right to "chastise" his wife with physical punishment, or perhaps he sought a compensatory form of power at home because of his problems at work. Regardless, John Heir's actions suggest that he sought to feel powerful by abusing his wife.

In another instance involving a white couple, Annie Hannewinckle charged Gust, her husband of twenty years, with assault and battery. The incident started over a debate about money while they were sitting on the front porch with their three children. Gust called Annie a "damn so and so," to which she responded that he should be ashamed of calling her a name and had "no reason to be growling like that."[8] Gust threatened her by yelling: "I'll show you what I am growling about," and then put his threat into action by hitting her.[9] Annie had openly questioned Gust's financial affairs as well as his language in front of their children. In doing so, she threatened his role as head of the household, his ability to provide for the family, and his decision making. Gust retaliated first by verbally insulting his wife and then by physically abusing her. The entire incident took place in the presence of the children, asserting his dominance and driving the lesson home that he was in charge.

In a similar situation, Lizzie Hill confronted her husband, Jeffery, which led to his reassertion of power through violence. Lizzie accused Jeffery of carrying on an affair with another woman, and she demanded that he end it. Jeffery defiantly told her that he would "have" the other woman and that Lizzie could do nothing to prevent it.[10] In the altercation, Jeffery demanded to know where his clothes were so he could go spend the night with his mistress. As Lizzie showed him, he hit and then choked her. Somehow during the attack, she escaped. Jeffery's adultery may have been many things, but it strongly suggests that he believed that he held power in his ability to beat and cheat on his legal wife, even if it made her miserable. He did not recognize marriage as a union intended to make both partners happy. His pleasure superseded her needs, and his dominance mattered more than her emotional and physical well-being.

Anxiety over men's loss of power over women and women's more public roles dominated the period, and some men lashed out in a desperate attempt to hold onto what had previously been a male privilege. Still, the fluidity in male and female expectations permitted some changes in the roles of men and women. Even if not witnessing a complete gender revolution, many women spoke out against their abusive partners and demanded that their families, the community, and the legal system change the existing notions of power, which now had to be renegotiated.

Table 3.1 Plaintiffs in Intimate partner violence Cases in Orleans Parish, 1880–1889		
Plaintiff	Number of IPV Cases	Percentage of IPV Cases
Abused Women	186	89%
District Attorney	13	5.7%
Community/Family Member	12	5.3%

As shown in table 3.1, the overwhelming majority (89 percent) of plaintiffs in intimate partner violence cases in the 1880s were abused women who brought their violent partners to court.[11] Abused women—not family members, the police, or other witnesses—pressed charges. This statistic supports the argument that women internalized messages from the Civil War and the need to renegotiate rights within their relationships with men. Consequently, the male right of chastisement lost favor as women asserted their right to be free from violence. From courtship to cohabitation to legal marriage, women demanded this right to be free from violence in every type of intimate relationship with men.

Courtship

As gender expectations were being redefined, courtship rituals shifted. In the antebellum period, southerners initially relied on family and community organizations, particularly churches, to help them on the path to matrimony. With a guardian's consent, men would call on intended partners, and, under the watchful eyes of a chaperone or parent, the couple would get to know each other. The man typically bestowed compliments and small gifts upon his intended until he declared his feelings. Then, the man and the woman's guardian arranged the marriage.

After the Civil War, courtship changed drastically. One of the most noticeable differences involves the role of love in romantic relationships. As historian Karen Lystra argues, intimate relationships in the postbellum era centered on the notion of love, and emotion mattered.[12] Women increasingly wanted men to prove their love, and many engineered challenges for men to solve as testament to their affection.[13] In the late 1800s, then, romantic love took precedence over other factors affecting women's reasons for marrying. Wealth, companionship, social status, and family consent still mattered to many women, but now to a lesser degree than love. Women expected reciprocity in the form of mutual affection.

The influence of new gender expectations further altered courtship rituals by permitting women to assert themselves in a variety of ways. For example, some white women in the rural South resurrected an old Irish tradition that allowed women to propose marriage in leap years, and they took advantage of it.[14] Twenty-year-old Thelia Bush from Louisiana noted in a letter, "there will be a great many more weddings before this year is out for you know this is leap year and the young ladies will have a fair chance to go to see the young men."[15] According to Bush, women not only proposed to men on leap year but also looked forward to it. Generally, brief breaks from a traditional hierarchy of gender or class act as a safety valve to release anxiety over power.[16] The leap year tradition in the postbellum South served that purpose. With masculine authority in abeyance, women could assert themselves in a controlled manner through the leap year proposals.

African American women who courted in rural areas often relied on family and the larger community. Religion was the backbone of much of the black community, and churches offered good meeting places for couples. Ruth McEnery Stuart's short story "Jessekiah Brown's Courtship," published in 1893, discussed courtship rituals among African Americans in rural Louisiana.[17] Jessekiah—also known as Ki or Brer Brown—was a forty-year-old bachelor of decent means.[18] Dressed smartly in a silk hat and with a "gorgeous walking cane," he "enjoyed the double distinction of being the fattest man and the oldest bachelor of his color on the plantation."[19] He courted women, brought them flowers, and talked to them on their front porches, but he dodged marriage for years. Older woman of the town teased Jessekiah, telling him that he would eventually settle down with "Fat Ann," a woman of similar stature, and the two were frequently thrown together at the Methodist church they attended. During the church's cakewalk one year, the congregation partnered Ki and Ann, much to Ki's chagrin. He resigned himself to marriage and asked God to bring him someone. After waiting a few months, he saw a woman along the levee and was smitten, only to discover that it was none other than Ann. He threw himself down the hill of the levee after the realization. In Ann's attempt to help, she quite literally stumbled over Ki, launching both of them into the river. They then began to talk. She commiserated with him over the loneliness of singlehood, and Ki was overwhelmed with emotion for Ann as he realized that God and the community had been right about the two of them all along. After an elaborate proposal he prepared, Ann agreed to marry him, and the community rejoiced in their relationship.[20]

Throughout the story, Jessekiah Brown depicts the central role the church played in courtship among African Americans. Jessekiah's clothes or financial status did not fully determine his standing in his peers' eyes. Rather, his faith and involvement as a Christian earned him a respectable status. His relationship with his peers, moreover, was conducted in and around the church and its functions. Sunday service and the cakewalk forced Ki and Ann to become more intimately acquainted with each other, and from that grew deeper emotions. Only through religion, the story argues, did Jessekiah find God's intended for him and experience true love. The story further illustrates the authority the community held. Their insistence kept him from marrying a beautiful, young woman he had previously courted and encouraged a fondness to grow between Ki and Ann. His peers felt that he "belonged" with Ann because of their similarities, such as their age and weight. In this way, the community taught Ki to keep within his "station" as determined by physical attractiveness and age. Partially due to limited opportunities to travel outside the watchful eyes of family, the rural South clung to tradition and older forms of courtship.

Courtship, however, changed more drastically in the city. Americans during the antebellum period had taken pride in local autonomy. Communities determined their own policies and value systems with little involvement from the rest of the country, but, as historian Robert Wiebe states, these "island communities" witnessed a gradual loss of influence and power.[21] With increasing numbers of women working, mechanized transportation, and recreational facilities, courtship no longer took place on the front porch, particularly among the lower-income socioeconomic classes. Parents generally could not control their children's movements or curb the desire for "mixed-sex fun."[22] Public places blossomed in urban areas, including New Orleans, and changed relationships between men and women.

In 1882, New Orleanian Peter Johnson expressed frustration over the shift. He saw his daughter with a man and ran to stop them from continuing their outing. Johnson testified, "I went up to the place where they were and caught them in the act. She broke and run. . . . I told him he need not run that all I wanted was my daughter."[23] Clearly, Johnson lacked complete power over his daughter and her relationships with men, and he went so far as to try to physically separate the two. Even if unsuccessful, his attempt demonstrated a desire to cling to older forms of influence in courtship. Parental worry over the loss of control was also depicted in children's stories. Charles Bennett's *The Frog Who Would a Wooing Go* is a southern tale about a frog who would not listen to his mother's advice on whom to marry. Instead of finding another frog, he pursues a mouse. The story ends with a cat eating his friend the rat, a kitten eating his intended the mouse, and a duck eating him. Obviously, the moral of the story was for children to listen to their parents about courting.[24] The change in courtship rituals created anxieties over parental authority, but in an urban setting families waged a losing battle and could not maintain the control they once had. Young women, particularly in cities, often took to deciding upon their spouses based on romantic love and without their family's consent.

Women entered the public sphere more and more frequently, increasing their contact with the opposite sex. Without the watchful eyes of parents, these women developed intense emotional bonds with men of their own choosing, adopting "shared identities" as couples.[25] This forging of bonds included a power dynamic. Many women, such as Lizzie Hill, whose story is recounted at the beginning of this chapter, went out with groups of female friends to listen to musical performances and met up with men. They rode streetcars and enjoyed the nightlife. But this desire for leisure time and "mixed-sex fun" placed women in vulnerable positions. As historian Kathy Peiss discusses, women often made less money than men and relied on their male companions to "treat" them to an evening of fun. Men paid for dinner, drinks, and dance tickets or whatever outing was planned, and they expected a return. As a result, "treating" often required some form of sexual compensation.[26] Women were then left with a "sexual debt."[27] Pressure for sexual favors created a situation in which women's autonomy could be threatened and their partners could become violent to maintain their sense of control. Some boyfriends ignored the new definitions of manhood and felt entitled to "chastise" or control their female partners.

In the summer of 1887, Eliza McRea of New Orleans had been seeing Willie Hennessey but refrained from becoming sexual with him. One evening, he followed her as she came out of her house. McRea testified: "[H]e said 'where are you going?' I told him I was going to my aunt's. He came up to me and asked if I was going to sleep with him. I said no. [Then] he hauled off and punched me in the eye."[28] Hennessey felt entitled to some sexual remuneration and a certain level of control over McRea. She, however, asserted herself, denying him complete power in the relationship. Instead of having sex with Hennessey as so-called payment for the outing or passively accepting the beating, McRea refused Hennessey on both accounts. She, moreover, believed that she was entitled to legal protection even if she had been "treated" by Hennessey, and McRea exhibited new gender expectations by displaying a level of autonomy and pressing charges against her abuser.[29]

Intimate partner violence during courtship often erupted when a woman disagreed with her boyfriend. Sometimes the disagreement could be as simple as not wanting to go out that evening. When John Green called on his girlfriend, Rosetta Williams, she told him that she did not feel up to leaving her New Orleans home. Green responded by grabbing her arm and hitting her. He seemingly could not tolerate "no" from the woman he was courting, which demonstrates Green's sense of power and privilege. Williams, however, illustrated new gender expectations. Her refusal to go out that evening suggests a right to act as she would like without being told what to do by her boyfriend. Williams's actions also indicate a right to be free from violence by having Green arrested for his abusive actions.[30] As evidenced by McRae and Williams, new courtship rituals did not maintain antebellum notions of male power and privilege.

Sometimes, intimate partner violence in courtship was less in the heat of the moment and more a premeditated act to exert power, but even in systemically abusive courtships, women demanded the right to be free from violence. In 1887, George Samuels followed Emma Conrad through the streets, harassing her on several occasions. After one intense verbal altercation, Conrad stopped by New Orleans's Fourth Police Precinct and asked an officer for protection. She said: "You would see me home. I am in trouble."[31] When pushed for more information, Conrad told the police officers that Samuels, who she said was her former boyfriend, was following her again and had threatened to beat her. A police sergeant named Klotter agreed to walk her home, and once they reached her house, Samuels arrived on the scene with a friend and yelled at Conrad. The officer sent him home and advised her that the best thing she could do was go to bed. Despite his assurances, Sergeant Klotter noticed that she was still very frightened. Conrad's fear was well founded. She later testified that Samuels returned two hours later with his friend, came into her home, snatched her from her bed, and beat her until she was unconscious.[32]

Samuels shadowed Conrad's movements all afternoon on May 20, 1886, intimidating and harassing her. His actions were a premeditated act of violence intended to break her emotionally and physically. He told her: "You got the best of me [by breaking up first]," and the loss of control sent him on a frenzied quest to regain the upper hand. His attempt to exert dominance did not stop at the beating. During the court testimony, Samuels's lawyer cross-examined Conrad and tried to clear his client of any responsibility by asking: "Are you not subject to epileptic fits?"[33] She flippantly responded, "Only when I get hit."[34] Despite months of emotional and physical abuse, Conrad believed that she had the right to be courted free from abuse. She expected the police to protect her from a potential act of violence from a man she had been seeing by demanding: "You would see me home."[35] When Samuels denied responsibility for his actions, she still held him accountable by pressing charges and remaining firm about his guilt in her testimony. The changes in gender expectations and courtship rituals, as Conrad demonstrated in the court case, meant that men could not wield unchecked violence against women.

As shown in the *Samuels* case, some men refused to accept a woman's decision to end a relationship and thereby cause the man to lose power. The case of Emma Starks, an African American woman, further illustrates this clash between old and new views of gender expectations. On November 10, 1881, Starks was enjoying an evening out with a female friend. They met up with the men they were seeing at the time, and the two couples gambled and danced at the Keno Room in New Orleans.[36] After a few hours, they left, and Starks spotted her ex, Andrew Williams. She knew that being in the company of other men would create an issue with Williams, and so the two women and two men went their separate ways. Starks and her female friend walked quickly together toward their homes until Williams ran up to them, punched Starks, and then tried to stab her. She pressed charges, which resulted in him spending four days in jail.

Throughout all of it, Starks displayed independence. She spent evenings out on the town, passed time in the company of different men, and filed suit against her attacker. In her testimony, she stated: "I used to have him," indicating a sense of ownership of her past lover.[37] Her case attests to the amount of power she held in the relationship as well as the desire to be free of his continued and unwanted abuse. Single women like Starks became more autonomous in the postbellum period, participating in leisure activities and the workforce. As they did so, many took pride in their emerging sense of self, and as women exerted this new autonomy, they upheld the right to be free from violence in courtship.

Engaged women asserted the same right to be free from abuse as did women being courted. In a similar situation to Emma Conrad's, Ada Wheeler attempted to break off her relationship with her fiancé, Morris Hamilton. She had been lying down on the porch of her house when Hamilton approached. He entered the house and asked her to come inside, but she refused. He barked back, "No, come inside. I don't want to tell my business to everybody."[38] Still, she would not accede to his wishes, and, in the presence of neighbors, Wheeler said: "Here Morris, there is your ring. I don't love you no more and I don't want to carry it [the engagement] out anymore."[39] He asked her if she truly meant it. After confirming that she did not love him, he pulled out a pocket knife, attacked her, and cut her hand.

Hamilton could not accept that his fiancée would leave him, at least not of her own will. He had developed strong feelings for Wheeler during their courtship, which exemplified how, by the late 1800s, men and women felt more free to demonstrate their affection, even outside of marriage. When he lost his shared identity with his fiancée, Hamilton turned to violence, endangering her life after hearing her emphatic claim that she had stopped loving him. Wheeler, on the other hand, exhibited new gender expectations by upholding romantic love as the primary reason for marriage. When she no longer cared for Hamilton, she ended the engagement. Wheeler also displayed the new gender expectations by acting with autonomy. She refused Hamilton's wishes to keep the argument private and refused that power in the relationship be his alone. When attacked, she pressed charges, and, despite his claim that someone else had forced her to do it, Wheeler insisted that she alone filed the complaint and wished to prosecute. Through their collective actions, the pair exhibited the new power dynamics that accompanied emerging gender expectations.

In New Orleans, courtship rituals changed in ways that gave women more independence in their intimate relationships with men. Women more frequently chose boyfriends and fiancés who reciprocated romantic feelings of love. Power, more importantly, could not be held solely by men. Women expected a say in a relationship free from abuse. When their partners violated these expectations, women often chose to end the relationship and demand punishment for these men who had transgressed the new gender roles.

Common Law Marriage

In the antebellum era, some states began to recognize marriages in which individuals privately exchanged vows or cohabitated openly as husband and wife. These common law marriages were often found in rural areas in the nineteenth century, where records were kept more sporadically than in cities, and among the poorer socioeconomic classes, who lacked the monetary means to contract a marriage. As the legal system sought to make marriage more accessible to the entire American population, courts generally followed the principle of "maxim semper prasesumitur pro matrimonio" (the assumption is always in favor of matrimony).[40] But, in the 1870s, common law marriages came under attack.

Purity reformers and evangelicals pushed to regulate marriage even more than it had been before.[41] Proponents of stricter marriage requirements felt that acknowledging common law marriage encouraged moral depravity by condoning couples living together and engaging in extramarital sex. Not surprisingly, they believed that the government in general and legislation in particular should be used to enact the change. The state, they argued, could and should intervene, even in what had previously been considered private affairs. Contemporary sociologist George Elliott Howard stated: "[Y]ou can make people better by law. . . . A good marriage law is prevention—social prophylaxis."[42] Some believed that denying the legality of common law marriage would be enough. Others supported stricter requirements for marriage celebrations, including who could officiate and how many guests should be present. The movement for marital reform gained a broad backing among religious conservatives and women's rights advocates, such as Elizabeth Cady Stanton. Stanton believed that stricter marital requirements would prevent unions without a woman's consent or full understanding, and, coupled with more liberal divorce laws, these changes would keep women from being trapped in bad marriages. Proponents of the social purity movement did not agree with Stanton's logic, but they worked together for marital change. Whether for women's interests or moral uplift, many Americans supported reforming the legal system's view of marriage.[43]

Detractors argued that increased regulation of nuptial celebrations would disproportionately influence poorer socioeconomic classes and people of color. Without funds to purchase the marriage license or pay the officiant, poor couples would continue to live together without the rights and privileges associated with the legal institution of marriage. This, critics of the proposals argued, would be to the detriment of society.[44] Most of their complaints stemmed not from a desire for equality but rather from fiscal conservatism. Property and children were at the top of their list of concerns. Children born in these unions would be illegitimate and deprived of the mandatory support of the father, and successions and property would also be denied to the widows and heirs. Financial responsibility for these children would then fall to the community or state. All of society, those opposed to marital reform argued, would suffer.[45]

People of color would also be impacted by the proposed changes. Although some African Americans rushed to have their marriages legalized and protected after the war, numerous others feared that white expectations would be imposed on their marriages if made legal, specifically the ability to end these relationships. Those who were wary of negative consequences kept their relationships outside of legal sanctions in what historian Nancy Bercaw calls "taking up and sweethearting."[46] Sometimes, a relationship involved simply a sexual or financial arrangement, but "taking up" or "sweethearting" could include a private vow between the couple, which was viewed in the African American community as a form of marriage. Courts often did not recognize this variation of marriage. Despite serious disapproval, many states enacted stricter legislation on what constituted a legal marriage, thereby outlawing common law marriages.[47]

Louisiana rarely recognized common law marriages even before the marital reform movement. As early as its territorial days, Louisiana passed legislation acknowledging marriage as a civil contract that was made when the parties were "willing to contract, able to contract, and did contract pursuant to the forms and solemnities prescribed by law."[48] The Civil Code remained vague about what was deemed a marriage "ceremony," but consent was crucial. If either party was forced by violence, if the woman was raped and not yet "restored to the enjoyment of liberty," or if either person misrepresented him or herself, then the marriage would be rendered invalid.[49] Marriage ceremonies, however, could not be performed by just anyone. Articles 102 and 103 of the code specify that only justices of the peace, parish judges, "minister[s] of any gospel, or priest[s] of any religious sect" could perform the ceremony, provided they abided by the law, including presenting a "special license issued by a parish judge."[50] Essentially, for marriage to be legitimate in Louisiana, the state required consent, licensure, and an approved official to perform the ceremony. By 1877, the state legislature of Louisiana added another article in the Civil Code requiring at least three witnesses (all over the age of twenty-one).[51]

In the late 1800s, Michigan, Missouri, Wisconsin, Minnesota, Arizona, Florida, Indiana, Utah, Colorado, Nebraska, Nevada, Kansas, Montana, Idaho, Texas, and (to some degree) Wyoming recognized common law marriage.[52] Louisiana—like much of the South—did not follow suit. Louisiana honored common law marriages created in states that legally recognized such unions, but common law marriages formed within the state of Louisiana rarely held up in civil court.[53] Still, even if judges did not formally recognize common law marriages, people continued to live as man and wife without a legal seal of approval. The practice remained entrenched despite attempts to dissuade or eradicate it.

The changes in common law marriage and gender expectations created an unstable power dynamic, namely common law husbands' inability to maintain their authority as women asserted themselves. In 1888, Mary Antoine sought to prosecute her common law husband, William Anderson, for abuse. She stated that they had been living together in New Orleans for nine years as husband and wife and had two children. One night, he choked her while she was sleeping. Antoine had the resources to leave with her two children, and she fled the home soon after the incident.[54] Since they had never legally solemnized the relationship, she could separate without seeking the court's intervention, but as often happens with intimate partner violence, her leaving proved the most dangerous phase of the entire relationship.[55] Married or not, Anderson spun out of control, not able to deal with his loss of power over Antoine. She testified that, on the evening of January 19, he found her at her friend's house and

> jumped into the room with a cotton hook in his hand. I ran and tried to get away from him. I got into the bed, he came after me, began to beat me with the cotton hook, he kept beating me until he hurt his hand with the cotton hook he then took the broomstick beat me with that then took me up bodily and threw [me] out of the door and as I started to get up, he kicked me.[56]

Anderson seemingly could not accept the end of his common law marriage and the subsequent repudiation of his "right" to control his common law wife, and so he found her and beat her again. She successfully escaped and sent a child to contact her aunt, who called for the police. Anderson did not internalize the new masculinity but rather upheld an antiquated view of manhood. To him, legal sanction of his marriage did not matter. Antoine was "his" and as such subject to his authority and methods of "discipline." Antoine, however, acted under the new views of womanhood in the postbellum period. She expected a certain level of protection and reciprocity. When he violated gender expectations by abusing her, she left. Although the exact catalyst that touched off the violence is unknown, the abuse clearly serves as an example of intimate partner violence based on a dynamic of competing gender expectations.

In a similar case, Elizabeth (Lizzie) Andrews pressed charges against her common law husband of five years, Major Anderson. He accused Andrews of having a relationship with another man, Daniel Jordan, and, despite her protests of innocence, Anderson choked her and pulled out a knife, insisting that he was going to kill her.[57] Andrews testified that her common law husband's actions were not isolated but that he had a history of violence and was extremely jealous. In her testimony before the New Orleans court, Lizzie Andrews stated: "The accused is a very jealous man and continually accuses me of being untrue and having criminal intercourse with other men. He has often ill treated me."[58] Through his actions, Anderson sought to control Andrews and ensure her fidelity through violence, but his actions violated gender expectations, leading Andrews to have her common law husband arrested.

The *Major Anderson* case illustrates how poor socioeconomic groups internalized the new views of gender and how the courts ruled on abuse in common law marriages. None of those involved in the suit—the black plaintiff, defendant, or witnesses—could read, write, or sign their names. All made their mark in the court records with an *X*. Although illiteracy cannot be the sole predictor of socioeconomic class, the inability to read and write indicates a lack of a rudimentary education and suggests that Andrews and Anderson did not belong to any middling or elite family.[59] Her living situation is suggestive of economic hardship, as Andrews and Anderson rented a room from Jane Green on Plum Street.[60] Instead of a bedroom, they lived in the kitchen and had been renting at that location for some time. Given her poor socioeconomic status, Andrews could have reinterpreted gender expectations differently, since those in power typically decide social expectations.[61] In a way, she did. Marriage, to Andrews, did not have to be legally recognized with a formal ceremony and license; instead, she accepted a common law marriage as a suitable and valid form of marriage. She insisted that she and Anderson lived as husband and wife, which showed an emotional commitment deeper than that of simple cohabitation. But, in another way, Andrews exhibited views similar to those of other women during the period. She internalized the new womanhood for women of color, and she refused to permit her common law husband the male privilege of chastisement any longer.

New gender expectations included a sense of reciprocity, particularly in working-class relationships. Working-class common law wives, for instance, expected assistance in the home, and some noted that their financial assistance to the family income entitled them to help with domestic chores. Others believed that the new gender expectations did not define women solely in terms of the home, but they still expected their husbands to contribute in some way. Jane Robinson, for example, certainly required respect and assistance with the housework despite middle-class ideals for white womanhood. In 1887, she filed assault and battery charges against her common law husband, Sam Carney. Carney wanted to go to sleep, but Robinson insisted that he take out the mattress and create a pallet for them to sleep on in their living room. After all, she argued, he had not gone to work, so he had not done anything to make him tired. If he did not help, she threatened that he would have to sleep in the bedroom with the children. Carney responded by yelling, "I will be God damn if I do," and then he began to curse and beat her.[62]

As part of the New Orleans working class, Robinson and Carney both found seasonal work to make ends meet. They could not afford a home with sufficient bedrooms but rather slept in the living room and had their children share a common bed. Despite their financial situation, Robinson wanted Carney to fulfill his obligation as a man and as a partner by assisting with the domestic chores. When he violated this understanding by not helping and by hitting her with "two licks in the face," she had him arrested.[63] She asserted a right to be free from violence and challenged his power.

The new gendered expectations infiltrated all socioeconomic levels and even relationships outside of marriage. Many women began to recognize their economic and domestic contributions, and they believed that power needed to be renegotiated in these relationships. In courtship and common law marriages, women held more legal rights than before because they were no longer subsumed under their husband's identity ("civilly dead"), as in the law of coverture.[64] Essentially, they could separate and manage their separate property as a single woman would. This situation could be interpreted as the women's ability to internalize a level of autonomy from their male partners, but during this period, even legally married women demanded the right to be free from violence.

Legal Marriage

For married couples, the new gender dynamic was noticeable. Even men recognized a different interaction between husband and wife, as evidenced by John McKowen. McKowen, from Louisiana, wrote to his sister Sallie Henry about his widowed mother's recent marriage and remarked:

> I hope that Mama is happy in her new home and is learning to boss her husband as every good wife, who resolutely intends to be happy in her own home, should, and I hope that her husband takes kindly to the bossing as every happy husband must do if he really wants to be happy in his married life.[65]

He based the ideal marriage around the concept of happiness for both the husband and the wife, not the husband alone. Moreover, McKowen linked happiness in marriage *not* to the complete submission of the wife but rather to a degree of female assertiveness. The wife held the position of "boss" in the home under new gender and marital expectations, and the husband should "kindly" yield to his wife's command of the household. If a wife became unhappy, she could seek a divorce; in fact, after the Civil War, unhappily married women increasingly sought divorce. Historian Carl Degler found that two-thirds of divorce petitions in the late 1860s were granted to women and argues that this shift in divorce signaled in part "another sign of women's drive for greater autonomy within their marriage."[66] Among Orleans Parish court cases for intimate partner violence from 1880 to 1889, legal marriages accounted for 65 percent of the cases while extramarital intimate partner violence made up only 35 percent.[67] Clearly, postbellum marriages did not resurrect an intact patriarchy and rather sought to renegotiate relationships between wives and husbands.

The role of the wife after the Civil War shifted to include visibility and participation in the public sphere. Using maternalistic rhetoric, women argued that their moral nature would be of benefit to the larger society and that the emerging gender expectations were not completely different from those of the antebellum period. Essentially, the glorification of white women as both domestic and moral forces remained. Both South and North engaged in memorial activities after the war including the creation of cemeteries, the relocation and burial of soldiers' remains, the building of monuments, participation in decoration days, and the establishment of Memorial Day as a national holiday.[68] In Memorial and Decoration Day speeches, men praised women not only for honoring the dead but also for their emotional and moral nature. In 1873, Confederate colonel Thomas Hardeman applauded these women's actions, saying:

These noble women come, when spring flowers bloom, to plant the memorial shrub and shed their tears of love over the humble mounds that tell where our heroes sleep. For this I give them honour and praise today.[69]

Hardeman lauded southern women in this speech for their sacrifice in the Civil War and for their continued love for the wounded and fallen soldiers. He noted that these women were "the perfection of beauty and glory of the land" because of their emotional fidelity to their men.[70] This is key to the new gender expectations. Women could hold an exalted status through their devotion to men but not independently of them. These southern women's reassurance in the wake of loss eased the grief of defeat and strengthened a weakened sense of manhood by emphasizing the sacrifice of southern men for the protection of southern women.

In spite of the conservative tone of women's roles, these women acted as public advocates, a role they had not often assumed in the past. They stepped out of the home and honored fallen men, even Confederate soldiers. Instead of being viewed as treasonous, women honoring the Confederate fallen were viewed as nonthreatening and helped pave the way for such tributes to be acceptable. Nurturing and moral behavior remained aspects of the new womanhood, but the older separate spheres ideal gave way to a more public female whose viewpoints and actions could have a larger impact. Although still defined maternally, women were now in an altered relationship with men even as they held onto older characteristics of womanhood.

Wives, especially those in the upper socioeconomic class, were encouraged to join benevolent societies and become leaders of their community. One Louisiana woman advised a female relative to do as much, since "this is an absolute cure for blues, is a strong anchor and fine encouragement for your husband, and in short makes you a good and valuable citizen rather than a hippo-condriac [sic] and drone and impediment to society."[71] Heading charities and other helpful organizations, then, made women useful assets to their husbands and to the larger society. Confining oneself to the home completely was not desirable or practical, and in their newer, more public role, women exerted more influence than before.

Women also became more visible in the public arena, especially in urban areas, by participating in what historian Kathy Peiss calls "cheap amusements."[66] For instance, women gathered in public squares to talk or listen to music, as Lizzie Muldaner did in New Orleans.[73] They sometimes went with their male partners, but women also participated in leisure activities with female acquaintances or sisters. Although most white women remained outside the workforce, more and more women had to earn an income, particularly women of color, in the wake of the economic recessions of the 1870s, 1880s, and 1890s.[74] The census of 1900 estimated that more than 20 percent of women worked and declared that "although far from customary," working women were "by no means unusual."[75] In Louisiana, the percentage was a little higher, reaching almost 28 percent.[76] Anna Marks from New Orleans testified in 1887 that her husband was unable to support them and that she had to work part time to earn money to buy shoes for their baby.[77] Necessity compelled her to find extra income for the household. Although Marks and Muldaner ventured outside the home for different reasons, their presence in the public sphere illustrates the increasing visibility of women in what previously had been considered male activities.

Many wives agreed that their husbands had no right to abuse them, but their repudiation of the male privilege of chastisement took various forms. Some New Orleans women showed a sense of agency by verbally standing up to their abusive husbands. A Mrs. Bax pressed charges against her husband, and in her testimony she stated that their argument had been over her treating him "coolly."[78] When her husband cross-examined her and asked if she would improve her attitude, she refused because, she reasoned, "he wasn't treating me properly and I wasn't going to do any better."[79] Like former nun Désirée Martin, Mrs. Bax seemed to expect a sort of reciprocity in male-female relationships.[74] When her husband did not seek to make her happy, she declared that she did not have to behave submissively. Instead, she argued with him and defended her cold treatment. Mrs. Bax implied that only when he acted as a loving and protective husband would she in turn conform to the role of a loving and submissive wife. Even if some husbands like Mr. Bax wanted obedience, society could not resurrect the expectation of complete female subordination in the postbellum period. The conditions of the Civil War made women recognize the negative consequences of upholding the antebellum feminine ideal, and new views of womanhood required a different type of marriage based more on respect and a give-and-take mentality.

Other women physically confronted their abusive spouses, believing that men's violation of new gender expectations warranted a like response. Virginia Wilson testified that her husband "rushed in and gave me a shove, and I shoved him back."[81] Wilson expressed the belief that he was subject to the same treatment that he showed her. Another woman, Mary Shields, stated that after her husband struck her, she hit him with a spoon she had in her hand.[82] When he then made a movement toward her, she "struck him in the mouth."[83] Shields's actions appear as self-defense, but she fought back rather than remain passive.[84] In a case involving an African American couple, the wife, Anne Dagan (alias Anne Williams), similarly fought back. When the court asked her why she beat her husband, Anne said, "I tell you sir, he got just what he deserved. I ain't no dog, and I ain't going to be thrashed in that way."[85] She explicitly stated that her husband had no right to strike her, believing that she possessed the right to be free from marital violence, and she took a stand to stop it. Despite what some historians claim, these New Orleans women did not seek to act like ladies to gain sympathy and successful prosecution from the court.[86] Physically violent behavior could be seen as unfeminine in most other situations, but in intimate partner violence, women could and did strike back without being judged negatively. After all, the husbands had first violated redefined gender expectations by being abusive toward their wives. Shields, Wilson, and Williams—like other women—openly refuted any male privilege of chastisement and did not hide their behavior from the court.

Of the 225 Orleans Parish cases of intimate partner violence in the 1880s, only three women expressed belief in the privacy of the family or the husband's right to chastisement. This accounts for approximately 1.5 percent of the cases of intimate partner violence—an astoundingly small minority.[87] In 1882, police dragged James Gillen to court for abusing his wife; Mrs. Gillen never sought to press charges. When asked to testify on the incident, Mrs. Gillen stated: "I didn't wish to prosecute him. . . . He wanted his way, and I wanted mine. It was my fault as much as his."[88] When the judge asked where she received her black eye, Mrs. Gillen responded, "It was done in the family. I didn't wish to go against my husband."[89] Despite a policeman having witnessed the abuse, Mrs. Gillen insisted that she was accountable and avoided a detailed description of the events, providing vague responses and upholding the concept of family privacy. She insisted that she did not want charges pressed since it was a family affair, even if she felt that she had a right to hold different views from her husband on certain issues. Although women such as Mrs. Gillen internalized some sense of guilt or privacy, clearly most women no longer accepted a complete patriarchy, including total female submissiveness. Gender ideals had changed too much for these women.

◆ ◆ ◆

Overwhelmingly, women internalized the change in gender expectations. Out of 225 cases examined from Orleans Parish during the 1880–1889 period, 98.5 percent asserted that their male partners did not have the right to raise a hand against them. Their testimony illustrates a large shift on an individual level about how women viewed intimate partner violence, and the fact that women constituted the majority of the plaintiffs, unlike in the antebellum period, further supports a different attitude about what had previously been a male privilege. By refusing to submit to physical and emotional violence, women renegotiated every type of romantic relationship with their male partners and influenced social attitudes. Their repudiation of abuse affected other members of society, the community, and the public at large. Fluid gender expectations, then, allowed for social reform on the issue of intimate partner violence.

Chapter Four

"You Can't Abuse Her in This House"

Family, Community, and Intimate Partner Violence in New Orleans

He [the accused] made a big excitement. The little girl called me. I went in as
quick as I could. He had [his wife] on the bed and was choking her. When I
came in he said, "I will kill you." I told my husband to go and call the policeman.
He did not come quick enough, and I went myself and got two policemen.
—**Hannah Anderson**, *State v. James Wilson*, 1887

At ten o'clock in the evening on July 26, 1887, Hannah Anderson awoke in her
New Orleans apartment to the cries from a nine-year-old girl begging for
someone to help her mother. Hannah quickly followed the girl. She arrived on
the scene to find a man choking his wife and threatening anyone who dared
stop him. Instead of turning a blind eye to uphold the privacy of family, Hannah hurried to intervene, calling to her husband for help.[1] Her actions and
demand for the police to do something suggest a rising level of awareness of
intimate partner violence and, more importantly, society's moral obligation
to stop it.

During the 1880s, the public intervened to protect all women, not just
those in keeping with the antebellum conception of a lady. The *Wilson* case
in 1887 New Orleans illustrates that point. Virginia and James Wilson separated multiple times during their sixteen-year marriage, and he reportedly
told her to become "a decent woman."[2] James never specifically testified as to
what Virginia did to make her an "indecent" wife, but when she refused his
sexual advances, he insinuated that she engaged in extramarital affairs. He
came over that summer night intent on reconciling the marriage and seeing if
they could live in the same house again. Virginia turned him away and acted
defiantly. She kept blowing out the matches he lit for his tobacco, and when he

shoved her, she shoved back. James possessively clung to his dominance and perceived power over her life by threatening: "I will kill you so you won't be of any service to me or anybody else."[3]

Far from demure and submissive, the abused woman, Virginia Wilson, did not exemplify the typical "proper" woman. She left her husband several times, fought back, refused his wishes, and found a job to provide single-handedly for herself and her daughter. Although Virginia, like other abused women, violated the antebellum notion of "true womanhood," this did not exclude her from societal protections. Hannah and the police intervened, throwing aside the concept of family privacy and male privilege, which suggests that the public agreed not only on a broader view of what was acceptable of a woman but also on new limitations to men's behavior.

The Wilson case involved at least three levels of intervention: family, community, and the law. The nine-year-old daughter sought help from Hannah Anderson, Hannah found watchmen, and the police and court used criminal statutes of assault and battery to enforce Virginia Wilson's right to be free from abuse. These multiple forms of intervention demonstrate a heightened public awareness about intimate partner violence that infiltrated every aspect of society. Greater awareness generated a level of visibility for a social problem prompting action, and public awareness changed the dominant message from accepting the male privilege of chastisement to ending intimate partner violence, making silence no longer acceptable. When this happened, people condemned the perpetrator and sought to protect a woman's right to be free from violence. Intimate partner violence came out of the shadows in the 1870s and 1880s as people discussed the problem and held the abuser accountable. Although laws in the majority of states did not change, judges responded by interpreting old assault and battery statutes to hold the batterer legally accountable. Rather than being solely a top-down issue, the shift also involved people taking a stand against intimate partner violence on an individual (as gender expectations and relationships shifted), then communal (as families and neighbors increasingly intervened), and finally state level (as courts responded and started prosecuting abusers).[4] Chapter 3 focused on individual responses; this chapter explores the community.

Family

At the core of this change lay a shift in gender expectations and the family power dynamic, which now allowed for greater family intervention in intimate partner violence. As previously stated, gender anxieties from the Civil

War undermined male authority, and women's experiences taught the need for a level of autonomy. The continuation of a male-led gender hierarchy consequently came with stipulations. In both the North and the South, women demanded a more reciprocal relationship between the sexes. Some insisted on equal rights, while others wanted legal protection. Whether radical or conservative in their goals, women sought to alter the power dynamics, particularly in marriage. When men became abusive, they violated the new understanding of heterosexual relationships governed by gender expectations in the postbellum decades, and consequently violent men forfeited their family members' respect and deference. As in the Wilson case, in which the nine-year-old daughter went in search of help, family members including siblings and children frequently witnessed intimate partner violence. Often, they became the first level of intervention. Those who interceded on their mother's, sister's, or daughter's behalf tended to do so without any remorse for rescinding their expected deference to the male head of the house. In return for the submission of one's wife and children, men had to be protective and refrain from violently chastising family members. Violating this new understanding meant that an abusive man could not command respect.

To uphold these new gender expectations, families in Orleans Parish sought to make the abuser stop his behavior, with some resorting to defensive acts of physical violence themselves. On September 27, 1883, Theresa Busch, a white woman, cooked a breakfast for her family when her husband, Herman, asked her to go somewhere with him. When she said no, he became angry and demanded the money she had in her pocket, but she kept refusing. Unable to accept defiance from his wife, Herman tried to enforce submission. Theresa testified:

> When I refused he caught a hold of me by the collar saying he would choke me.... Threw me down.... While in that position, Mary Senyetter, my daughter took a stick and beat him to make him let me go. He then jumped up got a hold of a piece of iron that we use as a poker and struck me in the face cutting my face.[5]

Theresa and Herman's daughter, Mary, had already married and moved out of the house, but she still intervened to stop her father from beating her mother. Instead of calling for help or yelling at her father, she grabbed an object and tried to force him to leave her mother alone, and in doing so, Mary reciprocated with the same behavior her father displayed toward her mother. Neither woman was submissive or obedient. Theresa defied Herman. Mary beat him. These women's actions seemingly threatened a traditional gender hierarchy, but by abusing his wife, Herman violated the new gender expectations and forfeited the respect of the community as a civilized man and consequently his authority.

Male family members in Orleans Parish intervened as well. New definitions of masculinity required men to police each other's behavioral performances, including intervening in other men's families. Uncivilized men engaged in abuse as a form of discipline or power, and to demonstrate their disapproval of brutish men, male witnesses felt the necessity to intervene. The *Joyce* case illustrates this point. William Joyce transgressed gender expectations when he abused his wife, Mary, and child, Katie. Mary left the home, refusing to live with her husband anymore, and she looked to her brother, James, for assistance. William sought his wife and daughter and eventually found them staying at James's house. On November 20, 1885, William demanded that his family return to him. He called to Katie, telling her to come to him, but she began to cry and hid behind her mother, who told her husband to leave. Mary insisted that she would not force their daughter to go with him, and William responded by yelling obscenities and grabbing Katie by the arm. Mary testified:

> I says, "You are looking for another term in the workhouse." He abused me and James says, "You can't abuse her in this house," and ordered him out. He [William] raised his hand to strike me. I told James to go out and get a policeman. As he was going out, William tripped him and beat him, and I went out to his assistance.[6]

The house belonged to James. As such, James insinuated that William did not possess any rights there, even access to his wife; rather, William was subject to the authority of the homeowner. Moreover, William's abuse violated the new limits to manhood, which meant that he had no right to force Mary and Katie to return with him. While James acted to protect Mary, she was not a passive victim. She told James to find an officer and seek legal help. She also went to help her brother when he was tripped by William, displaying loyalty to the man who recognized her right to be free from violence.[7] Brother and sister worked together, knowing that a man's rights did not extend to beating a woman, even if the woman was his wife.

While some sons learned abuse from their fathers and perpetuated the cycle of violence, others turned against their abusive dads. For example, the sons of an abused woman could and did file charges of assault and battery against their violent father. Ben Lee had a history of abusing his wife, Adelina.[8] Their child, Scott, filed suit against his father for one of the attacks in an effort to end the violence, and he succeeded despite the fact that he had not been present the night of the abuse to serve as a witness.[9] If not a witness or victim, then what right did Scott have to file criminal charges? His actions suggest that his knowledge of the abusive past and his position as a family member granted him the right to hold his father accountable, and the Orleans Parish Criminal District Court summarily recognized Scott's petition to press charges by finding the father guilty. In such a situation in which a father has forfeited respectability, his son could replace him as leader of the family, as the one who upholds the ideals of manhood.

Scott was able to use the court system because he was not a minor, but often young sons used a weapon as an equalizer, marking the level of determination family members had in ending intimate partner violence. On July 30, 1884, the *Daily Picayune* printed a story entitled "Misdeeds and Mishaps: Domestic Discords."[10] The article described an incident in the Hener family that "ended in a court scrape" because the father had created a "disturbance" by "beating his wife unmercifully."[11] The son tried to stop his father by hitting him with a blunt object, and consequently the police arrested both the father and the son. The son, whose age and first name were not disclosed, did not stand by and allow his father the privilege of chastisement but instead physically denied the deference typically due to the head of the family. This protective act came at a cost, however. Charged with assault and battery, the son paid a fine and spent some time in jail. More than an overture, the son's incarceration is a pointed criticism of his father's unmanly and uncivilized behavior. Family members could (and some did) silently witness spousal abuse, but when they intervened, they made deliberate choices that showed disapproval of intimate partner violence and of the abusive men whose violence transgressed their expectations for male behavior.

While the Hener case did not result in a fatality, sometimes a family member died in the attempt to stop the abuse. In July 1891, Elias Phips of rural Boone, Louisiana, saw his father come home drunk and beat his mother, prompting Elias to quickly grab a musket and shoot his father.[12] When the *Wheeling Register* published the story, the reporter believed that the abusive husband would die, and fourteen-year-old Elias sat in jail awaiting the court's judgment. The exact reason Elias used a gun can never be known for certain. Perhaps he felt that he could not stop his father without a weapon, or perhaps he simply became enraged at his father for his repeated violence. Whatever the reason, Elias Phips's actions demonstrate that male power had limitations. The father forfeited his position of authority and respect when he mercilessly beat his wife, and, in this case, he also lost his life.

Other family members risked their own safety when they tried to stop an abusive partner, which demonstrated their level of commitment to a loved one and to the right to be free from violence. In 1887, an African American woman, Mary Bassinger, took her children and left her abusive husband, Will. Mary surrounded herself with female relatives and rejoined them in her mother's home. As scholars have previously argued, these family links held immense value in the nineteenth century, especially for African Americans.[13] Many lived in interfamilial homes or in close proximity to their parents, siblings, or extended family members, and these relatives often served as support and protection.

In the *Bassinger* case, Will called for Mary to come talk to him at the gate, but she refused, saying that she wanted nothing to do with him. Will yelled, "If you don't come it will be worse for you."[14] Despite their separation, he felt that he was entitled to a level of compliance and submission from his wife, and in an effort to maintain his dominance he threatened her with violence. Will, however, compromised his rights by becoming abusive, and Mary's defiant behavior illustrates many women's view of marriage as one of reciprocity. At the very least, the wife possessed the right to live a peaceful life without the presence of abuse. After Will's verbal threat, Mary's mother came home and told him to leave or she would go to court and make a complaint. Undeterred, Will jumped the fence, yelling at the mother and claiming that she "harbored Mary for other men."[15] Mary's mother refused to address his jealous accusation but still tried to block his path, firmly declaring, "You are not going in there after her."[16] Will ran around her and into the room where Mary was hiding with the children and dragged Mary out of the house, beating her with a stick and then biting her hand. A neighbor alerted Mary's sister Cora, who was living nearby, that Mary was being attacked, and Cora quickly arrived, remarking, "That nigger got cheek enough to come into my mother's yard and beat you!"[17] Infuriated, Will attacked Cora with a knife, stabbing her in the back twice, and then went after Mary again. He pulled his wife onto the front steps and cut her twice on the face and once on the leg, leaving some wounds as long as three and a half inches.

Mary's mother's and sister's intervention went beyond a token overture. These women viewed their mother's home as a place of safety, even perhaps a bastion of female power. The household of women protected and empowered Mary so that when her husband came demanding their children, he was met with staunch resistance from all the female parties. As Cora testified, they did not believe that Will, despite being Mary's husband, had any right to set foot on the property, much less harm anyone in their family. Moreover, Cora degraded Will by calling him "nigger," and she physically challenged him, facing the danger of being stabbed. Neither Mary's mother nor Mary's sister believed that Will held power over anyone in the house, even if one of the women was his wife. After all, his behavior had cost him his children, his wife, respect from his in-laws, and authority over his family. Mary's female relations placed themselves in physical danger to protect Mary and her right to be free from violence, testifying to the lengths women were willing to go in order to stop the abuse.

Community

Family intervention was not removed from the larger society. Enough people had altered their notion of gender in the postbellum period such that the collective conscience shifted to expect limits on male power, including denying the male privilege of chastisement. By the 1870s, society had come to condemn intimate partner violence, and members of local communities felt the need and the right to step in and stop the abuse.

Community members had involved themselves in intimate partner violence sporadically throughout American history. In the colonial era, small communities generally concerned themselves when individuals disrupted the harmony of the settlement.[18] When they did, local councils sometimes banished the offender or demanded public repentance, and groups humiliated the abuser with colonial-era skimmington rides, parading the transgressor through the town as people made noise and yelled. Mary Beth Norton argues that colonial Americans accepted "moderate physical correction" of wives, but when a husband went too far, "it reflected negatively on him and raised the possibility others might intervene, not only to protect the wife from harm but also to instruct him in the responsibilities of household leadership."[19] In spite of records of community intervention, the colonial family remained a private entity, and a wife's identity was subsumed under her husband's identity and control.[20]

In the antebellum era, society occasionally intervened when a man assaulted his partner, but male dominance still ranked higher in priority than addressing intimate partner violence. Facing intense scrutiny from antislavery advocates, southern justifications of slavery included paternal benevolence, which argued that slave owners took care of and showed kindness toward those dependent upon them. In charge of potentially a wife, children, servants, and slaves, a man had the obligation to provide for them and not simply maintain the hierarchy through discipline. Restraint and even kindness then entered the dynamic, at least in theory.[21] How could a man control "unruly" members of his family, be aggressive, and simultaneously show restraint? Society and specifically men struggled with how to integrate these conflicting mandates.[22] When neighbors intervened in a situation involving domestic violence, they commonly argued that the couple had disturbed the peace, and sometimes both the husband and wife were arrested.[23] Ultimately, the southern community in general and the New Orleans community in particular wanted to restore balance and uphold the male hierarchy that had predominated in the antebellum era.

Reasons for community intervention shifted by the 1870s and 1880s. The most obvious reason to intervene occurred when the abuse took place in a public area. Public spaces expanded in the postbellum period as cities increased in size and municipal planners sought to regulate the burgeoning city landscape. As discussed in an article by contemporary sociologist and economist E. R. L. Gould, people required "adequate out-door breathing spaces" and "wholesome facilities for recreation."[24] New York City's Central Park served as an example of the new city planning and the creation of public spaces, but cities in other regions also set areas aside for people to interact and "breathe."[25] The city of New Orleans acquired the land for City Park in 1850 but left the space unimproved until 1886. New Orleans also purchased the land for present-day Audubon Park in 1871. In 1879, the local government named the area of Audubon Park "New City Park," and it served as the site for the 1884 World's Fair (the Cotton Centennial Exposition).[26] The city undertook major improvements after 1886 in order to make the land more decorative and an attractive park. To Gould and others, including the well-known public administrator and landscape architect Frederick Law Olmsted, "[u]ndoubtedly the most important requisite is small open spaces, well distributed over a city, but numerously located in populous districts."[27] In some neighborhoods, small pieces of land in the middle of streets (known as the neutral ground) and near canals sat empty and served as small "parks" where adults and children congregated. Regardless of the setup, public spaces served the entire public and required social policing given the purposes they served and the visibility of what occurred there.

In a neighborhood in Algiers (an area annexed into the city of New Orleans in 1870), William Teal, a white man, argued with his wife Elizabeth. She left the house, walking along a nearby canal, and, in full view of several neighbors, William hit her and knocked her into the canal. One witness, Mrs. Putnam, sought to help Elizabeth but was rebuffed when William yelled, "Do not, woman, you [come] over here to my house any more."[28] Other female neighbors went to Elizabeth despite his threats. Ellen Butler and Mrs. Leddey testified that they "heard a woman scream . . . her face bleeding. She was wiping the blood from her face with a towel. I asked Mrs. Teal to my house and we would put dry clothes on her; she went with me to the house and we changed her clothes."[29] Corporal Morgan, a police officer who lived nearby, was sleeping at the time of the incident but woke up due to the screaming coming from the streets. Morgan testified that he "saw a crowd of people," took an affidavit from Elizabeth Teal, and arrested her husband for assault and battery. He could have affirmed family privacy and the power of men to chastise their wives by charging William with disturbing the peace, but instead, Morgan arrested William for assault and battery, recognizing the importance of the incident and the neighbors' outrage over the spousal abuse. The public visibility of the violence necessitated the neighbors' intervention, and several stepped up. In their testimony, the witnesses all said that they felt the husband had no right to act as he did. Moreover, by defying William Teal's threats to leave his wife in the ditch, the neighbors' actions spoke against the supposed right of chastisement as well as for the social responsibility to address intimate partner violence.

Crowds frequently formed when members of the community overheard a domestic dispute. While some likely gathered out of simple curiosity, others intervened or went to find the local watchman. These actions illustrate large-scale societal disapproval and the responsibility to intervene. The long-held value of family privacy did not trump the right of a woman to be free from violence. In the post–Civil War period, an abusive husband could not claim the right to family privacy, because he lost much of his power by violating newly defined gender expectations. Sometimes, communities resorted to a form of vigilante violence against an abusive man to enforce expectations, but most interventions, even when numerous people were involved, sought to protect the female victim and hold the male perpetrator responsible.

On a Sunday during the summer of 1886, Louisa Johnson prepared to attend church when her estranged husband, Martin, came to her home in New Orleans. As the landlady attempted to block the entrance, Louisa tried to escape down a back alley but was caught by Martin and beaten "near to death."[30] Concerned, the landlady came with a crowd of others loudly protesting what Martin had done. Part of the crowd then took Louisa to a hospital while others alerted the police so they could make an arrest. In an attempt to avoid prosecution, Martin tried to claim that Louisa's injuries were from an accidental fall. Louisa and the witnesses denied any such possibility, and the court agreed with the plaintiff. As part of his sentence, Martin Johnson spent six months in jail for assault and battery. The crowd's involvement shows an attempt to regulate behavioral and gender expectations. They gathered after hearing of the abuse and refused to disperse. The crowd intervened by shaming Martin for using violence, by helping Louisa seek medical help, and by finding patrolmen. The group of neighbors found the abuser's actions unacceptable, but rather than seeking vengeance through extralegal violence, they sought to hold him legally accountable.

Sometimes, groups intervening in abusive relationships did resort to violence against the abuser, particularly if they lived in lightly populated areas where there was a shortage of police, which limited witnesses' ability to seek justice through the legal system. In one case, a white man named Winn owned a small amount of land in the small town of Collinsburg, Louisiana. Most people in the area knew of his notoriously cruel treatment of his wife. Winn not only beat her severely on multiple occasions, but he also had an African American mistress whom he called his "Sunday wife."[31] People constantly talked about his behavior as "cruel"; they said that he was in need of "justice."[32] Finally, in October 1877, a crowd decided to take justice into their own hands. They waited until he beat his legal wife again, and while he sat eating dinner with his wife bleeding on the floor of their home, someone shot him through the window. One white neighbor, Nancy Willard, declared the shooting "justice."[33] She went on to say, "I don't suppose any boddy [sic] cares. His every day Wife is a hard working woman and has got a crop of her own and workes [sic] it her self."[34] Winn's killer was never identified, in part due to the lack of concern by the townspeople.

In beating his wife, Winn violated social expectations—expectations held in common with larger urban areas. The townspeople intervened believing they had a right to do so, although their sense of justice included murdering the abuser. To them, Winn lost the privileges and rights of manhood by abusing his spouse and arguably by engaging in an openly sexual relationship with a black woman. Still, the extralegal violence took place after yet another incident in which Winn abused his wife, suggesting that the shooter acted because he or she believed that men did not have the right to beat their wives. Nancy Willard's comments about Winn indicate that the community had a broad base of support for depriving Winn not only of any respect or manhood but also his very life.

Crowds provided evidence for the broad base of public support for intervention by more than their sheer numbers; they also proved public support by their diversity, including people of different races. The Gillen case illustrates one instance of cross-racial alliance. Mr. and Mrs. James Gillen—a white married couple—had an argument in which James punched his wife in the eye in their New Orleans home.[35] Neighbors heard the screams of "Watch!" and "Murder!" and ran to intervene. One policeman estimated that a total of three or four hundred people of different races stood outside the house, yelling at the abuser, while six individuals carried Mrs. Gillen to safety at the local grocery. Officer Furloug testified: "She [Mrs. Gillen] was bloody and looked very bad, and I took her to the hospital. She told me Mr. Gillen did it and she wanted it stopped."[36] The level of intervention here was astounding. The wife's cries generated a large social response that crossed racial lines. In this case, a general view of intimate partner violence transcended color, allowing for groups to come together with a common purpose—to help the abused woman and punish the wife beater. James Gillen's supposed right to chastise his wife unleashed the wrath of the entire neighborhood. New Orleans has a history of some racial tolerance, at least more so than in much of the rest of Louisiana and the South, but during the 1880s race was becoming an increasingly divisive issue.[37] The enormous mixed-race crowd testifies to the city's broad disapproval of intimate partner violence and its belief that spousal "rights" and family privacy did not protect abusers.

Cross-racial alliances among women also formed in the face of intimate partner violence, since gender-based violence affected all regardless of race, ethnicity, or socioeconomic status. Just as New Orleans extended a limited definition of womanhood to African American women who were victims of intimate partner violence, white women and women of color collaborated and intervened to stop the violence. In a sense, a quasi-sisterhood sometimes emerged. In 1886, a white woman named Mary Hines filed charges of assault and battery against her husband, William. He had been yelling at the neighbors, and although she was sick, Mary told him to stop in fear that they would be evicted for disturbing the peace. William then turned his anger on his family. Mary tried to leave, but when he began hitting their child Margaret, she stayed. He then began beating his wife. Mary Hines stated in her testimony: "He beat me with a vase from the mantelpiece. He struck me, broke this rib with a rocking chair. He beat me everywhere, kicked me, thumped me, commenced to beat me with the chair.... I was weltering in my blood."[38] Fearful for her life, Mary screamed for help, knowing that their black domestic servant, Mary Cash, was in the next room. Cash quickly intervened and begged William to release his wife. Cash struggled with him, but he began biting her hand. Mary Hines testified: "She held his hand. He chewed on this finger all the time for fully fifteen minutes. He had it in his mouth. She begged him not to take the finger."[39] Despite trying to help, Cash could not stop the abuse, and when William quit biting her hand, she grabbed the child and sought outside help.

Key to the incident was Mary Cash. She physically struggled against a white man in an attempt to stop him from beating his wife, and she was an important witness in court. As a woman of color, she risked her job, her well-being, and possible retaliation by white supremacists for raising a hand against her white employer. Race mattered in the postwar South, but in this situation, these women prioritized gender over race. The quasi-sisterhood, of course, had limitations. In everything else, Mary and William Hines required Cash's submission, but Cash still helped Mary, even jeopardizing her own economic and physical health, which speaks volumes about the types of bonds, albeit tenuous, that could emerge in response to intimate partner violence.

Social awareness, however, had unpredictable consequences. Once manhood no longer included the privilege of chastisement, people sought to stop the violence as they saw fit, but those who intervened did not always behave in agreement the victim's wishes. Instead, neighbors, family, and the community tended to act according to the belief that the attacker should be legally punished even if the abused partner disagreed. Such an outcome might seem to deprive women of their agency in prosecuting batterers, but in sixteen cases initiated by witnesses, only two ended in nolle prosequi.[40] Although the abused partner may not have wanted her husband prosecuted, victims generally permitted the state to continue its prosecution without dropping charges. The fact that policemen, the district attorney, and neighbors could successfully file criminal charges suggests an awareness of intimate partner violence as a social problem, not simply an issue for the abused partners. For those trapped in the relentless cycle of abuse, New Orleans society attempted to solve intimate partner violence by mandatory arrest—a technique utilized in some states today.[41] Although it did not occur as frequently as victims themselves pressing charges, witnesses and officials could also intervene and prosecute on behalf of a victim, testifying to the overall dedication to eradicate intimate partner violence.

Exceptions

While many overwhelmingly recognized the importance of stopping the violence, some clung to the past and its notions of privacy, fearing society's erasure of privacy. To them, intervention appeared more like interference. They insisted that this unwarranted interference violated the veil of privacy that protected families and marriages from the demands of the larger public. Men more often than women advocated such a mentality, as they clung to male privilege and power. The push to end intimate partner violence, and women's demands for reciprocity and the right to be free from violence, chipped away at a gender hierarchy that empowered men. Men who feared the loss of family privacy hesitated to intervene. The 1886 *Traylor* case, involving an African American couple in New Orleans, illustrates some resistance to changes in gender and privacy.

On a Wednesday summer night, John Traylor came home to his wife, Mary, and accused her of having a man by the name of Jonnie Miller in the house. She insisted that no one was there and adamantly denied any hint of infidelity on her part, but John did not believe her. He began to hit his wife and threatened to kill her. At that point, Mary screamed, disturbing the neighbors, and they rushed into the Traylor home and saw John choking and beating Mary. One of the neighbors, Willie Kelly, testified: "I heard the woman screaming. He had her by the throat. The lady was down. He had her by the throat. She couldn't hardly hallar [*sic*]. . . . My father said, 'Shoot him.' I said, 'No, it may be his wife.' She got loose and ran back. She ran in the street."[42] Although his father thought differently, Willie Kelly limited the level of intervention in case the abusive man was in fact the woman's husband. Had there been evidence to suggest that John was someone other than Mary's husband, Kelly intimates, he would have shot him. To Kelly, the scene warranted use of a gun but only if the man was not her husband, and so he and his father stood in the doorway with their gun lowered. Willie Kelly may have feared legal consequences for entering someone else's home and shooting the abuser, or he may have wanted to affirm the precarious position of black manhood by not stopping the "domestic quarrel." After all, the legal ramifications of such actions could have landed Kelly in jail. Still, his refusal to do anything in the Traylor case suggests a certain amount of deference to husbands and their privilege of chastisement.

Some blatantly asserted a man's right to chastise his wife beyond the prying eyes of society. These men upheld not only family privacy but also male privilege. In 1888, Peter Carter witnessed a man beating his wife but refused to do anything. He testified in *State v. Warren Powell*:

> They got into a fuss in their room. I heard them. I did not interfere with them. He called [and] told me to come in. He said if I would not come in he would take me in. I tried to talk to him. He had a knife in his hand. I said, "For God's sake don't you use a knife!" He gave me his knife [and] hit her with his fist. She asked me not to let him beat her. He struck her two powerful licks with his fist.[43]

Carter refused to assist Annie Powell even as she begged for him to intervene. To Carter, his intervention would have actually been interference. To interfere meant that he would be acting *without any right*. From his viewpoint, stopping Warren Powell's attack would be destructive, particularly to the family and to male power. He would be meddling in the private affairs of a family and violating a husband's entitlement. After all, Carter stated, another man had been in Annie Powell's room, and she had cheated on her husband. To Carter, Annie's infidelity seemed to justify her husband's violence, and so he looked on as Warren beat Annie and she cried for help. Only when he was almost dragged into it did Carter, unwillingly, limit the level of abuse. His conscience finally registered concern when he saw the knife. Despite changes in gender expectations, social intervention, and male-female relationships, Carter upheld older notions of marital privacy and male privilege. As in the Traylor case, some male witnesses refused to intervene and punish abusers.

Some men clung to conservative definitions of family privacy and gender, even if the family included those not legally married. Social attitudes viewed family and marriage less rigidly than did the courts. If a couple cohabitated and presented themselves as partners, then community members recognized them, in everything but legal terms, as married and a family. People generally recognized that men in such situations possessed the same rights as legal husbands, but some believed that those rights included antiquated views of the male privilege of chastisement, as demonstrated in the *Mayfield* case. Louis Mayfield stopped by his house and grabbed a cup of tea before heading out to the local bars. On his way out the door, Annie Mayfield, his common law wife of five years, yelled, "You better come back instead of going out and drink all your money," but Louis left anyway and did not come back until eight that night.[44] He staggered into the house and passed out on the living room floor for a solid hour. When he awoke, Louis demanded to know where his tobacco was. Annie hesitated, and Louis screamed, "Do it when I command you!" He grabbed an oak whip and told Annie to get on her knees. As she did so, he began to beat her and told her to call him "master," which Annie did all the while she begged him to stop.[45] Finally, Louis did and shoved her out of the house with nothing on but a nightgown. Eventually, Annie found a way back into the house, but at this point, Officer Louis Deris came onto the scene after hearing a neighbor's screams of "Murder!" He saw Louis dragging Annie out by her leg from under the bed, where she'd gone to hide, and he intervened by arresting Louis and sending Annie to the hospital. Mrs. Washington Johnson, the neighbor who had alerted the police, testified:

> He was whipping the woman so long; he was whipping her until she could not speak. I told my husband that he was going to kill her; my husband told me I had nothing to do with that. Then he beat her so long that my husband had to speak to him. Then he cursed him and told him to mind his own business. He said it was his wife and he could do what he wanted. Then he dragged her in the yard to show my husband he could beat her good at that time. I got out and I halloared [*sic*] for the police.[46]

According to Mrs. Johnson's statement, both her husband and Louis Mayfield believed that men had the right to do as they wished without intervention. Only when the beating went on and on did Mr. Johnson decide to speak to the abuser, but still, he refused to go any further once he was told to "mind his own business."[47] Privacy to him stood as a pillar of the rights of manhood. He may not have gone so far as to whip his own wife, but he respected a veil of privacy to ensure a man's right to act without communal or legal interference. Louis Mayfield violently defended his power and his right to beat his wife; he asserted his dominance over Annie by beating her, forcing her to her knees, and making her call him "master." Louis Mayfield's actions here clearly illustrate intimate partner violence as an issue of power in a gendered hierarchy. To Louis, this gendered power extended beyond the legal definition of family to any relationship between a man and woman, and this belief resonated with Mr. Johnson. Louis sought to publically assert his manhood and the right of chastisement by abusing Annie in the front yard—in full view of all the neighbors. Not all men believed in such definitions of male privilege and privacy, but some definitely did.

The real intervention in the *Mayfield* case came from Mrs. Johnson, the police, and the court. Mrs. Johnson defied her husband and Louis Mayfied by running for a patrolman. Whatever the prior notions of men's power and dominance, the gender dynamic changed to some degree after the Civil War. Men had to respect limitations to what was previously considered a male privilege, and, like many women, the law agreed. To Mrs. Johnson, the abuse was wrong, and she took the responsibility to intervene in intimate partner violence. The officer arrested Louis Mayfield and pressed charges, since Annie was incapacitated at the hospital. The Recorder's Court charged Mayfield with assault with a dangerous weapon and intent to kill and placed him under a thousand-dollar bond. Finally, the judge who tried the case sentenced Mayfield to four months in jail after he had already served two months. From multiple perspectives, Louis Mayfield had violated gender expectations and Annie's right to be free from abuse. He had assaulted her with a dangerous weapon and acted in an uncivilized manner, and thus he was subject to punishment. Regardless of Louis Mayfield's or Washington Johnson's antiquated views of masculinity, male privilege, and the right to privacy, Mrs. Johnson and those who enforced and interpreted the law disagreed and enforced this new view upon those who clung to the past.

◆ ◆ ◆

As the country grew, rural areas gave way to more populated towns and cities. Communal intervention, while still important, became less effective as neighbors more often than not were strangers, and cohesive social groups stretched thin in a larger urban sprawl. People needed a more effective means of regulation and enforcement. In the last few decades of the nineteenth century, New Orleans and the rest of the South underwent a search for stability and new means of economic and social organization. The unregulated growth of corporations, labor issues, and Radical Republicans in politics pushed many Americans toward reform, even southerners who clung to tradition and the past. Increasing the power of the state offered an opportunity "to apply more effective social controls in the interest of an orderly and cohesive community."[48] In urban (and urbanizing) areas, vigilante justice became less necessary as law enforcement regulated violations, particularly crimes of assault and battery.

On each level, the people of New Orleans sought to intervene when men abused their female partners. They beat, shot, and embarrassed abusers. They provided escapes and protective measures for victims. From the family to the community, the public took a stance against intimate partner violence, and through their intervention and testimony they pressured the state to act on the problem. After all, as historian Robert Wiebe argues, bureaucratic and centralized measures were thought necessary to combat a host of societal issues efficiently and effectively.[49] People looked to the government to intervene, and under such stress, individual states reformed the legal response to intimate partner violence.

Chapter Five

"The Rule of Love Has Superseded the Rule of Force"

The Criminalization of Intimate Partner Violence in New Orleans

> In a ruder state of society, the husband frequently maintained his
> authority by force.... But [in recent times] the wife has been regarded
> more as the companion of her husband; and the right of chastisement
> may be regarded as exceedingly questionable at the present day. *The
> rule of love has superseded the rule of force.* (emphasis added)
> —**James Schouler,** *A Treatise on the Law of the Domestic Relations*

By the 1870s, legal writers on marriage began to change their views on divorce
and intimate partner violence. Prominent nineteenth-century legal scholar and
professor of law James Schouler wrote *A Treatise on the Law of Domestic Relations* in 1870, which was reprinted six times and revised into a student textbook
for law students.[1] In it, Schouler suggested a new dynamic between husband
and wife, which had implications for the "chastisement privilege."[2] Women
renegotiated new gender expectations after the Civil War, creating a reciprocal
marriage based on emotion rather than female submission. Schouler and other
legal scholars recognized this change and remarked that the antebellum male
right to chastise his wife was, at the least, "exceedingly questionable."[3] Women's
demands for protection clearly led to tangible, legal results.

In civil courts, married women increasingly sought and successfully
gained divorces from abusive husbands. With a total divorce, an abused
woman could claim her freedom without being economically devastated,
because courts generally awarded alimony and child support. In the 1870s,
the country began drastically revising divorce laws. By 1871, out of thirty-
seven states, "thirty-four permitted divorce on grounds of habitual drunkenness."[4] Temperance arguably had a significant impact on legislation, since the

majority of states recognized chronic alcohol use and physical abuse as legitimate grounds to end a marriage. Still, cruelty alone accounted for 13 percent of all divorces throughout the states during 1867–1871.[5] While not a majority, a sizeable number of judges throughout the country recognized abuse alone as reason enough to permit women a divorce; civil courts now viewed wives as semiautonomous individuals who had a right to be free from intimate partner violence.

Louisiana passed an act in 1877, strengthening a similar piece of legislation from 1870, declaring that "married persons may reciprocally claim a divorce on account of excesses, habitual intemperance, [and] cruel treatment."[6] No longer did wives need to have an additional reason besides cruelty to aid her petition for a divorce but instead could file because of abuse alone. In 1884, the Supreme Court of Louisiana put the new law to use by granting an abused wife separation of room and board. In the case of *Margaret Moclair v. James Leahy*, Moclair sued her husband for separate room and board under the charge of cruelty. She claimed that on two separate occasions after their marriage in 1881 Leahy had broken furniture, "used foul language, and struck her."[7] He also failed to provide for her, depriving her of food and medicine when she was sick. Despite prior decisions in favor of the husband, the Supreme Court of Louisiana overturned the lower courts, and Moclair's separation was granted with a provision that she could seek alimony and division of community assets in a separate case. The presiding judge, J. Poche, declared in the court's opinion: "A woman subjected to such treatment is justifiable in taking refuge with her parents and is entitled to the intervention of the laws enacted for the protection of ill-treated and abused wives."[8] Leahy failed to live up to his obligations under the new notion of masculinity as a husband and a man. He did not provide or protect his wife, and he acted brutally by verbally and physically abusing her. Consequently, the court felt that in such a situation a woman had the right to be legally separated from her husband.

Within three years, Louisiana courts moved from separations to full divorces in cases of abuse. In the 1887 case *Macado v. Bonet*, the Supreme Court of Louisiana granted the wife a full divorce from her abusive husband.[9] For years, Bonet verbally and physically abused Macado in the presence of their children, servants, and guests, and once he attempted to kill her by shooting at her with a pistol. Bonet claimed that Macado had been abusive as well—yelling, cursing, and breaking furniture. Typically, courts would not grant divorces, especially full divorces, when fault could be found with both spouses, and so the lower courts of Louisiana ruled in the husband's favor.[10] In the Supreme Court's opinion, J. Poche overturned the lower courts, saying:

To condemn a woman to live under the authority of a brutal husband whose
excesses and cruelty render her life with him absolutely unbearable, simply
because such conduct has driven her to desperation, culminating in endless quarrels with him, and in violent explosions, would be a denial of justice.[11]

The wife, then, did not have to play the passive role to be treated as a lady and
receive rights in the courts. Her husband's brutality alone constituted grounds
for divorce. Given the emerging views of manhood and womanhood, the shift
in the civil court system appears less surprising. The husband's failure to be
civilized meant that he had violated his obligation as a man and, given his
public marital vows, as a husband. Moreover, the new womanhood meant
that women possessed a certain degree of legal autonomy when victims of
intimate partner violence.

The legal precedent for prosecuting criminal cases of wife abuse originated
in 1871, when the Alabama Supreme Court ruled against a man charged with
assault and battery. George Fulgham, a black male, had been "disciplining"
one of his children when his wife, Matilda, tried to stop the abuse. George
then turned on his wife and beat her with a board. She in turn defended herself with a switch. The defense claimed that a husband had the right to chastise his wife and could not be convicted on assault and battery charges "unless
he inflicts a permanent injury or uses excessive violence or cruelty."[12] The Alabama Supreme Court denied this right, declaring the defense's argument as a
"relic of barbarism."[13] The court went on to state:

> And the privilege, ancient though it be, to beat her with a stick, to pull her hair,
> choke her, spit in her face, or kick her about the floor, or to inflict upon her
> like indignities, is not now acknowledged by our law.... [I]n person, the wife
> is entitled to the same protection of the law that the husband can invoke for
> himself.... Her sex does not degrade her below the rank of the highest in the
> commonwealth.[14]

A woman was not, Judge Thomas M. Peters argued, denied rights before the
court because of her sex. She, moreover, was not "the husband's slave" but
rather an individual recognized by the law, even within marriage. Just as
slaves once had no legal protection but gained political rights in the postbellum decades, women too gained legal personhood after the war. This pointed
reference to the Fulghams' relatively new status as a freedman and freed-
woman helped to define freedom for African Americans. Freedom, in part,
meant the right to not be abused by a partner. Moreover, the ancient privilege

of chastisement, just like the institution of slavery, was no longer accepted and indeed seen as morally wrong. Instead of protecting men who were violent against their female partners, criminal courts in the postbellum decades could and did rule against men charged with assault and battery as guilty of intimate partner violence.

Criminal Law and Legal Marriage

Before the Civil War, only two states passed legislation specifically addressing intimate partner violence—Georgia and Tennessee.[15] In Georgia's 1857 "Whipping Wife" law, the criminal code simply stated: "If a man shall whip, beat, or otherwise cruelly maltreat his wife, he shall be deemed guilty of misdemeanor and upon conviction shall be punished."[16] Tennessee's law was similar, but neither law contained specific penalties for violations. Even after the Civil War, criminal statutes in most states did not specifically mention intimate partner violence. Since most states did not pass legislation specific to the issue during the nineteenth century, criminalization and prosecution of intimate partner violence took place within the court system and was fleshed out by case law.[17]

By the mid-1870s, judges began to reinterpret criminal statutes already on the books to apply to wife beaters. Many state statutes on assault included a vague definition focusing on the intent to cause harm, regardless of the sex of the assailant or victim. This enabled a district attorney to press criminal charges against an abusive husband, and, given the demands from abused women, local communities, and organizations that the legal system address intimate partner violence, courts followed by successfully prosecuting and punishing wife beaters. In Louisiana, dockets for criminal court cases against abusive partners cited Section 796 of the Revised Statues of Louisiana, which contained genderless, open-ended definitions of assault and of punishment for assault, leaving both to "the discretion of the court."[18]

Following the criminal statute on assault, judges made rulings influenced by new social attitudes on gender and marriage. Recorder court judges in Louisiana questioned both the plaintiff and the defendant in assault and battery cases. Occasionally, the questions asked convey some bias. In 1884, for example, Adelina Lee gave testimony to the local New Orleans judge after her husband, Ben, beat and choked her until she passed out. Adelina stated: "He beat me all up and down my side. . . . I had been away from home all day to keep him from fighting me."[19] Her neighbor, Sarah Colbert, also gave testimony, stating: "I heard him ask her for something to eat and she said she had nothing. He threw the plate of victuals at her. He beat her and choked her until she was unconscious. She couldn't speak. I called watch and when the whistle blew on Clio Street he stopped."[20] Despite the plaintiff's account of the events, which was verified by a witness, the judge still asked, "Had he any right to beat you?"[21] The question suggests that the judge might have let the abusive husband go if the wife gave any indication that she had somehow provoked him. Adelina responded with one word: "No."[22] She clearly articulated that her husband had no right to beat her despite the judge's question, and Ben was sentenced to two months in prison and ordered to pay court costs.[23] The judge's question could also imply a racial bias. As the Lees were a black couple, the judge may have been seeking to rule out the possibility that Adelina had started the fight—black women were often stereotyped as more violent and less refined than white women. This line of questioning, however, resonates with antebellum cases in which white women were "guilty" of having supposedly provoked their spouses into beating them. He did not push beyond the one question about her potential culpability, however. Even if a gender or racial bias influenced his initial response to Adelina, the judge did not dismiss the case but heard her testimony and found the husband guilty. The *Ben Lee* case suggests that judges did sometimes have lingering views that were sympathetic toward the male privilege of chastisement but still were swayed by the testimony of victims seeking legal help.

As judges witnessed shifts in gender expectations, they began to employ different tactics in the courtroom instead of waiting for the legislature to change existing laws. As demonstrated in this chapter and the appendix, courts increasingly protected women's right to be free from violence, moreover in a way that extended beyond simple paternalism. A paternalistic approach would consider women as weak and in need of protection, thereby affirming male strength, but the courts went further by expressing the right of women to be free of violent attacks. Louisiana courts relied on an abused wife's sworn description of an incident, even though Section 1712 of the Louisiana Criminal Code denied the admissibility of a wife's testimony against her husband.[24] Consequently, examining case law in New Orleans as decided in the criminal court system provides vital information for understanding the state's intervention in the family and the application of new gender expectations.

One of the most frequent criminal charges in Orleans Parish, assault and battery, accounted for 40.4 percent of all criminal court cases in the parish between 1880 and 1889.[25] Assault and battery cases resulted from barroom brawls, unmannerly behavior, money issues, race-based attacks, boredom, jealousy, domestic conflict, and retaliation for verbal insults (to name a few). Sometimes an assailant only used his or her hand or fist, but often axes, cotton hooks, chairs, pots, knives, and guns were involved as well. The exact charge could be listed as "assault and battery," "assault and wounding," "assault with a dangerous weapon," or "assault with intent to murder," for example. While "assault with intent to murder" and those attacks resulting in life-threatening injuries are today usually filed as attempted murder, the court system in post-bellum Louisiana generally charged a person who sought to inflict any sort of harm on another party with assault and battery.[26] Of the assault and battery charges, cases that involved intimate partner violence made up approximately 4.2 percent.[27] While not a majority of cases, intimate partner violence–related assault and battery charges were far from negligible. In fact, the drastic rise in cases from the 1850s to the 1880s—an 800 percent increase—testifies to the newfound importance of addressing the social problem of abuse.[28]

While race mattered, by the 1880s the legal system did not perceive inti-mate partner violence cases as a means of racial control—at least not yet. Making up 27 percent of the total population of Orleans Parish in 1880, African Americans accounted for 33.5 percent of such cases during the 1880–1889 period.[29] Accordingly, African Americans made up a slightly but not significantly larger percentage of criminal charges for abuse, consider-ing the parish's racial makeup. In the 1880s, police and judges viewed the problem as a concern among whites, too; instead of race, gender remained the biggest factor influencing legal treatment of intimate partner violence. Courts did not overlook violence in a home, even if the couple was legally married. Rather, the states actively pursued and prosecuted uncivilized men for abusing their partners.[30]

The Orleans Parish courts witnessed a surge in cases involving partner abuse during the 1880s with a total of 225 cases, the high-water mark for such cases in the nineteenth century. The criminal courts had previously often relied on witnesses to verify the word of the plaintiff; otherwise, the case devolved into a he said/she said situation. In the 1880s, however, the courts began to waive the need for witnesses. Intimate partner violence frequently took place in the home, particularly the kitchen and bedroom, so a third party could be difficult to find. Rather than throwing out the wife's testimony or believing the man over the woman, as would be expected in an intact patri-archy, the Orleans Parish courts now gave priority to the wife's testimony in intimate partner violence cases. Most had no legal right to do so, but under criminal statutes of assault and battery, a judge could use his own discretion. Many interpreted this in the 1880s to include recognition of the wife's testi-mony, which chipped away at legal coverture.

In 1884, Adelina Lee pressed charges against her husband, Ben, for a sec-ond time. In her statement to the recorder's court, she relayed what happened:

I was in the yard washing and he went in the kitchen and we had some words about milk. He told me to hush and I told him I wouldn't and he hit me three times with his fist once in the nose once in the side of the face and once in the arm.[31]

No witnesses were present, nor were they required in this case. Adelina blatantly challenged the concept of a patriarchy and female passivity. She refused to "hush" when told to do so by her husband, and she pressed charges for spousal abuse. For his crime, Ben served ten days in the parish prison and had to pay court costs. Adelina's testimony was accepted as legal, and, despite her husband's denial of the incident, the judge believed Adelina and convicted Ben without questioning if she had provoked him this time. Sometimes, court documents indicated that a plaintiff would show her bruises or cuts, or that a judge would ask about obvious physical marks. The Lee case had no record that visible evidence was presented. Perhaps the transcriber neglected to mention such, but since Adelina went to the court three weeks after the incident, the judge seemed to have relied exclusively on testimony and prior history. Ultimately, the court recognized her legal right to use the courts and extended the rights of womanhood to Adelina even though she did not have a witness and even though she did not display complete submissiveness.

While women who were physically abused seemed to have better grounds for pressing charges than those who were not, women frequently discussed emotional and verbal abuse. For the courts, verbal abuse helped depict the batterer as a brute, but for the wives, the verbal, emotional, and physical abuse inflicted by their husbands all figured significantly into their grievances. With the changes in gender expectations, emotional happiness mattered to these women, and men were expected to reflect that new expectation in their behavior. In one instance in 1886, Emma Seldner sat on the porch talking with her mother and a female friend, until Emma's husband, Nicholas, started to yell at everyone. In her testimony, Emma stated that he "then came back and began abusing me and then he struck me a blow in my face."[32] Sophie Langs, Emma's mother, claimed that Nicholas "had never treated her [Emma] as a wife" and called Emma "a whoar [sic] and a dam bitch."[33] Emma spent more time discussing the name-calling than she did her husband punching her in the face, indicating that she seemed to prioritize the verbal abuse as the most significant grievance. She went on to describe how he had already called her mother "an old bitch" and did not respect any of her female family members.[34] While being hit mattered to Emma Seldner, so did the curse words. Some scholars may read this as Emma portraying herself as a lady who was offended by such language, but the court records show that Emma tried to choke her husband and possibly hit him with a brick while he was restrained and being taken away by the police.[35] To seek legal redress, women could have portrayed themselves as ladies and passive victims, but this was not always the situation, as evidenced by Emma.[36] Her testimony and actions reveal that she expected the right to be free from violence, both physical and emotional. The judge listened to everyone's testimony and found that Nicholas had acted as an uncivilized husband by insulting and beating his wife, and Nicholas ultimately spent three months in the parish prison.[37] Husbands, the court suggested in its ruling, could not resort to physical or verbal abuse without being subject to legal punishment.

Criminal Law and Extramarital Relationships

Women's sense of autonomy did appear slightly more marked in victims of intimate partner violence outside the legal institution of marriage. While intimate partner violence cases in legally recognized marriages accounted for 65 percent of the cases examined, they accounted for 79 percent of those in which the charges were dropped.[38] Nonmarital intimate partner violence cases, on the other hand, made up 35 percent of the total cases and only 21 percent of the nolle prosequi cases.[39] Although not an immense difference, the fact that unmarried women more successfully prosecuted their abusers does hint at a different ability to press charges between those legally married and those not. Legal reform in the crusade against intimate partner violence included addressing abuse in relationships outside of the institution of marriage.

Girlfriends and common law wives quickly realized that, aside from some benefits, such relationships came with limitations. Neither women nor men could utilize the civil courts to seek divorce, alimony, or maintenance for separate room and board. Because such unions were not regarded as "real" marriages, the legal system in Louisiana did not consider there to be any community property that needed to be divided, and women who were dependent upon their significant other's income in informal marriages tended to be more economically vulnerable.[40] Torts were sometimes, although rarely, a useful recourse, but generally the criminal courts offered the only legal solution for abused women in common law marriages.[41]

Courts actively prosecuted men who abused their female partners, whether the victims were in a common law marriage or simply courting, and the right to be free from violence extended to all women, as shown in *State v. William Green*. In April 1885, Lizzie Jones went out with a group of friends, but the night ended tragically with her admittance to the New Orleans

Charity Hospital. A man she was seeing, William Green, followed Jones and her friends for a while. At one point in the evening, he tried to join the group and become affectionate with her, but when his advances were refused, Green responded violently. Lizzie Jones testified:

> The accused attempted to put his arms around me. I objected and he struck me over the head with his coat that he was carrying in his arms. We had a few words there. When we left and walked up as far as Nashville Avenue . . . we had some more words. Then the accused broke a jailing off a box around a tree and struck me violently on my left side with it. He dropped the stick and struck me several blows with his hands. I told him I would have him arrested when he said they could only give him thirty days for it and when he came out he would kill me.[42]

Green's actions suggest that he felt entitled to a certain amount of compliance and intimacy from his girlfriend, and his supposed "right" permitted him to force her into submission. The courts, he believed, would only give him a slap on the wrist, recognizing a man's right to chastise his female partner, but, contrary to his belief, the courts found William Green guilty of assault and battery and sentenced him to four months in the parish prison.[43] Granted, courts generally responded in accordance with the severity of the assault and were more likely to punish someone based on the damage inflicted. His actions were indeed extreme, beating Jones with an object to the point that she was confined in the hospital for seven days and in bed at home for another ten days, but this case also showed the courts drawing a distinction between what was acceptable and what was not.[44]

Lizzie Jones's experience demonstrates that single women could and did use the legal system to deal with intimate partner violence, and the courts responded by prosecuting the abuser. Jones knew that she had the right and the ability to press charges against William Green for beating her—even if she had been romantically involved with him—and she warned him as much. The new womanhood brokered a different dynamic between men and women, one in which women expected the right to be free from violence. If men violated the expectations, then women could seek justice through the courts.

Sometimes, the courts continued prosecution when women attempted to have the charges dropped. In 1886, Henry Gibbons argued with his common law wife, Emma Connors, at their New Orleans home, accusing her of being out all night drinking. At one point, he threw a kettle at Emma, and in the conflict she landed on the furnace and burned her leg. A young African American child named Lizzie Missouri worked for the Gibbons family, who were white, washing their laundry. She witnessed the attack but did nothing at first. She knew that Henry had a history of being abusive, and Emma tended to drop charges. Although Lizzie may have not directly intervened, she shamed them by saying, "Look at you two fighting," and then ran to get a watchman despite Emma telling her not to do so.[45] Emma attempted to have the court drop charges as she had done in the past, but the state, in removing the choice from her, continued its prosecution. Emma's common law husband faced an arraignment, pled guilty, and served ten days in jail.

Female agency in intimate partner violence during the postbellum period was more complex than simply empowering the victim. Women could and did press charges of assault and battery against their abusers, and the majority of these women did not drop their suits. Sometimes, however, the victim's voice lost out to other men and women in the community. The fact that the court refused to drop the case suggests that the local judge and district attorney felt the history of abuse necessitated the state intervening and mandating consequences. Ultimately, the legal system in the *Gibbons* case took it upon itself to address the social problem of intimate partner violence, even without the consent of the abused woman. Intimate partner violence had become a public concern, and the high level of awareness about the problem required the law to act when evidence of abuse was presented to local authorities.

Courts even extended legal protections to women engaged in interracial relationships despite the growing stigma against interracial couples. In 1886, Kate Siddell, who was white, pressed charges against her African American boyfriend, Richard (Dick) Sheldon. He monitored her activities on the day of October 7 and waited outside the building where she rented a room in New Orleans. The owner, Josephine Bernard, told Siddell that Sheldon was outside, and Siddell tried to make him leave. Sheldon hit her, knocked her down, and then hit her again with a stick.[46] After he was arrested, Siddell went to the station to give a statement, and he ran up to her, yelling: "You damn white bitch." After his outburst, she pressed charges. Bernard served as a witness and testified that Sheldon's black girlfriend, Ernestine Kent, had also pressed charges against him for assault and battery, and he had served a month of jail time.[47] Given the overwhelming evidence and the prior conviction, Sheldon pled guilty and was sentenced to a month in jail. Interestingly, the court's sentence for Sheldon was comparable to those in relationships of the same race.

In another interracial relationship, the court upheld a woman of color's right to be free from violence when the abuser was white. Interracial relationships, especially between white men and black women, had a long history in New Orleans, with the practice of *plaçage* and a significant free person of color population before the war. In 1887, Ellen McClellan, a black woman, pressed charges against her estranged husband, Gerhart Koester, who was white. Before taking a trip to Texas, Koester "asked an improper question."[48] When McClellan declined his sexual overtures, he demanded that she sit on his lap, which she again refused. Koester then took out his pistol and fired off five shots, with one hitting McClellan in the leg. He was arrested and sentenced to four years in prison. Three days after the criminal trial, the local civil court granted McClellan a legal separation. In the civil trial, McClellan testified about Koester's prior arrests for physical abuse in July of that year as well as his verbal cruelty in calling her a "damned nigger whore."[49] While Koester's actions could be viewed as attempted murder and therefore more extreme than the crimes in the *Sheldon* case, Koester was guilty of intimate partner violence, which led to the court granting a legal separation and imprisoning him.

During the 1870s and 1880s, New Orleans courts intervened in intimate partner violence similarly across race, ethnicity, and socioeconomic class. Women, regardless of rank or color, possessed the same rights of womanhood, at least as they applied to protection and intimate partner violence. Officers called the victims "ladies" when they referred to them in the court transcripts, even if the woman was not white or if she was from the lower classes.[50] The rhetoric of protection and changing gender expectations created a narrow but definite space for strengthening female identity.

The Whipping Post Debate

By the 1870s, the alternative of the whipping post emerged as a punishment for wife beaters. Only Maryland passed legislation before the turn of the twentieth century permitting abusers to be whipped, and the law was largely symbolic and infrequently used.[51] Still, many states debated the merits of a whipping post specifically for wife beaters, and newspapers throughout the country carried coverage denouncing or praising the idea.[52] The *Wheeling Register*, for example, openly supported such legislation. Whipping an abuser was the "natural punishment," especially because

> four times out of five the poor bruised woman will come to testify in his favor. . . . She does this because she and her children will suffer hunger and cold if he loses his wages by imprisonment. He will go to a comfortable prison; she will suffer vastly more than he. . . . There is something in nine and thirty well laid on that lingers in the memory, and helps to make drunken husbands well behaved.[53]

Interestingly, the *Wheeling Register* recognized the complexity of intimate partner violence and the problems that arose in holding the abuser accountable. Prison sentences compounded the victim's difficulties, since she would be without a vital source of income. With the majority of women remaining out of the workforce until the 1980s, many women depended upon their partner's wages.[54] Even in working-class families, men had larger incomes than their wives, given the lack of pay equity. The whipping post offered what appeared to be a solution to the social problem without compounding the victim's sufferings with a long imprisonment of the family breadwinner and subsequent loss of income.

Other states took notice. In 1879, Missouri and Kentucky legislators introduced a whipping post bill, which led to heated discussions. In Louisiana, the *Daily Picayune* printed an article in 1881 declaring that if a man beat his wife, he should be sentenced to a whipping post, and according to the *Daily Capitolian-Advocate* in 1886, Louisiana senator Charles C. Cordill declared that he would propose whipping post legislation "at a future date."[55] Although this never materialized, the whipping post garnered some support in Louisiana.

The mid-1880s witnessed a notable increase in legislative debates largely due to the highly publicized account of the second use of Maryland's whipping post law.[56] In 1882, a lower Baltimore court sentenced a white man by the name of Frank Pyers to fifteen lashes and six months in jail.[57] Described as "a thick-set, muscular man of about 30 years, who was formerly the brakeman on the Baltimore and Ohio Railroad," Pyers had been convicted for beating his wife and causing her to miscarry.[58] Even after the public whipping, Pyers protested his innocence and stated that no white man deserved such treatment.[59] He tried to sneer or smile during his incarceration, but when he returned to his cell and was treated for the lacerations, he told the doctor, "That's a damn hard punishment."[60] Pyers spent the rest of the day in tears "from the realization of his degradation" and remained in a "dazed and half stupid condition."[61] Reportedly, Henry Myers, another white man convicted for assault and battery of his wife and sentenced by Maryland's whipping post law, sat frightened in his cell as he heard Pyers receiving his lashings. Having supposedly broken the spirit of the abusers, the local sheriff claimed the whipping post a success.

This punishment attracted so much attention at that point because the second abuser whipped was white, whereas the first Maryland flogging had been of a black man. With a white man publicly whipped, discussions on the merits of the whipping post filled newspapers. Some, such as the *Philadelphia Inquirer*, claimed that it was necessary "for the brutal and cowardly ruffians who beat their wives."[62] The abuser would "be reclaimed and society have restored to it a human being in place of the wife-beating brute."[63] Still, while several legislatures debated whipping post bills and newspapers bandied about its usefulness, advocates for abolishing corporal punishment won in the majority of states, and the whipping post did not become a legal method for curbing intimate partner violence in the vast majority of states. Legal remedies, then, rested primarily on whether the courts would try to punish assailants for assault and battery.

Nolle Prosequi

Overwhelmingly, women exhibited agency in using the legal system to uphold the right to be free from violence, but not all married women could be completely defiant. Approximately 17 percent of the intimate partner–related assault and battery cases were marked as "nolle prosequi," a term that meant the plaintiff dropped charges.[64] Women stopped prosecution of the cases for a number of reasons, varying from economic need to fear. Sometimes, the ideal that a woman had the right to be free from violence lost out to the reality of everyday life. Annie Hannewinckle, a white woman, testified when her case went to trial that she did not wish to prosecute anymore by stating, "I want peace that is all."[65] Since her husband had not made bail and had been sitting in a New Orleans jail for over a week, she felt he had served enough time. Any more time in jail would not be necessary for him to learn his lesson, Annie concluded. Moreover, she needed him out of jail so he could contribute to the family income; immediately after her wish for peace, Annie said: "For every dollar he made, I made half."[66] Annie argued that she contributed to the family, almost a point of pride, but still her income paled in comparison to his. As a family dependent on two incomes, she required his help to provide for the children, and this economic need caused her to enter a nolle prosequi plea.

Similar to the *Hannewinckle* case, Mrs. Blondeau had her husband, Gaston (both were white), arrested for slapping her after a dispute over money, but five months later she dictated a letter to the district attorney asking for the case to be dismissed.[67] She wrote:

I am unable to appear in court tomorrow at 9 a.m. as I am expecting to be confined every day at any moment. I do not want to prosecute my husband, and I beg you to have mercy on me and my two children and excuse him as this is the first time that it happened, and he is my only support. If you punish him myself and children will be the sufferers. He is good to us and it will not happen again. I made the affidavit in passion, and I am sorry for it now hoping you will grant me this favor.[68]

Gaston had served nineteen days in jail before he made bail and had been back at home for the last few months of his wife's current pregnancy. Mrs. Blondeau articulated a common problem with breaking the cycle of violence when the husband is the breadwinner—namely, her family depended on her husband's income. If Gaston sat in a New Orleans jail, he did not bring in money, and his wife and children suffered. With a third child due "at any moment," she relied on her husband even more. When faced with the choice of getting by financially or starving by forcing her husband to stand trial for beating her, she chose the economically prudent route. Solving the problem of intimate partner violence has always been a complicated issue, and unless other social issues are remedied, unintended consequences often result from legal attempts to address intimate partner violence. Mrs. Blondeau begged for mercy for herself and her children when faced with the prospect of losing Gaston's income. She would consider it a favor were the district attorney to no longer press charges. Clearly, women understood that charging their partners with criminal assault and battery could impact them and their children negatively, so they occasionally dropped charges, not because they believed the men had the right to hit them but because other social inequities forced them to make tough decisions.

Women also dropped charges because they feared the response of their partners when they were released. In 1888, Cecila Carter's husband, Ike, asked her for money. She gave him a dollar, but when he asked for more, she refused. He responded by hitting her "hard enough to make a gash."[69] Initially, she had him arrested for assault and battery, but when he made bail later the same day, she rushed into the court and begged for them to stop prosecution. The Orleans Parish court recorder asked her why, and she plainly stated: "Because I had made a charge against him and I thought he might do something to me for it." A wife could have her husband arrested for abuse, but the maximum sentence barring severe physical impairment was three months' imprisonment. Eventually, he would be released. If the abuser harbored a grudge, he could repeat the beating to "teach" her not to press charges again. Similarly, in 1888, J. O. C. Wallis arrived at his New Orleans home and beat his wife. She went to the local police station and asked Corporal Lethegue to press charges. After her husband made bail, she went to the recorder, saying, "I attach no blame to him whatever it says in my testimony."[70] Despite being beaten and sustaining two major cuts on her forehead, Mrs. Wallis told the judge that she did not want to prosecute any longer. It is likely that his presence influenced her to change her decision. Intimidation and threats of repeated abuse caused women to stop proceedings.

Some women feared what criminal proceedings would do to their public image. While wealthy wives possessed other means to remedy intimate partner violence, they still utilized the criminal courts, but such a resource came with drawbacks for even the well-to-do. On Tuesday, March 25, 1884, Augustus Richards attempted to throw away the dinner his wife, Martha, had cooked. When she tried to prevent him from doing so, Augustus choked Martha and then attacked her with a gimlet knife, saying: "I will make a Kate Townsend out of you."[71] Kate Townsend was a well-known New Orleans madam who ran an upscale brothel, perhaps the most expensive in New Orleans at the time. In 1883, Townsend was stabbed to death by her lover, leading to a frenzy of newspaper coverage. The comment, then, was not only a clear threat but also intended as an insult by likening Martha to a madam. Martha was able to ward off the blow by raising her hand, but the knife nevertheless cut her thumb. Ultimately, Augustus threatened Martha's life, hit her, and compared her to an infamous New Orleans prostitute who had met a bloody end. She pressed charges, but Augustus quickly made the $500 bail, which suggests that the Richards family was well situated financially.[72]

Although many cases involved poorer couples, Martha was not atypical for the period. Legal professor Carolyn B. Ramsey recognizes that "wealthy and middle-class husbands were compelled to appear in court on domestic assault and battery charges more often than scholars have realized," and their charges "were deeply distressing to the men involved" to the point that "prominent male defendants sometimes filed libel suits."[73] The public character and name of people mattered, and the public status of a husband could influence his wife to drop charges. On May 2, Martha personally wrote to the district attorney asking him to cease prosecution, arguing: "By doing this a family scandal will be avoided and a favor will be conferred on."[74] Martha may have dropped charges for other reasons, such as pressure from her husband, but her letter claimed that the primary reason was to avoid "a family scandal."[75] She feared for the reputation of her family if Augustus stood trial, even though he had threatened to stab her to death. Complicating the desire to end the violence, women from wealthy socioeconomic classes sometimes had to choose between the family name and seeking help from the criminal courts.

Divorce laws and economic inequality in the nineteenth century tended to fuel a woman's dependence on her spouse, and, given the psychological and emotional component in intimate partner violence, battered women sometimes took abusive husbands back.[76] Occasionally, a case failed because a husband became apologetic, swearing that he was a changed man and pleading for another chance.[77] Odelia Nelson experienced the difficulties involved in extricating oneself from a violent marriage. She lived in fear of her husband, Henry, and testified to the New Orleans court: "He is always threatening my life; he is always beating me. . . . He choked me himself."[78] Odelia pressed charges against him after one incident in February 1887. While in jail, Henry promised his undying love and never to harm her again, as he wrote: "I am sick and if you love me like I love you, you would come and get me out of this place. . . . You is my wife and you is the only one that will do for me and I will never ill treat you like I have been doing. I will respect you as long as I like."[79] But, when Odelia was not moved enough to drop charges, he wrote a longer and more emotional letter.

> My dear wife Odel,
> I love you and I will stick to you as long as I live but I will never be means to you as I was before. . . . You is my wife and I will die for you because you is good and kings for me. I was fighting for you Monday when I seen that you did not come I says I am shore [sure] that my wife is sick. My dear wife I am grieving myself to death about you. I am in all that rain and on them wet stones suffering. I hope that when I will come out that I will treat you better than before and I will worke and give you money and help you along and try to like what you like. Wife and husband I love you and I will stick to you tell I die. If you please my dear wife come Friday and bring something to eat and do not bring my close [clothes]. All the people in here treat me like a dog. My knees is sore from scrubbing. Please kiss little Charlie.[80]

Henry sought to manipulate his wife's emotions and elicit sympathy by describing his hard conditions in jail and his sickness. He also tried charming her by resurrecting any lingering emotional attachment she may have had, a tactic commonly used by batterers. Henry appears to have believed that if only Odelia would remember how much she loved him, she would feel sorry for him and release him from jail. And so he praised her for being "kings" to him. Henry even claimed that he would go so far as to die for his wife because she was so good to him. He promised profusely that he would change everything—the abuse, stinginess with money, and dislike of her personal interests. If all else did not work, perhaps his last line would. Henry ended by asking Odelia to kiss their son for him, showing that he indeed was repentant and would uphold the southern masculine role of being a kind and protective father and husband. The case subsequently ended as nolle prosequi. Manipulating several different emotions and engaging in the cycle of abuse by apologizing and promising to change, batterers could influence wives to drop charges, complicating the ability to challenge intimate partner violence.

Despite these difficulties in bringing charges against abusers, nolle prosequi results made up only a small percentage of the total cases.

Of all the assault and battery cases I examined, however, only three women expressed belief in the privacy of the family or the husband's right to chastisement. These cases account for less than 1.5 percent of all intimate partner violence cases, and only 8 percent of those that ended in *nolle prosequi*.[81] As previously discussed, in 1882, police dragged James Gillen, a white man, to an Orleans Parish court for abusing his wife. Mrs. Gillen never sought to press charges, but the watchman in the neighborhood arrested James anyway. When asked to testify on the incident, Mrs. Gillen stated: "I didn't wish to prosecute him. . . . He wanted his way, and I wanted mine. It was my fault as much as his."[82] When the judge asked where she received her black eye, she responded: "It was done in the family. I didn't wish to go against my husband."[83] Despite the police having witnessed the abuse and pressing charges, Mrs. Gillen insisted that she was accountable. She avoided providing a detailed description of the events, giving only vague responses, and she insisted that she did not want charges pressed because it was a family affair. Eventually the court consented. The case ended without finding the abusive husband guilty.

In a similar case involving a black couple, Celestine Clark charged her husband, George, with "assaulting and wounding" in 1887.[84] When required to testify, Celestine hesitated. The New Orleans court pushed her by asking if she had given him cause for the beating, and she replied, "Yes, sir, I was in the fault."[85] When asked what caused George to become violent, she stated, "Little family fracas." Celestine appears to have internalized the message that her disobedience necessitated George's physical attack. Moreover, she seemed to think that family disagreement served as enough of an explanation to the court for what had happened. To her, the court did not need to know the details of the incident, but rather it should uphold the ideal of family privacy and allow her to drop the charges. The case ended in nolle prosequi.

Similarly, in 1888, the New Orleans police arrested Warren Powell for assault and battery. Warren broke into his wife Annie's bedroom and caught her being intimate with another man.[86] A witness convinced Warren to put down the knife in his hand, so instead Warren used his fist to punch his wife twice. When asked to testify, Annie refused to blame him. She said, "I was in fault. He came in and caught me in bed with a man. I am the only one in fault. I did not ask my step-father to have him arrested. I gave him some back talk."[87] She held herself deserving of the violence since she had "back talk[ed]" and committed adultery. Despite her pleas and her adultery, the court convicted Warren and sentenced him to twenty-four hours in jail. The state found his behavior unacceptable and acted without the wife's consent for the betterment of society. Although women such as Mrs. Gillen, Celestine Clark, and Annie Powell internalized some sense of guilt or family privacy, most women still did not believe that a patriarchy entailed total female submissiveness. The majority of women in the cases denied responsibility for the violent incidents. Gender ideals had changed too much to resurrect such antiquated views, and the courts recognized the shift.

Intimate partner violence was and is overwhelmingly a gender-based problem, but men can be victims of abuse, too. They faced a far less sympathetic community and court, however. These men struggled with their own masculinity in having their wives hauled before court for assault and battery, and the courts seemed to question a man's prosecution of his wife. Men could not resurrect a complete patriarchy, but masculinity still meant that they had to hold onto their position and not be physically dominated by other persons, particularly their own wives. In 1884, a New Orleans police officer dragged Sarah Hodges, an African American woman, to the station for assault and battery. Her husband, Elijah, had asked for dinner when his wife took an ax and hit him in the face. Elijah sustained injuries including a cut lip and two loosened teeth, but he insisted that did not want to press charges.[88] Sarah pled not guilty and was found not guilty despite the serious physical damage her actions had caused.

Similarly, in 1888, Jennie Robinson struck her husband, Henry, in the stomach with a stone, knocking the wind out of him. He pressed charges but admitted his reluctance to do so. The New Orleans judge asked, "You are not very anxious to prosecute this woman?," to which Henry replied, "No, sir."[89] These men reluctantly found themselves testifying about their wives' abuse. The judges, in turn, reluctantly heard the cases and did not prosecute husband beating like they did wife beating. The testimony is brief. The wives did not even seek to cross-examine the plaintiffs, and the courts decided exclusively on what the husband said. These cases should have resulted in easy convictions, but judges acted in accordance with social views toward abused husbands. How could a husband be a "real" man if he could be beaten by a woman? The question seemed to boggle newspaper reporters and judges. Consequently, men did not commonly achieve success prosecuting their wives for assault and battery, at least in New Orleans. The *Hodges* and *Robinson* cases show the difficulty of pressing criminal charges for male victims of intimate partner violence, given the prevailing gender expectations in society and the court system.

◆ ◆ ◆

In both the criminal and civil courts, social attitudes guided legal decisions. In ruling on intimate partner violence, judges rejected the husband's right of chastisement. After all, by the 1870s, "[t]he rule of love [had] superseded the rule of force."[90] Abusive men flagrantly disregarded new gender expectations, and they invoked public outcry for violating their role as husband. Instability between partners threatened the foundation of civilization. Society tore down the veil of privacy for the betterment of the whole, and people demanded that something be done to bring abusive men in line with modern views of gender and marriage. Following case law clearly shows the shift in mentality and the reform in the legal system. In the postbellum decades, women pressed charges against abusive partners for assault and battery and sued for legal separation or divorce more commonly than in the past. And intimate partner violence–related criminal court cases had a 92 percent conviction rate for cases that went to trial.[91] Clearly, the courts viewed intimate partner violence as wrong and within the state's right to regulate. The new gender expectations presented women with an opportunity to seek legal redress for abuse, and to succeed.

Chapter Six

"It Will Be Done to Maintain White Supremacy"

The Decline of Intervention in the South

[T]he good [Negroes] are few, the bad are many, and it is impossible
to tell what ones are . . . dangerous to the honor of the dominant race
until the damage is done. . . . If it is necessary every Negro in the
state will be lynched; it will be done to maintain white supremacy.
—**James K. Vardaman,** 1897

At the turn of the twentieth century, James K. Vardaman served as state senator
and governor of Mississippi, and in the senatorial and gubernatorial elections
he touched on issues important to many southerners in the 1890s, particularly the supposed threat blacks posed to whites morally, politically, and economically.[1] Vardaman was not alone in his desire to "fix" southern society by
strengthening white control over African Americans. White southern Democrats in general utilized race and the failure of populism in the last decade of
the nineteenth century, and through their fear mongering, race became the
dominant issue in the South, surpassing every other problem the region faced,
including intimate partner violence.[2] Quickly, those in power began to deny
the existence of intimate partner violence in white communities and instead
created a fiction that the problem only occurred in the black community.

The Tenuous Cross-Racial Alliance in the 1870s and 1880s

Under Radical Reconstruction, the federal government supported local
Republican governments and tried to punish white supremacists who violated Republican rule or African Americans' rights. The 1870 Enforcement

Act in particular enabled the federal government to arrest and indict individuals for depriving African Americans of political or civil rights. Consequently, the measure led to crackdowns on the Ku Klux Klan, and about two thousand people were charged in both 1872 and 1873 under the act.[3] One of the men arrested after the Colfax (Louisiana) massacre, in which some 150 African American men were murdered, took his case to the US Supreme Court, and in the ensuing *United States v. Cruikshank* (1875) the Supreme Court backed away from Radical Reconstruction and overturned the conviction of two white men who had participated in the massacre. The ruling stated that the Enforcement Act, which based its legal standing on the Equal Protection clause of the Fourteenth Amendment, did not apply to situations involving "one citizen against another" but only to state actions.[4] States consequently were left to handle violators of African American rights without intervention by the federal government. Prosecution of violent white supremacists practically ceased after *Cruikshank*, and the level of brutality against African Americans increased, with few victims finding justice. Even before the Compromise of 1877 that ended Reconstruction, the federal government had tired of Reconstruction and become amenable to reconciliation.

When whites were questioned about racial relations in the South, such as in the 1880 *Report and Testimony of the Select Committee of the United States Senate to Investigate the Causes of the Removal of the Negroes from the Southern States to the Northern States*, they often played down the violence. For example, Andrew Currie of Shreveport, Louisiana, spoke of elections in the 1870s and denied having seen any violation of the Fifteenth Amendment at the voting booth or elsewhere. He discussed many points, including how often Republican speeches were publicly given and how "marvelous" he believed them to be.[5] When asked about his participation in the state militia during the Bossier riots in 1868, Currie argued with Senator William Windom about the number of deaths.[6] Windom claimed that *Executive Document Number 30, House of Representatives, Forty-Fourth Congress, Second Session*, in its 868 lines on Bossier Parish, provided evidence that at least 230 African Americans had been killed, while Currie fervently insisted on only 5. When pressed, Currie flippantly replied: "You do not seem to appreciate the truth." Windom retaliated in kind by stating: "I do not, from some quarters, because I hear it so rarely."[7] Despite inquiries into race relations and race-based crimes, southern whites had, for all intents and purposes, regained control of the South with the withdrawal of federal troops after 1877.

By the late 1870s, power shifted from Republicans to Democrats in the South, and the Reconstruction Amendments and Enforcement Act were deliberately being misconstrued by southern whites. The case of a black woman, Mrs. John Simms, illustrates just how much. A local election in Wilson, North Carolina, took place in 1878. Mrs. Simms told her husband, John, to vote for Republican James Edward O'Hara, but on his way to the polls John was attacked by a group of white men on horseback, beaten, and forced to drink liquor until intoxicated. The white men then made certain that John voted for the Democrat. Fearing what he had done, John hid in the woods for several days, and when he returned home he confronted an angry wife, who beat him with a hickory stick. Local officials heard of the spousal abuse and arrested Mrs. Simms, not simply for assault and battery but also for infringing on her husband's Fifteenth Amendment right. Rather than try the group of white men, the state twisted the situation to prosecute a black woman, further reinforcing white supremacy. North Carolina's case against Mrs. Simms attracted attention and support throughout the South. An article printed in the *Daily Picayune* stated: "The Democratic House will cheerfully appropriate the fees of special counsel in this case [for the prosecution of Mrs. Simms]."[8] With power shifting back to white male Democrats, intimate partner violence became co-opted to serve white racist ends.

The pivotal factor that transformed southern society and was utilized to consolidate white power was the failure of populism. Multiple economic depressions in the postbellum years hurt farmers still struggling to recover from the Civil War. Exports, which the South depended upon, dropped while credit tightened. Consequently, smaller landowners found that surviving financially had become more and more difficult. They formed organizations such as the Grange and the Farmers' Alliance to discuss productive farming methods. Others recognized that real change could only occur if a political body was formed, a goal that was realized with the establishment of the Populist Party in 1891. The Democratic Party felt threatened by the reforms proposed, such as the subtreasury plan, as well as by the loss of rural whites, who were leaving the Democratic Party for the Populist Party in large numbers.[9] Consequently, the Democratic Party adopted some of the Populist platform, and in a joint attempt to win the presidential election of 1896 by combining the two parties, the Populist Party lost all cohesion and crumbled as a political group.[10] Democrats used the failure of populism to reinforce white solidarity, blaming black farmers, who had also been strong supporters of populism, for the massive fraud and political corruption that characterized the age. Thomas Watson went so far as to say:

[M]y opinion is that the future happiness of the two races will never be assured until the political motives which drive them asunder, into two distinct and hostile factions, can be removed. There must be a new policy inaugurated, whose purpose is to allay the passions and prejudices of race conflicts and which makes its appeal to the sober sense and honest judgment of the citizen regardless of his color.[11]

White Democrats exploited the populist failure to divide the races further and ensure support for a platform of white supremacy.[12] Many rural whites subsequently returned to the Democratic Party, and with white supremacy unifying white men across socioeconomic classes, southern whites inaugurated an era of racial oppression that sought to deprive African Americans of the rights gained under Radical Reconstruction.

The Rise of an Oppressive Racial Order

The last decades of the nineteenth century gave rise to the oppressive racial order known as the Jim Crow era, but, as C. Vann Woodward argues, this shift was a choice rather than an inevitability.[13] White southerners chose to deny African Americans civil and political rights, but this did not occur immediately upon the end of Reconstruction, nor was it the only alternative.

In part, the movement started by a process of "othering." From 1850 to 1890, federal census records qualified African Americans based on the darkness of their skin. For much of the nineteenth century, censuses used two major categories for African Americans: black and mulatto (the latter term being a source of much historical debate, but for census purposes, a "mulatto" was characterized by a light skin tone).[14] Then, in 1890, there was a remarkable change in the national census forms, which now showed further differentiation of African Americans. The official categories were black (3/4 or more black), octoroon (1/8 or any smaller trace of black), quadroon (1/4 black), and mulatto (3/8 to 5/8 black).[15] How census takers were to determine the percentage or color of skin tone is not specified. Some undoubtedly relied on individuals to self-report, while others made their own judgments. While the accuracy of such census data is surely suspect and ultimately of little relevance, what matters here is that people in the postbellum decades believed in a spectrum of blackness, and with this, a specific set of rights depending on the lightness of one's skin color. The fact that the designation "mulatto" was of value in the 1870s and 1880s is not to be overlooked. Mixed-race individuals were tangible examples of race as fluid rather than polarized. Rights for mulattos, particularly in major urban areas like New Orleans, were more likely to be enforced and protected in the 1880s than for people categorized as black. Even interracial marriage was technically legal (at least in the state of Louisiana) between 1870 and 1894, at which point Louisiana reenacted its anti-miscegenation law in Article 94 of the Civil Code and subsequently a 1908 law to outlaw even the antebellum practice of concubinage between people of different races.[16]

Despite this initial racial fluidity after the war, the 1890 census report claimed: "These figures are of little value," which led to reforming the census.[17] The 1900 census simply consolidated racial categories into white and black, but this mentality facilitated depriving African Americans of equal protection of the laws under the Fourteenth Amendment. In 1890, Louisiana's legislature enacted the Separate Car Act, which was challenged by Homer Plessy in New Orleans. Plessy's trial became a focal point for segregationists seeking to maintain social stability through racial control and to undercut interracial cooperation in the wake of labor unrest. To many white locals, Plessy's octoroon status had to be understood as just black—as a means of polarizing race and curtailing any advancements in racial equality.[18] The US Supreme Court ultimately ruled on the legality of the Separate Car Act in *Plessy v. Ferguson* (1896), and the case became a precedent for state-sponsored segregation under the infamous "separate but equal" rationale stated in the opinion.[19]

Whites also sought to consolidate authority by stripping African American men of newly acquired legal rights, such as voting. The vote was viewed as an integral part of citizenship and a means to achieve total equality. After reclaiming the majority of political offices, white Democratic southerners legally deprived African American men of the vote by enacting "color-blind" laws. Politicians could not exclude individuals from voting solely because of race, not with the Fifteenth Amendment in effect, but they could find loopholes. Mississippi pioneered this southern strategy to disenfranchise black men. In the 1890 Mississippi Constitution, politicians limited voting through a number of ways. Specifically denying the vote to women, "idiots," "insane people," "and Indians not taxed," the 1890 Mississippi Constitutional Convention also stipulated that voters had to pay a poll tax of two dollars (ostensibly for public schools) and "be able to read any section of the constitution of this State."[20] Literacy tests and poll taxes circumvented the Fifteenth Amendment by not using race as a category for exclusion, but the intended target group felt the impact nonetheless. In 1867, 70 percent of African American men in Mississippi were registered to vote. By 1892, only 6 percent of black males in the state were still registered.[21] Because of their "color blindness," the laws could and did disenfranchise poor whites as well. To remedy the situation and maintain white solidarity, Mississippi created a grandfather clause enabling those individuals whose ancestors had voted before the Civil War exemption from the new voting regulations. This clause aimed to maintain the vote for all white men while the state continued its campaign to eliminate the political rights of African Americans.

In 1890, the Colored American Citizens of the United States formed and issued a proclamation to the president asking the federal government to intervene. Among the many injustices faced by African Americans, the organization pointed to disenfranchisement as the most significant issue. Participants at the organization's 1890 convention argued that the situation in the South made African Americans' position "worse than abject slavery."[22] Still, nothing was done. Groups subsequently tried to mount legal challenges. In 1898, the US Supreme Court heard *Williams v. Mississippi*, which challenged Mississippi's new voting requirements. Instead of ruling in favor of African Americans, the Supreme Court stated in its opinion that the Mississippi statutes "do not on their face discriminate between the races, and it has not been shown that their actual administration was evil, only that evil was possible under them."[23] The judges acknowledged that officials could pervert the state's legal requirements to vote, but this, they argued, did not mean that the state of Mississippi intended any form of racial discrimination. Lacking intent, Mississippi supposedly had not violated the Fourteenth Amendment, and the "color-blind" laws remained in place.

Alabama, Virginia, and South Carolina soon debated Mississippi's methods for disenfranchising African Americans. Alabama's 1901 Constitutional Convention illustrates this goal. President of the convention John B. Knox gave a speech on the "importance" of the meeting.[24] He argued that "the southern people, with this grave problem of the races to deal with, are face-to-face with a new epoch in Constitution-making."[25] Crediting Mississippi for being a "pioneer" in the process, Knox declared that Alabama had to act "within the limits imposed by the Federal Constitution, to establish white supremacy in this State."[26] Virginia's 1901 Constitutional Convention began in much the same way. At one point in the proceedings, newspaper editor and constitutional convention delegate Carter Glass claimed: "Discrimination! ... [T]hat exactly is what this Convention was elected for ... with a view to the elimination of every negro voter."[27] Including wife beating as a measure to disenfranchise would, Virginia legislators believed, aid in the goal to "eliminate the darkey from our body politic."[28]

Upholding part of the Compromise of 1877, the Supreme Court allowed the South to deal with African Americans as each state saw fit, and without federal intervention southern states quickly deprived black men of their right to vote. Alabama even devised new techniques by requiring a potential voter to be "regularly employed in some lawful occupation" and imposing a character evaluation whereby a person had to demonstrate that he understood "the duties and obligations of citizens under a republican form of government."[29] The combination of laws, fraud, and extralegal violence throughout the South effectively limited the franchise. By the early 1900s, African American voters in the South had virtually disappeared.

In order to limit the rising aspirations of the black community, southern whites also argued that black men were a threat to white women, leading white women to prioritize race over gender. As in the antebellum era, white women often capitalized on their ability to exert influence through their whiteness by accepting a patriarchal society. Moreover, the fear of black men raping white women—referred to as "the New Negro Crime"—caused many whites to panic. Against the supposed menace of the "black fiend," white women sided with white men in the campaign to instill racial dominance over all African Americans.[30] Newspapers helped create this panic by frequently publishing stories with gruesome details about alleged rapes of white women or children by black men.[31] "An Arkansas Young Lady Assaulted, Mutilated, and Murdered," which was printed in the Duluth Daily Tribune, reported on a young white female named Ada Gross who was from a respectable family. Gross's body was found not far from her parents' home "riddled with buckshot," her face "hacked by a hatchet in a terrible manner."[32] Instead of waiting "for the slow process of the law," friends and family members went after the accused and cut off his head, arms, and legs before burning him.[33] Stories like this reinforced racial stereotypes of African Americans as primitive and hypersexual, and they created terror in both white and black communities. Ultimately, they helped maintain white solidarity and dominance.[34]

The "new wave of racial violence" emerged not during Reconstruction but in the 1890s as the number of lynchings surged.[35] Terrorist mobs targeted Republicans, African Americans, drunkards, and wife beaters in an effort to coerce community members into upholding their racial and social values; lynchings at the turn of the twentieth century significantly had a "blatant connection" with race.[36] Despite attempts by W. E. B. Du Bois and Ida B. Wells to refute the racialized view of African Americans as hypersexual and violent, such stereotypes persisted.[37] People labored under the assumption, Wells argued, that white women would not consent to sex with black men, which meant that any actual sexual interaction between the two had to be rape.

Racial solidarity and the supposed protection of white womanhood required stereotyping blacks as bestial. Even white women who consented to sex with black men faced ostracism and legal consequences, which encouraged some white women to falsely cry rape when their interracial liaisons were discovered. Their male partners, of course, often met with violent reactions once the relationship became public. Ida B. Wells declared that white women were often wrongly "paraded as a victim of violence" to justify racial violence, and when some white women refused to claim rape, they were "compelled by threats if not violence, to make the charge against the victim [their sexual partner]."[38] The rhetoric of protecting white womanhood proved so strong that it cloaked racially motivated crimes against African American men. Even when fabricated, claims of a black man raping a white woman incited white southerners and provided a socially acceptable excuse to lynch a black man.

White women who had previously campaigned to protect women regardless of race redefined womanhood as an exclusively white status by the late 1890s. Despite progressive reformer Rebecca Felton's earlier pleas to extend womanhood tenuously to women of color, she gave a speech in 1897 that touched on the fear of black men's supposedly aggressive sexuality. Felton cried: "If it needs lynching to protect woman's dearest possession from the ravening beasts—then I say 'lynch'; a thousand times a week if necessary."[39] Black women, on the other hand, were left without legal or social protection from sexual assault. In January 1890, two white men from Georgia raped an African American teacher, Victoria Day. Black newspapers were the only media outlets to cover the story, and despite Day having reported the assault to the local authorities, the police did little about it.[40] Black activist publications like the *Washington Bee* and the *Sentinel* (Atlanta) demanded justice from the governor of Georgia, but their demands fell on deaf ears. The rapists, despite being identified, never faced trial.

In other attempts to limit intimate relationships between the races, miscegenation laws proliferated around the South in the postbellum period, declaring interracial sexual relations and interracial marriage illegal.[41] Historian Peggy Pascoe argues: "Miscegenation law was . . . the foundation for the larger racial projects of white supremacy and white purity."[42] Miscegenation kept the races separate, stating that the mixing of white and black bloodlines was "unnatural."[43]

With these shifts in legal and social views on race, womanhood was no longer extended to African American women. In 1891, Rosy Adams was witness to the changing attitudes toward women of color in the legal system in New Orleans. Rosy and her husband George (both black) verbally argued until George stabbed Rosy with a penknife. The recorder judge asked, as is typical in most such cases, if the defendant was the plaintiff's husband. She answered "yes." The judge pushed the question further, "your legal husband?"[44] After clarifying her marriage as a legal one, the judge then asked Rosy if she had tried to "do anything to him," and after hearing a "no," he asked another question about her potential culpability, demanding: "Did you have any weapons in your hand?"[45] Again, Rosy Adams declared "no," insisting that she had not provoked her husband or been mutually violent. The judge's apparent disbelief that Rosy had not been violent was a marked departure from most of the questions typical in cases from the 1880s. No testimony from the husband suggested that his wife had been aggressive, and, given that women in the 1880s often freely admitted to hitting or throwing things without it affecting the court case, the repeated line of questioning demonstrates a different mentality toward black women seeking legal redress for abuse. Even though she had displayed no violence and was the victim of a knife attack, Rosy Adams met with a hostile line of questioning that went beyond understanding the event under scrutiny. Although no reason was given, only a few months later she withdrew her complaint before any formal trial could be held. For women of color, womanhood no longer was a status the courts would freely grant, even if the white-dominated legal system did have an incentive to prosecute black men.

Rolling Back Reform on Intimate Partner Violence

Race dominated most issues in the South by the 1890s, including intimate partner violence. Many people began to believe that intimate partner violence only occurred in the black community because whites were supposedly so superior and civilized that they had eradicated the crime. Newspapers furthered this idea and claimed that intimate partner violence was rampant in African American households. The *State* (Columbia, SC) asked in one headline, "Is Wife Beating Still in Vogue?" The writer argued that since the subject "of negro farm hands . . . whip[ping] their wives . . . comes up for general conversation in a matter of fact way," only the black community faced this problem anymore.[46] After all, the *State* went on to say, "there is yet a lot of semi-barbarity among these [African American] people."[47] Because intimate partner violence was already considered a barbaric crime, it provided an easy means to uphold white supremacy and regulate African Americans. Racial order rested, in part, on the arguments that whites and blacks were enormously different and that whites were far more advanced. To deprive African Americans of the political and civil rights granted under Reconstruction, a threat had to be fabricated—a threat of being outnumbered by supposedly uncivilized beings. As one legislator in Virginia declared, "It was a question of self-preservation . . . a question of maintaining white civilization," whose supporters "never hesitated to vindicate the moral right of brave white men who should not be overwhelmed by an inferior race."[48] How could whites claim to be better than blacks if some male members of their race still engaged in the barbarity of wife beating? Politicians and newspapers endeavored to validate racial superiority by relegating intimate partner violence to being exclusively an African American problem.

Articles suggesting the connection between the black community and intimate partner violence appeared as early as the mid-1880s. One article stated that such violence was "terribly on the increase among members of *that* [African American] race."[49] White men, the article intimated, did not engage in wife beating nearly as much as their black counterparts. By the mid-1890s, newspaper descriptions shifted from calling black wife beaters "brutal" and "uncivilized" to using racialized descriptors, including "blood-thirsty Negro," "bad nigger," "bad Negro," "the coon," and "notorious hoodlum."[50] While negative portrayals of abusive husbands were common in newspapers during the 1870s and 1880s, racist depictions of African American abusers surged during the 1890s, coinciding with the rise of an oppressive racial order in the South that ran the gamut from racial violence to segregation to disenfranchisement. Gender no longer outranked race in the court records. Rather, race took priority in almost every issue, including intimate partner violence.

While abuse still undoubtedly occurred in white marriages, the image presented indicated that intimate partner violence was rare among whites.[51] Newspaper articles seldom mentioned race in the title of an article, particularly if the abuser was white, but by the 1890s a few headlines identifying race sprinkled the papers, such as "White Wife Beater."[52] This article told of Sam Bell, who beat his wife to the point that she was expected to die from the abuse. Given the infrequent coverage of intimate partner violence cases among white couples, the headline suggests that the situation was uncommon. In 1904, another newspaper covered the arrest of two white men who had abused their wives. The headline read "Alleged Wife Beaters Arrested on Warrants Sworn Out by Wives—Said to Have Been Drunk."[53] This was one of the first to include the word "alleged" in front of a crime that men had committed. Moreover, the men in this instance were charged with a lesser crime, disturbing the peace, rather than assault and battery, despite testimony that they had beaten their wives and children. African American abusers, on the other hand, were still reported as, for instance, "A Bad Wife Beater: Negro Convict Made an Assault on the Guard."[54] Now, more than before, race mattered in the legal treatment of intimate partner violence.

Associating intimate partner violence with African Americans also served as an excuse for white southerners to lynch black males. In 1893, an article in the *Idaho Daily Statesman* discussed a lynching of an African American man and described it as southern "justice." David (also known as Dave) Jackson supposedly had committed the crime of wife beating near Covington, Louisiana, and was summarily lynched. Once northern and western newspapers started publishing the incident as a racially motivated act, locals denied knowledge of the lynching.[55] Southern papers claimed that no one even realized that Jackson was missing from the jail. The *Daily Picayune* reported that Deputy Sheriff George Cook testified at the coroner's inquest and that he "knew nothing" about Jackson's removal from jail.[56] The lynching, he claimed, was mysterious. No one supposedly had reason to suspect anything until Jackson's body was found in a river. The coroner ruled the death a murder by persons unknown, and the case remained unsolved.

In her 1895 publication *The Red Record*, noted anti-lynching activist Ida B. Wells referenced Dave Jackson's murder. In her chapter titled "Lynched for Anything or Nothing," she said:

> In nearly all communities wife beating is punishable with a fine, and in no community is it made a felony. Dave Jackson, of Abita, La., was a colored man who had beaten his wife. He had not killed her, nor seriously wounded her, but as Louisiana lynchers had not filled out their quota of crimes, his case was deemed of sufficient importance to apply the method of that barbarous people.[57]

Seeing through the claim of wife beating, Wells condemned southern society and its lynchings. She noted that the reason for the lynching was not intimate partner violence but rather racial animosity on the part of a "barbarous people."[58] Despite northern scrutiny from whites and blacks alike, locals vociferously denied any wrongdoing. Instead, they used intimate partner violence as an excuse for white racial violence and claimed that Dave Jackson had been at fault for the crime of wife beating and "was a mean and notorious negro."[59]

The crime of intimate partner violence was also used by whites to disenfranchise African American voters. Mississippi's 1890 Constitution targeted crimes the drafters believed were specific to the black community, including theft, rape, bigamy, burglary, and wife beating, and used these crimes to deny black men the right to vote.[60] That same year, South Carolina's legislature passed a law that had the same effect as Mississippi's new Constitution.[61] Intimate partner violence qualified as misdemeanor assault and battery, and, believing that it was no longer an issue in the white community, Mississippi and South Carolina legislators included it in the list of crimes that excluded someone from the right to vote. A decade later, Alabama followed other southern states by targeting supposedly black crimes to disenfranchise African American men. Some politicians wondered if that strategy would be effective. President of the Alabama Constitutional Convention John Burns resolutely declared, "The crime of wife beating alone would disqualify sixty percent of the Negroes."[62] Legislator William Knight agreed, commenting that wife beating by itself "would settle the vexed question of negro suffrage" in Hale County, Alabama.[63] Clearly, Burns, Knight, and other white politicians believed that intimate partner violence was so prevalent in the black community that it could be used to disenfranchise most black voters. Voting disqualification based on intimate partner violence, then, deliberately served as a means of enforcing white supremacy, and the legal system had an incentive to prosecute black abusers and not white ones.

By the 1890s, southern courts were responding by prosecuting white abusers less frequently than before. The 1896 *Annual Report of the Chief of Police* of Columbus, Georgia, for instance, reported a 100 percent decrease in arrests for wife beating compared to the previous year.[64] In Columbus, then, no crimes of intimate partner violence supposedly took place, or, more likely, white abusers were ignored and black women refused to go to the police for protection, given the prevailing racial climate. The Orleans Parish local courts show a similar but far less drastic decline.

Table 6.1 Intimate partner violence Cases in Orleans Parish by Decade, 1880–1900			
Decade	Total Number of Cases	Percentage Change	Guilty Verdicts
1880–1889	225	N/A	75%
1890–1900	168	-25.3%	60%

In the 1890s, 168 intimate partner violence cases were brought to court in Orleans Parish, but clearly, as in Columbus, Georgia, some factor had generated a decline in the prosecution of intimate partner violence trials. Had legal intervention truly solved the problem within a decade or two? Were practically no men abusing their wives in the late 1890s?

Table 6.2 Race of Defendants in Intimate partner violence Cases in Orleans Parish By Decade, 1880–1900			
Decade	African American	White	Immigrant (Irish, German, Italian, Arab)
1880–1889	33.5%	56%	10.5%
1890–1900	64%	26.5%	9.5%

Due to limited identifiers in the court cases, the movements of couples, and the inaccuracy of census reporting, the race of the defendants could not be determined for many of the nearly 400 postbellum intimate partner violence cases from Orleans Parish. In the 1880s, the racial/ethnic background of the defendants could be identified in 101 of the 225 cases (45 percent), and in the 1890s, the racial/ethnic background of the defendants could be identified in

53 of the 168 cases (31 percent). Still, of those cases from the 1890s in which race *could* be determined, African American men made up the larger portion of the defendants.

When taking into account the percentage of the overall population of Orleans Parish in the 1890s, there is a disparity between the percentage of parish residents who were African American and the percentage of black defendants in intimate partner violence cases. In 1880, black men and women made up 57,617 of the total population of 216,030 (or approximately 27 percent).[65] The percentage of men tried for intimate partner violence in the 1880s who were African American was 33.5 percent (see table 6.2), only slightly higher than their percentage of the total population (27 percent). The 1900 census recorded 77,714 African Americans in New Orleans out of 287,184 total (still 27 percent).[66] And yet the percentage of intimate partner violence cases involving black male defendants for the same decade went up to 64 percent of all such cases, more than double their percentage of the total population. The prosecution of black men for abuse increased substantially between the two decades in terms of both raw numbers and percentage of all such cases. The change clearly reflected a shift in attitudes about intimate partner violence as well as the legal response. Fewer total cases meant a decline in the desire to prosecute, or the diminishing importance of intimate partner violence as a social issue. A rise in black men being tried, moreover, indicates the racialization of the criminal offense. Intimate partner violence became a problem of the black community and prosecution a means of racial control.

In a search of southern newspapers from 1890 to 1900, twenty-seven articles covering court cases involving intimate partner violence mentioned the race of the abuser, which testifies at least to the fact that the problem still existed. Of those twenty-seven, twenty (74 percent) were about cases in which the perpetrators were black.[67] Moreover, in *Ratliffe v. Beale*, a case about the constitutionality of jury selection and disenfranchisement practices in Mississippi, the Mississippi Supreme Court argued:

> By reason of its [African Americans'] previous condition of servitude and dependence, this race had acquired or accentuated certain peculiarities of habit, of temperament, and of character, which clearly distinguished it as a race from that of the whites—a patient, docile people, but careless, landless, and migratory within narrow limits, without forethought, and its criminal members given rather to furtive offenses than to the robust crimes of the whites.[68]

African Americans, the court stated, were supposedly prone to petty crimes, and these were used as new methods of disenfranchising black men. The list of misdemeanors that Mississippi, South Carolina, Alabama, and other southern states used as color-blind methods to deprive African American men of the right to vote included, among offenses such as rape and bigamy, the crime of "wife beating."[69] The courts, then, agreed with southern politicians and newspapers that intimate partner violence was a problem in the black community. Given the solidification of the Democratic Party and the racial concerns of the decade, white supremacist views influenced legal intervention as well as social attitudes in intimate partner violence. As domestic abuse became racialized as a black problem, concern dwindled except as another means to disempower African American men.

Denying the legal personhood of black men had implications for the recognition of all women as autonomous individuals in a marriage. Some southern states resurrected antebellum cases as precedents to deny women the right to be free from violence. The 1890 case of *Commonwealth v. Sapp*, for instance, rejected the testimony of white women against their husbands. William Sapp had sprinkled arsenic on a piece of watermelon in full view of his wife and then given it to her to eat. She filed charges against him, but the only evidence the prosecution had was the wife's testimony. Given that fact, the entire case rested on her word. Rather than permit her voice to be heard, an appeals court in Kentucky affirmed the right of privileged communication between husband and wife. Citing a legal scholar, the appeals court's opinion declared:

> The great object of the rule is to secure domestic happiness, by placing the protecting seal of the law upon all confidential communications between husband and wife, and whatever has come to the knowledge of either by means of the hallowed confidence, which that relation inspires, cannot be afterwards divulged in testimony.[70]

Marriage, the judges argued, required a veil of privacy. *Sapp* conceded only rare instances permitted a wife to testify against her husband, but this was not one of them.[71] For precedent, they cited the 1852 *State of North Carolina v. Hussey*, which allowed wives to give witness against their husbands only if permanent injury had occurred.[72] Since William's wife in *Sapp* did not eat the poisoned watermelon piece and did not die, her testimony was not permitted.

Sapp influenced other cases by denying women the right to act as witness against their husband. This impacted even civil trials. Citing *Sapp*, *Fightmaster v. Fightmaster* (1901) ruled a wife as ineligible to stand trial against her husband in divorce cases that involved physical abuse.[73] Often, if lacking witnesses, wives found that they were unable to press charges against abusive spouses and were sometimes unable to obtain a divorce. By the turn of the twentieth century, some states not only stopped criminal prosecutions for intimate partner violence but also ceased to grant divorces for physical abuse alone.[74] Turn-of-the-twentieth-century courts in the South showed a regression from the legal intervention against intimate partner violence that had prevailed during the 1870s and 1880s.

Popular literature of the time reflected the shift in intimate partner violence, although few authors wrote about spousal abuse, and those who did tended to do so indirectly. Unlike the majority of writers during the period, Alice Moore Dunbar-Nelson published a short story that dealt directly with intimate partner violence in the South. Paying close attention to female victimhood, she painted a terribly bleak picture of women who suffered from abuse. Published in 1899, her collection *The Goodness of St. Rocque and Other Stories* included the short story "Tony's Wife." Set in New Orleans—Dunbar-Nelson's birthplace—the story centered around a working-class Italian-German couple. They owned a small shop on Prytania Street that sold everything from oysters to coal. Described as a "great, black-bearded, hoarse-voiced, six-foot specimen of Italian humanity," the husband, Tony, treated his common law wife brutally.[75]

The woman remained nameless in the story, only called Mrs. Tony, and was depicted as "meek, pale, little, ugly, and German" with "drawn in sleek, thin tightness" and a "pinched, pitiful face, whose dull cold eyes hurt you, because you knew they were trying to mirror sorrow, and could not because of their expressionless quality."[76] Mrs. Tony worked doggedly during her relationship. She ran the store, dealt with customers, cleaned house, shucked oysters, and even made lace to sell to the locals for additional income.

The abuse was no secret, but, despite widespread awareness, no one intervened to stop it, not even Mrs. Tony's mother. The young neighborhood children, upon noticing the bruises, only muttered, "Poor Mrs. Tony."[77] When her husband became sick, Mrs. Tony begged him to formalize their marriage with the priest, but he refused. Upon Tony's death, his brother inherited the shop and all its cash; Mrs. Tony was forced to leave the home and shop with nothing but "her bundle of clothes."[78] Despite having acted as an obedient wife and endured Tony's abuse, she received no protection from spousal abuse or poverty.

In "Tony's Wife," Dunbar-Nelson illustrates the vulnerability not only of women in common law marriages but also of immigrant women of the lower socioeconomic classes. Mrs. Tony was at a disadvantage for not being legally married. Without the state's recognition of her common law marriage, she inherited nothing, leaving her economically devastated. She also faced prejudice because of her working-class status and ethnicity. Despite New Orleans's large immigrant population, discrimination against "nonwhites," particularly Italians and Germans, rose during a period when nativism dominated.

Dunbar-Nelson also drew from other elements of her personal life. During her engagement to her first husband, the poet Paul Dunbar, Alice was raped by Dunbar, and he continued to abuse her both verbally and physically after their wedding.[79] She endured four years of such treatment before separating in 1902, and only with Paul's death did she achieve complete freedom from the abusive marriage. Arguably, her affluent status enabled her to secure a life separate from him, including another home, but Dunbar-Nelson could not dissolve her marriage because of changes in southern treatment of intimate partner violence. Like Mrs. Tony in the story, many southern women in the last decade of the nineteenth century lost social support and legal recourse for addressing abuse. The options for women facing intimate partner violence in the South worsened after the 1890s.

◆ ◆ ◆

"Tony's Wife" presented the reality experienced by many southern women at the end of the nineteenth century. As intimate partner violence became racialized, all abused women suffered. The racialization of intimate partner violence meant that African American women received legal assistance only as a method of maintaining white, male power. Often, intervention took place as an excuse to disenfranchise or lynch black men, and attention to African American abusers helped whites label people of color as barbaric and primitive. Black women fortunate enough to have money could seek separate room and board and perhaps (if legally married) a full divorce, but they were denied any other civil or criminal action.

The shift impacted white women as well. The racialization of intimate partner violence necessitated the denial of the very real presence of violence among white couples. After all, southerners claimed, intimate partner violence had been eradicated in the white community, so what need was there to raise awareness or legal resources for white women? In instances when white men were found to be excessively violent, courts funneled such cases to a local branch of the Society for the Prevention of Cruelty to Children or to family courts, which prioritized family stability above fixing the problem of intimate partner violence.[80] Intervention became unnecessary in white couples, since, one newspaper claimed, intimate partner violence was a "rare crime," and women resented interference given "the fact that the women whipped by their husbands seem to enjoy it."[81] Socially and politically, white men benefited, and their dominance was secured for another few decades. Women, regardless of race or socioeconomic class, lost. On the most intimate level, women remained vulnerable to the dynamics of power, concentrated in the hands of men, until the women's liberation movement of the 1970s. For the better part of a century, the veil of privacy would protect the white southern male privilege of chastisement.

Epilogue

Gender and Intimate Partner Violence in the Early 1900s

The man, a drunk and wasted earnings . . . the Mother, a good
woman. . . . The woman was afraid to talk, knowing that it would
mean a beating from her husband if he found she said a word against
him. . . . [He was] put on probation to show he was a better man.
—**Louisiana Society for the Prevention of Cruelty to Children,**
case no. 5606, 1911

On January 13, 1911, a caseworker arrived at 2731 Charters Street in New
Orleans on reports of domestic troubles in the family. The caseworker took
notes on the investigation, remarking on the intemperate husband as well
as the obedient and dutiful wife.[1] The submissive and ultimately "feminine"
gender performance of the wife, then, entitled her to some sort of intervention, but as alcohol was deemed the culprit to the abuse, the husband was
ordered to act in a more respectable (ergo "manly") way. No one—not family
members, the community, the caseworker, or the court—sought to punish
the abuser. Rather, the first and foremost goal centered on keeping the family
unit together, despite evidence of repeated violence. The South's racialization
of intimate partner violence in the 1890s had already made legal reform but a
mere sham, aimed at upholding white supremacy; but with the ascendancy of
science and growing reliance on expertise in the early 1900s, the response to
intimate partner violence shifted, again, in the South and finally ended in the
North. In New Orleans and the rest of the nation, intimate partner violence,
especially in legal marriages, fell once more under the veil of privacy.

At the turn of the twentieth century, progressives believed that experts in
individual fields could determine the most effective solutions to the problems American society faced, and these professional authorities increasingly
provided new policies for a host of social ills. Courts across the nation relied
on psychologists and social workers to fix problems in marriages, thereby

effectively transferring the issue of intimate partner violence from the
authority of the courts to the realm of science. Family counselors during the
period, instead of holding the abuser accountable, looked to the individuals
in the marriage to find internal conflict that manifested itself in violence.
Often, this meant that the victim of intimate partner violence faced anything
from psychotherapy to instruction on sexual hygiene—all aimed at changing
the woman.

The Field of Science and Views of Gender

The ideological trend in psychology and social work at the turn of the twentieth century tended to view gender expectations conservatively. Experts in science increasingly vocalized their disapproval of changing relations between
the sexes as advocated by the suffrage movement and the National Women's
Party (NWP). Granting women the right to vote, in particular, drew the ire
of some experts. American biologist William T. Sedgwick pronounced the
"feminist propaganda" of suffragists as the "best example of biological bosh."[2]
Sedgwick and other anti-suffragists such as W. L. George argued that the
equality of the sexes denied the "natural" biological principle in which the
male asserted dominance over the female. Moreover, they claimed, such "revolutionary" ideas "would mean degeneration and degradation of the human
fibre," including "total destruction of wifehood and the home."[3] If women
continued to demand change, they argued, society would suffer. Women voting would upset the "natural" balance of power between the sexes and bring
chaos to society by destroying the most basic social unit—the family. To
biologists and others in the medical and scientific profession, nature dictated
the relationship between men and women. The home supposedly needed a
dominant male.

Natural law and resistance to the modern woman formed the basis of
many scientific arguments on the roles of the sexes. Another doctor, Abraham
Myerson, stated in his 1920 book, *The Nervous Housewife*: "The husband dif-
fers from the wife in this fundamental, that essentially he is not a house man
as she is a house woman."[4] The book discussed women who suffered from
physical and mental complaints that resulted from different neuroses. Myerson found several reasons for female disorders, with most caused by tension
resulting from modernity. He found that strain suffered by women who had
adopted "manly" behaviors and dress—a concept he called "feminism"—was
a common problem that led to a multitude of diseases that harmed marriages.
Myerson proposed a solution to marital problems, saying:

If only one will is expected to be dominant in the household, the man's, then there can arise no conflict. If the form of the household is unaltered, but if the woman demands its control or expects equality, then conflict arises. If a woman expects a man to beat her at his pleasure, as has everywhere been the case and still is in some places, if she considers it just, brutality exists only in extremes of violence. If she considers a blow, or even a rough word, an unendurable insult, then brutality arises with the commonest disagreement. In other words, it is comparatively easy to deal with a woman expecting an inferior position. . . . [I]t is very much more difficult to deal with her modern sister.[5]

To Myerson, abuse was a relative term that only younger women of the modern generation identified as a problem. If women accepted "natural" gender roles, then domestic harmony would reign. Although he did not advocate spousal abuse as pointedly as others did, Myerson weakened anti–intimate partner violence arguments by claiming that recent changes in women's expectations had created the problem, not the abuse itself.

Some extended the rationale of the law of nature and argued that male domination in the home meant resurrecting and protecting the male privilege of chastisement. In 1913, Dr. William F. Waugh, dean of Bennett Medical College and chief surgeon of the Jefferson Park Hospital in Chicago, declared "wife beating as a wholesome and proper discipline."[6] Like George and Sedgwick, Waugh believed that marriage rested on "natural" biological differences between the sexes. Once a man married, Waugh advised, "rule her. . . . When she awakens your jealousy, beat her; she needs it."[7] For Waugh, fear and power rested as the cornerstones of every good marriage. If a wife feared her husband, she would be devoted and the marriage would be a success (defined as stability, not harmony). Women in marriage, to these experts, did not need protection or legal recognition as autonomous individuals because doing so would compromise the husband's position and thereby the marriage itself. Abuse, then, served as a method to maintain a supposedly good marriage based on natural law.

Other articles at the turn of the twentieth century also tapped into the scientific community's fascination with masculinity and men's primitive roots; these specialists sought to redefine gender expectations based on male dominance and female obedience. American psychologist G. Stanley Hall and others in the profession like Waugh believed that industrialization and civilization placed manhood in danger. Men became sick and developed nervous "diseases" such as neurasthenia from becoming too civilized and consequently too effeminate. To recapture their masculinity, Hall advised men to embrace their primitive heritage during childhood and emerge as adults with a defined, aggressive masculinity.[8] Waugh agreed, stating: "There is a constantly thickening coat of varnish of civilization formed over the man and the woman, but underneath it they are identical with the cave man and the cave woman, unchanged at heart."[9] Men and women were ultimately, Waugh argued, no different from cave dwellers from centuries earlier, and for the sake of their own mental health they should accept their primitive instincts and the "natural" order of society. This included men's privilege of chastisement, since spousal abuse was, Waugh declared, "natural." His argument, and medical authority in general, helped to gain societal acceptance of curtailing anti–intimate partner violence efforts by supporting conservative gender expectations and placing wife beating beyond the scope of the law. Experts, utilizing their professional authority to redefine gender expectations yet again, were at the root of rolling back reform. Although such medical and scientific views facilitated the retreat from intervening in instances of wife beating and punishing the abuser, the real damage to anti–intimate partner violence efforts came with the alliance between the medical profession and the family courts.

The Growth of Psychology and Social Work

Psychology and psychotherapy gained momentum in Europe during the mid-to late 1800s, but the United States did not develop this scientific specialization until closer to the turn of the twentieth century.[10] The field of psychology in America was shaped in large part by an advocate of aggressive masculinity, Stanley G. Hall, and in the 1880s clinics, medical literature, and professional degree programs began to proliferate. Hall founded the American Psychological Association in 1892 and served as the first president to promote the interests of psychologists and consolidate professional authority. Influenced by Sigmund Freud's work, some American practitioners inaugurated the *Journal of Abnormal Psychology* in 1906, which was dedicated exclusively to Freud's theories and psychoanalytic methods. The popularity of psychoanalysis led many professionals to fear that nonmedical laypersons would begin practicing the art, thus diluting the medical authority the rising field sought to establish. To keep professional authority exclusive to psychologists, practitioners created the American Psychoanalytic Association (APsaA) in 1910. The APsaA quickly issued training requirements and guidelines for the emerging specialty, and psychology and psychotherapy gained considerable influence in the first two decades of the twentieth century.

Social work, closely related to the growing field of psychology, blended reformers' goals with psychology. Social work initially sought "to bring about social reconstruction . . . [with] the family as its unit."[11] The individual mattered only to the extent that he or she could be brought to "the best adaptation within the present social order."[12] Social workers in the early 1900s, then, largely carried out their work in accordance with the notion of the family and family stability; as Dr. Ernest Mowrer and Harriet Mowrer argued, family was "an asset to social organization and well-being."[13] Starting in 1898, universities began to offer classes on helping children and families through home visits. With its newly formed expertise in marriage, the field of social work, along with psychology, dominated new solutions for intimate partner violence.

These fields grew so rapidly that specialized clinics, offering such services as family therapy and marriage counseling, started appearing as early as the 1910s and 1920s. To solve problems, whether personal or social in origin, these specialists used a counseling method that taught people to reflect on their inner conflicts. Even victims of violence were told to find suppressed desires, usually sexual, and come to terms with them. Typically, suggestions for personal change accompanied the treatment, which sent abused women on a host of personal makeovers intended to please their husbands. None sought to punish the abuser. Mental healthcare workers wanted to reconstruct the family instead by having abusers examine themselves and change their own attitude or behavior in order to better the relationship. Success, the Mowrers agreed, resulted when an individual had achieved "conformity of overt behavior to the dictates of the group."[14] Essentially, a stable family mattered more than individual needs.

Further Rolling Back Legal Reform

In 1910, the US Supreme Court reaffirmed the role of medical experts in establishing the sanctity of the family by removing intimate partner violence from the domain of the courts. Jessie Thompson sued her husband, Charles, in Washington, DC's, civil court, attempting to collect $70,000 in damages for assault and battery inflicted when she was pregnant. Despite undeniable proof of abuse, Jessie lost the case. Wives of the time generally did not succeed in torts against their spouses, but the Supreme Court's ruling went beyond denying Jessie the right to collect money for damages caused by her husband. Many states previously passed legislation allowing married women to contract business independently, provide testimony against their husbands in felony cases, and hold possessions as individuals. These laws permitted women some level of economic and legal autonomy, but in the 1910 *Thompson* case, the justices declared: "At the common law the husband and wife were regarded as one. The legal existence of the wife during coverture being merged in that of the husband."[15]

The various late nineteenth-century changes establishing the legal autonomy of a married woman did not, according to the *Thompson* decision, include a woman's right to sue her own husband, even if she suffered permanent physical damage as a result of abuse. The Supreme Court argued that the right of a wife to sue her husband would set a "radical" precedent and lead to "destruction by the statute of the unity of the married relation."[16] Essentially, such a legal right would destroy the institution of marriage. Moreover, Judge William Day claimed, it would "open the doors of the courts to accusations of all sorts of one spouse against the other and bring into public notice" domestic issues.[17] With *Thompson*, the highest court in the country reaffirmed the privacy of family and set back decades of work in combating intimate partner and family violence. The Supreme Court categorized intimate partner violence as a private issue that was beyond the scope of the criminal and civil court system. Allowing the public into a couple's relationship, the *Thompson* decision stated, to promote "the public welfare and domestic harmony is at least a debatable question."[18] The statement insinuated that marital peace could best be achieved by protecting family stability by protecting privacy, which hindered the ability to hold abusers accountable. Legal reform regressed, and, after four decades of opening, the veil of privacy fell back over the family finally in the North.

Heavily cited in the years following, *Thompson* established a legal precedent for rolling back the wave of marital violence reform.[19] The state of Minnesota heard a similar case in which a wife attempted to sue her husband for damages. In *Drake v. Drake* (1920), Minnesota's courts decided against both the husband's and the wife's claims. The husband sought to enjoin his wife for "nagging" him, but the Minnesota court found the examples vague and without legal basis.[20] The wife countered that her husband was a habitual abuser and that the level of violence entitled her to a divorce. The court dismissed her argument as well, claiming that nagging and intimate partner violence were "matters of no serious moment" because, if only the couple slept on it, the events "would silently be forgiven or forgotten."[21] The court declared that the public had no right to intervene in the couple's supposedly petty problems and that women, despite recent legislation granting them economic rights, were subsumed under their husband's identity according to the common law definition of coverture. *Drake*, like *Thompson*, confirmed spousal immunity from torts, the common law definition of married women as coverture, and the privacy of family, but *Drake* also reduced wife beatings to "trivial family disagreements."[22] Serving as a legal affirmation to social attitudes, *Thompson* and *Drake* illustrate that American interest in addressing intimate partner violence had officially ended by 1920.

Even as the criminal and civil court system declined to address intimate partner violence, abuse still posed a threat to the stability of the family unit, and, as a result, many states created a new type of court to deal specifically with issues relating to the family and to give experts the power to solve the various problems categorized as marital discord. The country's first family court emerged in Buffalo, New York, to deal with a wider range of family problems, and these courts proliferated such that by the late 1920s there was at least one family court in each state.[23] Family courts primarily sought, as historian Elizabeth Pleck observes, to "preserve the family, act in the best interest of the child, and offer a curative rather than punitive approach to family problems."[24]

Despite Judge Day's claims in *Thompson* that women could seek divorce in civil courts, the creation of family courts facilitated the retreat from addressing intimate partner violence even there. The new courts actually decriminalized violence between family members. After all, progressives believed that family violence was caused by preventable conditions, such as poverty. Abuse, then, was not a suitable focus for the new courts. Increasingly, they started to rely upon professionals in science and medicine, who influenced the discussion on spousal abuse by asserting their expertise. Some criminal courts explicitly denied the right of anyone to interfere in domestic abuse issues by the first decade of the twentieth century, but when most courts began referring cases of intimate partner violence to family courts, the impact was the same.[25] Intimate partner violence was sidelined as a lesser issue, or as a result of poverty or immorality.

Family courts utilized these new social and mental healthcare workers and their methods, often assigning newly trained psychologists and social workers to handle cases. Abuse was the most widely given reason for court-mandated psychological therapy in the 1920s.[26] Psychologists, however, did not seek to treat the abuse but rather sought to uncover the reason for the conflict. In their analyses, psychologists cited Sigmund Freud's views on subconscious desires and repressed sexual urges as reasons for marital discord. Professionals pointed to sexual adjustment and loose gender roles as the two most frequent underlying problems leading to intimate partner violence. The solution, then, was to teach women to be obedient and dutiful wives.

One Chicago case sent for therapy involved a Mr. and Mrs. "A," who had been married for eleven years. After the birth of their sixth child, Mrs. A left her husband and returned to live with her parents, claiming that Mr. A was abusive. She told the caseworker that she believed returning to her husband "would only mean more children for whom they cannot provide adequately."[27] To solve the problem, the caseworker provided the wife with birth control and sexual hygiene information. No attempt was made to counsel the husband. To the courts and the psychologists, the solution lay not with stopping the violent husband from abusing his partner but with honing the wife's ability to limit their family size and keep her genitals clean enough to satisfy her husband's olfactory and sexual desires. She had to change, and the family had to be maintained.

In another long-term case, the courts and social workers followed a Mr. and Mrs. B for eleven years, trying to keep the couple together. The husband and wife found themselves in the Chicago family court after being denied a legal separation. As in many of the other cases, the wife claimed that her husband abused her and had a violent temper, and the husband accused his wife of bad housekeeping and nagging. The caseworkers visited the home and found the house "in a terrible condition, the bed was unmade, everything was dusty and dirty, and the children were dirty and half-dressed."[28] Mrs. B asked for help to leave her husband, since the abuse and conflict were too much for her to endure any longer. The caseworkers refused. Instead of helping a victim of abuse, they found the party at fault to be the wife. The caseworkers called her selfish and jealous. They told her that she nagged her husband excessively and needed to "realize her responsibility as a wife and mother" by serving her husband's meals on time and by learning good housekeeping, "if she wishes to command the respect of her husband."[29] Here, as in the other cases, the medical profession wielded authority to shape public policy and ensure that the family remained together. This new goal directed interventions, and women found the courts less capable of providing a real solution. No longer did legal intervention provide assistance for a separation, for criminal punishment, or for counseling of the abuser. In the view of social workers and the new family courts, intimate partner violence mattered less than the preservation of the marriage.

The new trend in medicine and the law also took responsibility away from the abuser and redirected blame toward the wife. Victim blaming pointed to a larger issue. If the legal, medical, and social resources for abused women did not seek to solve the problem, then what purpose did they serve? By the 1920s, they effectively acted as a method of controlling gender expectations and dynamics in marriage. Many men resented the changes in women's roles, from women's increased participation in the workforce to their demands for the right to vote, and punishing wife beaters chipped away at what had been for centuries a male privilege. Rolling back the reform to end spousal abuse helped, in some way, to resolidify male authority in the home. At the very least, men were not being demonized or punished for their violence, which reaffirmed a basic level of power over their female partners. Mental professionals and legal officials further upheld conservative gender expectations by training women in the standards of good housekeeping and submissiveness.[30] Reclaiming an aggressive, powerful masculinity effectively eroded some gains women had made in the late 1800s, particularly the right to be free from violence.

By the first decade of the twentieth century, scientific experts were directing new public policies that dealt with family violence. These influential experts contested gender expectations again, claiming that natural law required men to be dominant and women to be submissive. Violence in a marriage, some argued, was simply a method of control, to be interpreted as the male privilege of chastisement rather than a violation of a woman's right to be free from violence. The criminal and civil courts resurrected the concept of family privacy and relegated intimate partner violence to the family courts, psychologists, and social workers.

Family courts and the medical profession helped to establish a new method of "treating" intimate partner violence. Abusers no longer were the focus, but rather the victims came under scrutiny. In court-mandated therapy, mental health professionals examined the intrapsychic tensions of the individual. After all, Harriet Mowrer claimed, domestic conflict came from "disorganization of the personality [and] leads to greater emphasis upon the personal development and social experiences" of the couple.[31] Often, however, the only partner who attended counseling sessions was the wife, which meant that treatment revolved around changing her. These women, health professionals claimed, needed to become good housekeepers and sexually available to their husbands, and so counselors led wives down a long, never-ending path of self-excavation, asking what they could change to make their marriage better. In doing so, medical professionals co-opted efforts to end intimate partner violence.

Conclusion

Between 1846 and 1920, men and women continued to contest the definition of womanhood. How did society expect a woman to behave? What rights did a woman have? How would power be distributed in a woman's relationship with a man? These questions yielded different answers over the years, as competing images of manhood and womanhood clashed and the varying gender expectations that had dominated across the decades influenced the sociolegal response to intimate partner violence and abused women.

Examining intimate partner violence during the postbellum decades reveals an interplay of complex factors. As historian LeeAnn Whites writes, "gender matters."[32] In the lives of these women, the social construction of gender had real, tangible consequences. The fluid definition of womanhood permitted some sense of agency to claim women's right to be free from violence in the decades after the Civil War, but by the 1890s in the South and the 1920s in the North, society's view of women enabled men to use nonlethal violence against their female partners without fear of punishment. This had serious implications for women's emotional and physical well-being.

Social expectations for men and women are significant because they affect people's lives. These gender ideals are more than just abstractions that provide mental exercise; they matter because they can influence who has the fundamental right to be free from violence. People interpreted and reinterpreted gender, and they interpreted and reinterpreted the proper method for addressing battered women and abusive men. Sometimes, society recognized the right of a woman to be free from violence and demanded government intervention to punish the abuser. Other times, people thought that women caused the violence, and the courts utilized intimate partner violence as a measure of social control. Gender expectations as well as legal reform influenced social responses to problems, and those social views on gender both advanced and reversed progress.

The history of intimate partner violence did not follow a linear progression toward eradicating the problem. The issue did not emerge from the shadows for the first time in the 1960s and 1970s. Instead, Americans in the late 1800s addressed the problem of intimate partner violence and pursued some sense of justice for victims, if only for a few decades. The problem of intimate partner violence was brought out into the open and confronted. Women made concrete advances in the 1870s and 1880s toward the right to be free from violence. Abusers faced social condemnation and legal punishment for their actions. But then, in the 1890s, intimate partner violence was permitted to slip back under a veil of privacy and silence. Like a wave, the reform crested and receded, negatively altering women's position before the courts and in their relationships with men. Turn-of-the-twentieth-century solutions to intimate partner violence became a perverted method of social control, posturing as a righteous cause but all the while privileging one group at the cost of another. Rather than showing steady momentum toward a solution to gender-based violence, the erratic history of intimate partner violence illustrates the drawbacks of perceiving the passage of time as the equivalent of progress. Such a mentality glosses over the lived realities of actual people, such as abused women in the early twentieth century, and in doing so perpetuates a harmful myth of progress. This conclusion perhaps does not offer solace to the modern-day movement against intimate partner violence, promising that things will get better over time, but it does encourage more critical analysis of the multifaceted problem of intimate partner violence and the way shifting beliefs about gender have shaped American society's reactions and responses.

Appendix

State	Year	Case	Ruling
A.1. Intimate Partner Violence and State Supreme Court Cases in the Rest of the South			
Alabama	1870	*Turner v. Turner*	If husband pulls hair or strikes wife, the courts regard this as cruelty and permit divorce *a mensa et thoro*.
	1871	*Fulgham v. State*	Use of weapon for moderate correction of wife no longer legal.
	1876	*Anonymous* (names withheld; 55 Ala. 428)	Court decides in favor of wife for divorce due to husband's "ill usage" and "cruelty"; child custody given to wife.
Georgia	1870	*State v. Miller*	Husband guilty of wife beating (no sentenced mentioned).
	1880	*Georgia v. Sampson*	Husband guilty of wife beating (no sentence mentioned).
	1881	*State v. Bush*	Husband guilty of wife beating, jail time.
	1885	*State v. Hutchins*	Husband guilty of wife beating, 8 months in chain gang.
		State v. Saunders	Husband guilty of wife beating, 6 months in chain gang.
		State v. Garner	Husband guilty of wife beating, 20 days.
		State v. Russell	Husband guilty of wife beating, 20 days.
	1887	*State v. Brooks*	Husband guilty of wife beating, 25 days.
		State v. Anderson	Husband guilty of wife beating, 20 days.
		State v. Bankston	Husband guilty of wife beating, 25 days.
	1888	*State v. McFarland*	Husband guilty of wife beating, $50 or 6 months.
	1889	*State v. Gage*	Husband guilty of wife beating, 9 months.
		State v. Garrett	Husband guilty of wife beating, 12 months.
	1890	*State v. Angling*	Husband guilty of wife beating, 6 months.

State	Year	Case	Ruling
Kentucky	1883	*Richardson v. Lawhon*	No longer recognized right of chastisement.
Maryland	1874	*State v. Bly*	Husband guilty of assault and battery, jail time.
	1883	*State v. Foote*	Husband guilty of assault and battery, 60 days and 7 lashes (appeals court upheld whipping post sentence).
	1884	*State v. Lyons*	Husband guilty of assault and battery, 24 hours.
	1885	*State v. Meyers*	Husband guilty of assault and battery, 1 year and 20 lashes.
		State v. Pyers	Husband guilty of assault and battery, 6 months and 16 lashes.
	1889	*State v. Hebert*	Husband guilty of assault and battery, 5 days, 15 lashes.
Mississippi	1882	*State v. Turner*	Wife ruled competent witness against her husband for assault and battery.
North Carolina	1868	*State v. Rhodes*	Repudiated "rule of thumb" but upheld male privilege of chastisement.
	1870	*State v. Marbery*	Stricter limitations on interpretations of abuse v. chastisement.
	1874	*State v. Oliver*	Ruled that men did not have right to correct partners.
	1877	*Taylor v. Taylor*	Abuse of wife (whipping in this case) cause for divorce.
	1878	*State v. Driver*	Supreme Court ruled husband guilty of assault and battery but 5-year sentence of lower court extreme.
	1879	*State v. Pettie*	Husband guilty of assault and battery, 2 years in jail.
	1884	*State v. Huntley*	Ruled wife beating jurisdiction of courts, not justice of the peace.
South Carolina	1880	*State v. McKittrick*	Ruled wife beating jurisdiction of courts, not justice of the peace.
Tennessee	1889	*State v. Bradford*	Husband guilty of assault and battery on wife, sentenced to workhouse.
Texas	1879	*State v. Owens*	Wife ruled competent witness against her husband for assault and battery.
	1886	*Bramlett v. State*	Husband guilty of assault with intent to murder, 2 years in jail.

State	Year	Case	Ruling
Virginia	1890	*State v. Hauser*	Husband guilty of assault and battery, jail time.
West Virginia	1877	*State v. MacGruber*	Husband guilty of assault and battery, 30 days and $10.
		State v. Dargen	Husband guilty of assault and battery, 30 days and $5.
	1881	*State v. Little*	Husband guilty of assault and battery, 30 days and $5.
	1884	*State v. Hill*	Husband guilty of assault and battery, 30 days.

All cases involving "State" are criminal court cases. Cases involving two individual names are divorce cases. As seen in the table, the vast majority of southern states addressed intimate partner violence in the 1870s and 1880s by criminalizing "wife beating" or revoking the male privilege of chastisement. Aside from Tennessee and Georgia, all other states (including Louisiana) used assault and battery criminal statutes already on the books and admitted the wife's testimony, which had previously been excluded.

All Louisiana Supreme Court cases were civil and not criminal, thereby dealing with the dissolution of marriages rather than criminal punishment for abusers.

A.2. Intimate Partner Violence and Louisiana State Supreme Court Cases, 1840–1900			
Decade	**Year**	**Case**	**Outcome**
1840 to 1861	1840	*Headen v. Headen*	Granted separation on grounds of repeated cruelty.
	1841	*Rowley v. Rowley*	Rejected separation but permitted claims to monetary compensation for lost property and control over paraphernal estate.
	1849	*Armant v. Her Husband*	Granted separation of room and board for repeated physical ill treatment.
	1851	*Sarah Jane Leake v. T. P. Linton*	Granted separation of room and board, not full divorce, no claim to paraphernal property.
	1857	*Henrietta Trowbridge v. C. T. Carlin*	Rejected separation.
	1860	*Marie Lauber v. Joseph Mast*	Rejected separation of room and board but permitted wife's control of paraphernal property.
	1860	*Mary McVey v. Joseph Holden*	Rejected separation and wife's claims for control of property.
1861 to 1890	1866	*Mrs. E. A. Halls v. J. A. Cartwright*	Rejected separation on grounds of habitual intemperance, cruelty, and dereliction of duty.
	1882	*Marie L. Cass v. Charles L. C. Cass*	Rejected of separation for cruelty and public defamation.
	1882	*Cordelia Terrell v. J. R. Boarman*	Rejected separation of room and board due to insufficient evidence of cruelty.
	1884	*Margaret Moclair v. James Leahy*	Granted right to separation of room and board; alimony and property claims left open for further suits.
	1885	*Aurore Blanchard v. Henry Baillieux*	Granted separation of room and board; custody of children granted to wife.
	1887	*Mack v. Handy*	Granted separation of room and board on grounds of habitual intemperance chiefly but granted a year for possibility of reconciliation.
	1887	*Machado v. Bonet*	Granted separation of room and board for endangering her life.

Decade	Year	Case	Outcome
1890 to 1900	1897	*Dunlap v. Dunlap*	Granted separation of room and board for mental cruelty but not ill treatment of the child.
	1897	*Amy v. Berard*	Rejected separation for reciprocal ill treatment.
	1898	*Holmes v. Holmes*	Granted separation of room and board for cruelty and adultery.
	1898	*Lane v. Bursha*	Rejected separation of room and board in hopes of leaving open a path to reconciliation.
	1899	*Gagneaux v. Desonier*	Granted separation and alimony.

Although by no means are the cases at the state supreme court level indicative of the day-to-day rulings in the legal system, the tables above provide a snapshot of contested cases that did lead to important legal precedents in all of the southern states.

Notes

Introduction

1. *State v. Peter Molloy*, First District Court #7987 (1852).

2. *State v. Martin Johnson*, CRDC #8562 (1886).

3. *State v. James Reynolds*, CRDC #17008 (1891).

4. *State v. Jefferson Green*, CRDC #14826 (1891).

5. Linda Gordon, *Heroes of Their Own Lives: The Politics and History of Family Violence; Boston, 1880–1960* (New York: Viking, 1988); and Elizabeth H. Pleck, *Domestic Tyranny: The Making of Social Policy against Family Violence from Colonial Times to the Present* (New York: Oxford University Press, 1987).

6. *Fleytas v. Pigneguy*, 1836, 9 La. Reports, 419.

7. Reva B. Siegel, "'The Rule of Love': Wife Beating as Prerogative and Privacy," Yale Law School, Faculty Scholarship Series, no. 1092, 1996, at http://digitalcommons.law.yale.edu/fss_papers/1092. States in the antebellum period generally (although not always) prosecuted men who killed their female partners. Some states also intervened when men became violent toward their female partners. Georgia and Tennessee, for example, passed laws criminalizing intimate partner violence in the 1850s. Some, such as Louisiana and Michigan, fined abusers in severe cases of abuse, but these states did not recognize the right of a wife to be absolutely free from violence. Victoria Bynum examined the Piedmont area in North Carolina in the antebellum era and found that thirty-nine women had sworn out peace warrants against their abusive husbands in three counties from 1850 to 1860. See Victoria E. Bynum, *Unruly Women: The Politics of Social and Sexual Control in the Old South* (Chapel Hill: University of North Carolina Press, 1992). "Lesser" forms of abuse, such as slapping or inflicting nonpermanent injuries, were not seen as criminal and were not prosecuted. This was not the case after the Civil War.

8. The West during the 1870s was still being settled, and as territories or newly recognized states the West is more difficult to assess, particularly using newspapers and court cases. A few historians have examined intimate partner violence in the West during the period using petitions for divorce from Oregon that reached higher courts. For more information, see David Peterson, "Wife Beating: An American Tradition," *Journal of Interdisciplinary History* 23, no. 1 (Summer 1992): 97–118; and David Peterson del Mar, *What Trouble I*

Have Seen: A History of Violence against Wives (Cambridge, MA: Harvard University Press, 1996).

9. Many historians of women's history have shown that these "spheres" were in reality not as rigid as previously supposed. Rather, the "spheres" were fluid, as Paula Baker argues in "The Domestication of Politics: Women and American Political Society, 1780–1920," *American Historical Review* 89, no. 3 (June 1984): 620–47. Acknowledging that fact, I use the term "sphere" not to counter those arguments but rather to emphasize the expectation of gender performance. Carl Degler, in "What Ought to Be and What Was: Women's Sexuality in the Nineteenth Century," *American Historical Review* 79 (1974): 1467–90, and Helen Lefkowitz Horowitz, in *Rereading Sex: Battles over Sexual Knowledge and Suppression in Nineteenth-Century America* (New York: Alfred A. Knopf, 2002), have been instrumental in showing how Victorian America did not necessarily live up to the widely circulated ideals. However, the enforcement of these ideals by families, communities, and those in power (courts, legislatures, etc.) is key in this discussion.

10. Gail Bederman, *Manliness and Civilization: A Cultural History of Gender and Race in the United States, 1880–1917* (Chicago: University of Chicago Press, 1995).

11. A few examples are: the *Columbus (GA) Daily Enquirer*, May 11, 1870; *Daily Picayune*, March 30, 1871; *Morning Republican* (Little Rock), July 9, 1873; *Wheeling (WV) Register*, June 18, 1875; and *Daily Picayune*, August 30, 1882.

12. *Wheeling (WV) Register*, May 4, 1881; *Savannah Tribune*, December 12, 1876; *Macon (GA) Weekly Telegraph*, September 12, 1876; *New Orleans Times*, August 8, 1874; *Morning Republican* (Little Rock), August 23, 1873; *Macon (GA) Weekly Telegraph*, April 30, 1872; and *Daily Picayune*, October 31, 1871.

13. In situations of sexual assault, especially when the accused assailant was white, African American women had little or no recourse for crimes against their person. Often, women of color were blamed for the rapes because white social expectations considered them hypersexual and incapable of saying "no" to sex. Deborah Gray White examines this mammy versus jezebel myth of black women in *Ar'n't I a Woman? Female Slaves in the Plantation South* (New York: W. W. Norton, 1985), and Crystal Nicole Feimster analyzes the lack of protection for African American women against sexual assault in the New South in *Southern Horrors: Women and the Politics of Rape and Lynching* (Cambridge, MA: Harvard University Press, 2009). Darlene Clark Hine also explores the rape of African American women and what she calls the "culture of dissemblance" in "Rape and the Inner Lives of Black Women in the Middle West," *Signs* 14, no. 4 (Summer 1989): 912–20.

14. *State v. Huntley*, 91 N.C. 617 (1884). The majority opinion denied precedent in *Hussey* and argued that the wife could in fact testify against her husband. *Huntley* also argued that justices of the peace had no jurisdiction for intimate partner violence, because such assault and battery was not trivial. The judges used mental suffering as evidence of the severity of wife beating.

15. *Fulgham v. the State*, 46 Ala. 143 (1871). Although there is a major case before *Fulgham—State v. Rhodes*, 61 N.C. 453 (1868)—I start with *Fulgham* because *Rhodes* still recognized the primacy of the family and state intervention only in severe cases of spousal assault. *Fulgham* goes further than the North Carolina Supreme Court case to argue

that wife beating was not acceptable. For more information on the *Rhodes* case, see Laura F. Edwards, "Women and Domestic Violence in Nineteenth-Century Carolina," in *Lethal Imagination: Violence and Brutality in American History*, ed. Michael A. Bellesiles (New York: New York University Press, 1999), 114–36.

16. For example s of similar cases that followed *Fulgham*, see *Knight v. Knight*, 31 Iowa 451 (1871); *Commonwealth v. McAfee*, 108 Mass. 458 (1871); and *Shackett v. Shackett*, 49 Vt. 195 (1876).

17. Although *Fulgham* involves an African American couple, the repudiation of the male privilege of chastisement extended to every race, ethnicity, and socioeconomic class. For information on white elites being charged with wife beating, see Carolyn B. Ramsey, "A Diva Defends Herself: Gender and Domestic Violence in an Early Twentieth-Century Headline Trial," *St. Louis University Law Journal* 55 (2011): 1347, University of Colorado Law Legal Studies Research Paper no. 12-12, at http://ssrn.com/abstract=2096360.

18. A few examples are: *State v. Stagno Salvador*, CRDC #2041 (May 12, 1893); *State v. Jeffery Hill*, CRDC #7593 (September 30, 1885); and *State v. James Gillen*, CRDC #2911 (September 8, 1882).

19. *Charlotte Observer*, August 25, 1896; and *Wheeling (WV) Register*, November 26, 1893.

20. Historian Elizabeth Pleck, for instance, found that "[b]etween 1889 and 1894, fifty-eight out of sixty men arrested for wife beating in Charleston, South Carolina were black." See Elizabeth Pleck, "Wife Beating in Nineteenth-Century America," *Victimology: An International Journal* 4 (1979): 65.

21. For a seminal work in the field of gender history, see Joan Wallach Scott, "Gender: A Useful Category of Historical Analysis," *American Historical Review* 91, no. 5 (December 1986): 1053–75.

22. Judith Butler, "Imitation and Gender Insubordination," in *The Judith Butler Reader*, ed. Sara Salih (Malden, MA: Blackwell, 2003), 119–37.

23. Bynum, *Unruly Women*, 3.

24. Jesse Lemisch is the New Left historian who coined the influential phrase "history from the bottom up." See his *Jack Tar in the Streets: Merchant Seamen in the Politics of Revolutionary America* (Manchester, NH: Irvington Publishers, 1968); see also Lenore E. Walker, *The Battered Woman* (New York: Harper and Row, 1979), xi.

25. Michelle L. Meloy and Susan L. Miller, *The Victimization of Women: Law, Policies, and Politics* (Oxford: Oxford University Press, 2011), 12.

26. Evelyn Brooks Higginbotham, "African-American Women's History and the Metalanguage of Race," *Signs* 17, no. 2 (Winter 1992): 253.

27. C. Vann Woodward, *Origins of the New South, 1877–1913* (Baton Rouge: Louisiana State University Press, 1951); Grace Elizabeth Hale, *Making Whiteness: The Culture of Segregation in the South, 1890–1940* (New York: Vintage Books, 1999); and Alecia P. Long, *The Great Southern Babylon: Sex, Race, and Respectability in New Orleans, 1865–1920* (Baton Rouge: Louisiana State University Press, 2005).

28. US Census Bureau, *Report on Population of the United States at the Tenth Census: 1880* (Washington, DC: Government Printing Office, 1885).

29. "The Louisiana Railway Accommodations Act," Louisiana Legislature, Act no. 111 (1890): 153–54. Passed July 10, 1890, the act went into effect ninety days later.

30. Historian Michael J. Klarman's *From Jim Crow to Civil Rights* argues that law, particularly concerning the *Brown v. Board of Education* case, was and is largely influenced by social values. Klarman also discusses how judges rule (based on personal values or the letter of the law) and argues that, while a blend of both, judges rely on personal beliefs when the law is "less clear." See Michael J. Klarman, *From Jim Crow to Civil Rights: The Supreme Court and the Struggle for Racial Equality* (Oxford: Oxford University Press, 2004), 5. Legal scholars Austin Sarat and Thomas Kearns agree that social views are the impetus for change in the legal system. They write: "Law, in the instrumentalist account, mirrors society. Changes in law tend to follow social changes, and often intend to do no more than make those changes permanent." See Austin Sarat and Thomas R. Kearns, "Beyond the Great Divide: Forms of Legal Scholarship and Everyday Life," in *Law and Everyday Life*, ed. Austin Sarat and Thomas R. Kearns (Ann Arbor: University of Michigan Press, 1993), 21. Historian Richard Polenberg argues differently about the influence of the courts. He intimates that the courts affect the larger society and impose changes and views. See Richard Polenberg, *Fighting Faiths: The Abrams Case, the Supreme Court, and Free Speech* (Ithaca, NY: Cornell University Press, 1987). Legal scholar Reva Siegel uses a "preservation through transformation" argument, stating that judges tended to allow for some social change while upholding the older hierarchy by readapting their rulings along alternative lines aiming to largely preserve the status quo. See Siegel, "The Rule of Love."

31. Clifford Geertz, *Local Knowledge: Further Essays in Interpretive Anthropology* (New York: Basic Books, 1983), 211.

32. For historians who examine the cultural aspect of courts, see Mindie Lazarus-Black and Susan F Hirsch, eds., *Contested States: Law, Hegemony, and Resistance* (New York: Routledge, 1994); Richard Wightman Fox and T. J. Jackson Lears, eds., *The Power of Culture: Critical Essays in American History* (New York: Routledge, 1996); and Ariela Julie Gross, *Double Character: Slavery and Mastery in the Antebellum Southern Courtroom* (Athens: University of Georgia Press, 2006).

33. Edwards, "Women and Domestic Violence," 114–36.

34. Jerome Nadelhaft, "'The Public Gaze and the Prying Eye': The South and the Privacy Doctrine in Nineteenth-Century Wife Abuse Cases," *Cardozo Journal of Law and Gender* 14, no. 3 (2008): 549–607.

35. Peterson del Mar, *What Trouble I Have Seen*; and Robin C. Sager, *Marital Cruelty in Antebellum America* (Baton Rouge: Louisiana State University Press, 2016).

36. Population numbers are derived from the 1900 US Census. At this time, St. Landry included Acadia Parish as well.

37. Long, *The Great Southern Babylon*, 3.

38. LaKisha Michelle Simmons, *Crescent City Girls: The Lives of Young Black Women in Segregated New Orleans* (Chapel Hill: University of North Carolina Press, 2015), 14.

39. Edwards, "Women and Domestic Violence." North Carolina and Georgia quickly targeted wife beating. For instance, in *State v. Rhodes* (1868), North Carolina ruled against anything more than "moderate correction" of a spouse, and by the 1890s, North Carolina had a constitutional amendment disfranchising wife beaters. Both Georgia and West Virginia had several state supreme court cases punishing men for abusing their wives. Arkansas, on the

other hand, had no express legal consequences for intimate partner violence and fewer court cases, some newspaper stories on the subject, and no state supreme court cases. See table A.1 in the appendix.

40. State of Louisiana, *Official Journal of the Proceedings of the Constitutional Convention of the State of Louisiana, Held in New Orleans, Monday, April 21, 1879* (New Orleans: James H. Cosgrove, 1879), 7. The 1879 Convention was conciliatory and spoke of "working together [with the North] to promote a great national interest," avoiding any sectional tension, but a few remarks do mention "self rule," which asserted rule by locals citizens or what was referred to as "home rule" (232).

41. See Richard von Krafft-Ebing, *Psychopathia Sexualis*, trans. Charles G. Chaddock (Philadelphia: F. A. Davis, 1892), for a contemporary work on the pathologization and subsequent criminalization of homosexuality.

42. For more analysis on Texas and Virginia courts' rulings on the limits to the "male privilege of chastisement," see Sager, *Marital Cruelty in Antebellum America*.

Chapter One

1. *Fleytas v. Pigneguy*, 1836, 9 La. Reports, 419.

2. Ibid.

3. Ibid.

4. For more on mastery and manliness, see Craig Thompson Friend and Lorri Glover, eds., *Southern Manhood: Perspectives on Masculinity in the Old South* (Athens: University of Georgia Press, 2004); and Mark C. Carnes and Clyde Griffen, eds., *Meanings for Manhood: Constructions of Masculinity in Victorian America* (Chicago: University of Chicago Press, 1990). Stephanie McCurry discusses "martial manhood" as being part of the mastery of family. See Stephanie McCurry, *Masters of Small Worlds: Yeoman Households, Gender Relations, and the Political Culture of the Antebellum South Carolina Low Country* (New York: Oxford University Press, 1995).

5. Bertram Wyatt-Brown, *Honor and Violence in the Old South* (New York: Oxford University Press, 1986), 25–39.

6. J. D. B. De Bow, ed., *De Bow's Commercial Review of the South and West: A Monthly Journal of Trade, Commerce, Commercial Polity, Agriculture, Manufactures, Internal Improvements and General Literature* (New Orleans: Weld and Company, 1850), 205.

7. *Civil Code of the State of Louisiana*, 1825, 18–19 (inclusive of the 1827 act).

8. Amy Greenberg focuses on the lack of emotion in "restrained manhood," while W. J. Cash and Bertram Wyatt-Brown believe that southern men acted from emotion. See Amy Greenberg, *Manifest Manhood and the Antebellum American Empire* (Cambridge: Cambridge University Press, 2005); W. J. Cash, *The Mind of the South* (New York: Alfred A. Knopf, 1941); and Bertram Wyatt-Brown, *Southern Honor: Ethics and Behavior in the Old South* (New York: Oxford University Press, 1982). Ted Ownby, in *Subduing Satan: Religion, Recreation, and Manhood in the Rural South, 1865–1920* (Chapel Hill: University of North Carolina Press, 1990), argues similarly but about the postbellum South.

9. "Probability," *Daily Picayune*, February 18, 1841.

10. Nonfatal duels resulted in $200 fines for challengers and two years of imprisonment, and $100 fines for those challenged. For more information, see John Hope Franklin, *The Militant South, 1800–1861* (Cambridge, MA: Belknap Press of Harvard University Press, 1956), 58.

11. "A Synopsis of the Speech of Mr. Soule in Defence of Thourett," *Daily Picayune*, August 30, 1840.

12. For more information, see Franklin, *The Militant South*; Dickson D. Bruce Jr., *Violence and Culture in the Antebellum South* (Austin: University of Texas Press, 1979); and Jack Kenny Williams, *Dueling in the Old South: Vignettes of Social History* (College Station: Texas A&M University Press, 1980).

13. Darlene Clark Hine and Earnestine Jenkins, eds., *A Question of Manhood: A Reader in U.S. Black Men's History and Masculinity* (Bloomington: Indiana University Press, 1999), 1.

14. For more information, see Eugene D. Genovese, *Roll, Jordan, Roll: The World the Slaves Made* (New York: Pantheon Books, 1974).

15. Variations of this oral myth can be found; see John W. Roberts, *From Trickster to Badman: The Black Folk Hero in Slavery and Freedom* (Philadelphia: University of Pennsylvania Press, 1989), 61; Jeanne Campbell Reesman, ed., *Trickster Lives: Culture and Myth in American Fiction* (Athens: University of Georgia Press, 2001); and Richard M. Dorson, *American Negro Folktales* (Greenwich, CT: Fawcett Publications, 1967).

16. Sybil Kein, ed., *Creole: The History and Legacy of Louisiana's Free People of Color* (Baton Rouge: Louisiana State University Press, 2000), 209. For more information on free people of color in antebellum New Orleans, see H. E. Sterkx, *The Free Negro in Ante-Bellum Louisiana* (Rutherford, NJ: Fairleigh Dickinson University Press, 1972); Loren Schweninger, "Antebellum Free Persons of Color in Postbellum Louisiana," *Louisiana History* 30 (1989): 345–64; Robert Reinders, "The Free Negro in the New Orleans Economy, 1850–1860," *Louisiana History* 6 (1965): 273–85; and Gary B. Mills, *The Forgotten People: Cane River's Creoles of Color* (Baton Rouge: Louisiana State University Press, 1977).

17. Michael S. Kimmel, *Manhood in America: A Cultural History* (New York: Free Press, 1996).

18. Schweninger, "Antebellum Free Persons of Color," 4. Schweninger also estimates that at least 126 free people of color owned between five and ten slaves and that 263 free people of color owned real estate by 1860. Financial success, then, was possible for some.

19. Barbara Welter, "The Cult of True Womanhood, 1820–1860," *American Quarterly* 18, no. 2 (Summer 1966): 152. See also Nancy F. Cott, *The Bonds of Womanhood: "Woman's Sphere" in New England, 1780–1835* (New Haven, CT: Yale University Press, 1977).

20. Coventry Patmore, *The Angel in the House* (London: Macmillan, 1863).

21. I intentionally place the word "spheres" in quotation marks because the stated ideal was not reality of women during the period. Many historians have addressed the expectations of domesticity, such as Welter, "The Cult of True Womanhood"; Cott, *The Bonds of Womanhood*; and Carroll Smith-Rosenberg, "The Female World of Love and Ritual: Relations between Women in Nineteenth-Century America," *Signs* 1, no. 1 (Autumn 1975): 1–29. Others have shown the more fluid makeup of the domestic "sphere." See Baker, "The Domestication of Politics"; Barbara Leslie Epstein, *The Politics of Domesticity: Women, Evangelism, and Temperance in Nineteenth-Century America* (Middletown, CT: Wesleyan University

Press, 1981); Lori D. Ginzberg, *Women and the Work of Benevolence: Morality, Politics, and Class in the 19th-Century United States* (New Haven, CT: Yale University Press, 1990); and Nancy Isenberg, *Sex and Citizenship in Antebellum America* (Chapel Hill: University of North Carolina Press, 1998).

22. "A Hint to Girls," *Daily Picayune*, January 21, 1841.

23. See Isenberg, *Sex and Citizenship*.

24. Historians debate the regional aspects of southern womanhood. For more information, see Marli F. Weiner, *Mistresses and Slaves: Plantation Women in South Carolina, 1830–1880* (Urbana: University of Illinois Press, 1997); Catherine Clinton, *The Plantation Mistress: Woman's World in the Old South* (New York: Pantheon Books, 1984); Anne Firor Scott, *Southern Lady: From Pedestal to Politics, 1830–1930* (Chicago: University of Chicago Press, 1970); and Elizabeth Fox-Genovese, *Within the Plantation Household: Black and White Women of the Old South* (Chapel Hill: University of North Carolina Press, 1988).

25. For more information on women's work and gender expectations, see Jeanne Boydston, *Home and Work: Housework, Wages, and the Ideology of Labor in the Early Republic* (New York: Oxford University Press, 1990).

26. Ibid., 56.

27. White, *Ar'n't I a Woman?*, 29.

28. Ibid., 29.

29. Judith Kelleher Schafer, *Becoming Free, Remaining Free: Manumission and Enslavement in New Orleans, 1846–1862* (Baton Rouge: Louisiana State University Press, 2003), 1–14.

30. Arnold R. Hirsch and Joseph Logsdon, *Creole New Orleans: Race and Americanization* (Baton Rouge: Louisiana State University Press, 1992): 103–7.

31. Emily Clark argues that the conception of the quadroon and the focus on *plaçage* and black women in prostitution lead scholars to ignore a substantial number of African American women who married and held respectable positions in the city. See Emily Clark, *The Strange History of the American Quadroon: Free Women of Color in the Revolutionary Atlantic World* (Chapel Hill: University of North Carolina Press, 2013); see also Reinders, "The Free Negro in the New Orleans Economy," 274.

32. Clark, *The Strange History of the American Quadroon*, 96.

33. Mark Fernandez argues that Louisiana is not as atypical as most historians claim by showing examples of other states blending and borrowing precedents. See Mark F. Fernandez, *From Chaos to Continuity: The Evolution of Louisiana's Judicial System, 1712–1862* (Baton Rouge: Louisiana State University Press, 2001). Texas, for example, blended Spanish influences into a common law system and recognized community property. Also, other states such as Mississippi started recognizing the right of married women to own property by the 1840s.

34. For more information on the emergence of the civil law system in Louisiana, see Agustín Parise, "A Constant Give and Take: Tracing Legal Borrowings in the Louisiana Civil Law Experience," *Seton Hall Legislative Journal* 35, no. 1 (2010): 1–35.

35. Parise notes that there is some debate about the exact influences on the *Digest* of 1808, but strong evidence for source documents exists, in part, from later assessments of the *Digest* with notes and annotations, such as John W. Cairns, "The de la Vergne Volume and the Digest of 1808," *Tulane European and Civil Law Forum* 24, no. 1 (2009): 31, 74. See Parise, "A Constant Give and Take," 9nn39–45.

36. Parise, "A Constant Give and Take," 16.

37. Ibid., 17.

38. Ibid.

39. Fernandez, *From Chaos to Continuity*, 33.

40. Ibid., 41-42, 48.

41. For more information on the development of Louisiana's modern criminal law, see J. Denson Smith, "How Louisiana Prepared and Adopted a Criminal Code," *Journal of Criminal Law and Criminology* 41, no. 2 (July–August 1950): 125–35.

42. For more information on Louisiana law and slavery, see Judith Kelleher Schafer, *Slavery, the Civil Law, and the Supreme Court of Louisiana* (Baton Rouge: Louisiana State University Press, 1994).

43. Gross, *Double Character*.

44. For more on southern courts' reaction to behavior that threatened patriarchy, see Laura F. Edwards, "Law, Domestic Violence, and the Limits of Patriarchal Authority in the Antebellum South," *Journal of Southern History* 65, no. 4 (November 1999): 733–70.

45. See Laura F. Edwards, *The People and Their Peace: Legal Culture and the Transformation of Inequality in the Post-Revolutionary South* (Chapel Hill: University of North Carolina Press, 2009).

46. Siegel, "The Rule of Love."

47. Edwards, "Women and Domestic Violence," 116.

48. *Bradley v. State*, I. Mississippi (I Walker) 156 (1824).

49. Ibid.

50. *State v. Hussey*, 44 N.C. (Busb.) 123 (1852).

51. Ibid. States in the antebellum period generally (although not always) prosecuted a man who killed his significant other. Some states did intervene when men became violent to their female partners. Georgia and Tennessee, for example, passed laws criminalizing intimate partner violence in the 1850s. Most, such as Louisiana, fined abusers in severe cases of abuse, but these states did not recognize the right of a wife to be absolutely free from violence. "Lesser" forms of abuse such as slapping or injuries that were not permanent were not seen as a problem, and were not prosecuted. This was not the case after the Civil War.

52. *Civil Code of the State of Louisiana*, 1825, 18–19 (inclusive of the 1827 act).

53. Ibid.

54. For more information on the system of concubinage or *plaçage* (when involving a free woman of color), see Long, *The Great Southern Babylon*.

55. "Rowley v. Rowley, 19 La. 557 (1841)." Rowley v. Rowley should be in italics.

56. Ibid.

57. *Rowley v. Rowley*, 19 La. 557 (1841).

58. Other states gradually enacted laws upholding married women's property rights in the antebellum period, notably Mississippi in 1839, but these pieces of legislation tended to be limited until new acts passed after the Civil War. For more information on married women and property rights before the Civil War, see Angela Boswell, *Her Act and Deed: Women's Lives in a Rural Southern County* (College Station: Texas A&M University Press, 2001); and Joseph A. Custer, "The Three Waves of Married Women's Property Acts in the

Nineteenth Century with a Focus on Mississippi, New York, and Oregon," *Ohio Northern University Law Review* 40 (2013-2014): 395–440. For more on married women's property acts after the war, see Suzanne D. Lebsock, "Radical Reconstruction and the Property Rights of Southern Women," *Journal of Southern History* 43 (1977): 195–209.

59. Rowley v. Rowley, 19 La. 557 (1841).

60. *Bienvenu v. Buisson*, 14 La. Ann. 386, 1859 WL 6096.

61. Ibid.

62. *Trowbridge v. C. T. Carlin*, 12 La. Ann. 882 (1857), WL 4951.

63. Robin Sager also found duty as the main focus in divorce cases in Virginia during the antebellum period. See Sager, *Marital Cruelty in Antebellum America.*

64. Loren Schweninger, *Families in Crisis in the Old South: Divorce, Slavery, and the Law* (Chapel Hill: University of North Carolina Press, 2012), 127.

65. Ibid.

66. "Before Recorder Baldwin," *Daily Picayune*, April 30, 1850.

67. "Recorder's Court, Second Municipality," *Daily Picayune*, March 19, 1840.

68. "The City: Friday Evening," *Daily Picayune*, June 24, 1854.

69. Bynum, *Unruly Women.*

70. George Fitzhugh, *Sociology for the South; or, The Failure of Free Society* (Richmond: A. Morris, 1854), 297; and George Fitzhugh, *Cannibals All! or, Slaves without Masters* (Richmond: A. Morris, 1857), 39.

71. Fitzhugh, *Cannibals All!*, 84. It was common in the 1850s to compare the North's free labor economy and the South's slave economy in order to demonstrate which region was superior. For more information, see Frank Towers, *The Urban South and the Coming of the Civil War* (Charlottesville: University of Virginia Press, 2004); and Genovese, *Roll, Jordan, Roll.*

72. Fitzhugh, *Cannibals All!*, 84.

73. New Orleans Temperance Society, *An Address to the Citizens of New Orleans on the Subject of Temperance* (Boston: Toy, Printer, Office of the Lafayette City Advertiser, 1841), 14.

74. Ibid., 15–16.

75. "The City," *Daily Picayune*, October 11, 1854.

76. State v. Xavier Simeon, FDC #14520 (June 7, 1860).

77. Ibid.

78. State v. John George Mayers, FDC #9229 (September 3, 1854).

79. "The City," *Daily Picayune*, August 12, 1859. The reporter indicated the couple's Irish heritage by making stereotypical assumptions about the dinner the O'Flahertys would be having after paying the fine, namely boiled potatoes. Census records from 1860 also show a Patrick O'Flaherty married to Bridget with two young children in New Orleans's Third Ward and born in Ireland.

80. Ibid.

Chapter Two

1. Morgan's memoir is published in Sarah Morgan Dawson, *A Confederate Girl's Diary* (New York: Houghton Mifflin, 1913). This chapter's epigraph is from page 25. For more

information on Morgan, see Giselle Roberts, ed., *The Correspondence of Sarah Morgan and Francis Warrington Dawson, with Selected Editorials Written by Sarah Morgan for the Charleston News Courier* (Athens: University of Georgia Press, 2004).

2. Lisa Tendrich Frank, *The Civilian War: Confederate Women and Soldiers during Sherman's March* (Baton Rouge: Louisiana State University Press, 2015), 10.

3. Drew Gilpin Faust, *This Republic of Suffering: Death and the American Civil War* (New York: Vintage Books, 2008), 3–31.

4. Ibid., 3.

5. Joseph D. Hunstock to Henrietta Lauzin, November 26, 1864, Clinton, Louisiana, Gras-Lauzin Family Papers, ms. 5, Louisiana and Lower Mississippi Valley Collections, Hill Memorial Library, Louisiana State University, Baton Rouge.

6. Ibid.

7. William Tecumseh Sherman to Mayor James M. Calhoun, E. E. Rawson, and S. C. Wells, September 12, 1864, Atlanta, Georgia, Civil War Era NC, North Carolina State University, Raleigh, at http://cwnc.omeka.chass.ncsu.edu/items/show/23.

8. Ibid.

9. Mark Grimsley, *The Hard Hand of War: Union Military Policy toward Southern Civilians, 1861–1865* (Cambridge: Cambridge University Press, 1995).

10. J. David Hacker, "A Census-Based Count of the Civil War Dead," *Civil War History* 57, no. 4 (December 2011): 306–47.

11. "My God! What Is All This For?," Wolf C116, American Song Sheets, Duke Digital Collections, Duke University Libraries, Durham, NC, at http://library.duke.edu/digitalcollections/songsheets_bsvg100466/, accessed October 26, 2013.

12. John P. Nugent to his mother, Ann Nugent, November 18, 1862, Gilder Lehrman Collection, Gilder Lehrman Institute of American History, New York, GLC03135.01.05.

13. Mary Phinney, Baroness von Olnhausen, *Adventures of an Army Nurse in Two Wars* (Boston: Little, Brown, 1903), 355.

14. Faust, *This Republic of Suffering*, 37.

15. Quoted in ibid., 36.

16. In *Occupied Women*, E. Susan Barber and Charles F. Ritter explore the myth that rape during the Civil War was infrequent in the chapter titled "'Physical Abuse . . . and Rough Handling': Race, Gender, and Sexual Justice in the Occupied South." See LeeAnn Whites and Alecia P. Long, eds., *Occupied Women: Gender, Military Occupation, and the American Civil War* (Baton Rouge: Louisiana State University Press, 2009), 49–64.

17. Drew Gilpin Faust, *Mothers of Invention: Women of the Slaveholding South in the American Civil War* (Chapel Hill: University of North Carolina Press, 1996), 36.

18. Ibid., 3.

19. Ibid., 78.

20. As quoted in Eric T. Dean Jr., *Shook Over Hell: Post-Traumatic Stress, Vietnam, and the Civil War* (Cambridge, MA: Harvard University Press, 1997), 54.

21. Ibid., 55.

22. See Silas Weir Mitchell, *Fat and Blood: And How to Make Them* (Philadelphia: J. B. Lippincott, 1877).

23. Ibid., 39.

24. As quoted in Phillip Shaw Paludan, *"A People's Contest": The Union and the Civil War, 1861–1865* (New York: Harper and Row, 1988), 333.

25. Dean, *Shook Over Hell*, 100.

26. Ibid., 110–11.

27. *Daily Picayune*, April 21, 1861. See also Arthur W. Bergeron Jr., "Louisiana's Free Men of Color in Gray," in *Louisianians in the Civil War*, ed. Lawrence Lee Hewitt and Arthur W. Bergeron Jr. (Columbia: University of Missouri Press, 2002): 100–119.

28. For more information on free people of color in New Orleans, see Schweninger, "Antebellum Free Persons of Color," 345–60.

29. James G. Hollandsworth, *Louisiana Native Guards: The Black Military Experience during the Civil War* (Baton Rouge: Louisiana State University Press, 1995), 3–5.

30. Ibid., 8.

31. Ibid., 6–7.

32. Ibid.

33. Ibid., 47.

34. Ibid.

35. Ibid., 107.

36. J. Matthew Gallman, *The North Fights the Civil War: The Home Front* (Chicago: Ivan R. Dee, 1994), 117.

37. Emily Bliss Thacher Souder, letter of July 16, 1863, in *Leaves from the Battlefield of Gettysburg: A Series of Letters from a Field Hospital and National Poems* (Philadelphia: C. Sherman, Son and Company, 1864), 144.

38. Ibid., 27.

39. Kate Cumming, *Kate: The Journal of a Confederate Nurse*, ed. Richard Barksdale Harwell (Baton Rouge: Louisiana State University Press, 1959).

40. See Whites and Long, *Occupied Women*, 49–64.

41. Laurel Thatcher Ulrich employed the term "deputy husband" in her influential work *Good Wives: Image and Reality in the Lives of Women in Northern New England, 1650–1750* (New York: Alfred A. Knopf, 1982). She argued that colonial women could act in their husbands' places for economic transactions if needed. Since the publication of *Good Wives*, the term "deputy husband" has been employed elsewhere in similar contexts in American history. Laura Edwards, for instance, uses the phrase in her book *Scarlett Doesn't Live Here Anymore: Southern Women in the Civil War Era* (Urbana: University of Illinois Press, 2000), 77. Drew Gilpin Faust and Marli F. Weiner explore the impact of the Civil War on southern women. Both recognize that plantation mistresses did in fact use excessive physical force when dealing with slaves by themselves, even if they saw this to be a failure on their part. See Faust, *Mothers of Invention*; and Weiner, *Mistresses and Slaves*.

42. Dawson, *A Confederate Girl's Diary*, 24.

43. "The City," *Daily Picayune*, March 3, 1863.

44. Ibid.

45. The *Daily Delta* (New Orleans) and Sarah Morgan often referred to Butler as "Picayune" Butler—an insult referring to him as petty, cheap, or worthless. Other historians have found similar reactions among elite, white southern women. See Frank, *The Civilian War*.

46. Adelaide S. Dimitry, *War-Time Sketches, Historical and Otherwise* (New Orleans: Louisiana Printing Company Press, 1911), 4. See also James G. Hollandsworth, *Pretense of Glory: The Life of General Nathaniel P. Banks* (Baton Rouge: Louisiana State University Press, 1998).

47. "The City," *Daily Picayune*, February 22, 1863.

48. Alecia P. Long, "(Mis)Remembering General Order no. 28: Benjamin Butler, the Woman Order, and Historical Memory," in Whites and Long, *Occupied Women*, 17–32. For more information on Butler's occupation, see Chester G. Hearn, *When the Devil Came Down to Dixie: Ben Butler in New Orleans* (Baton Rouge: Louisiana State University Press, 1997).

49. "Register of Contrabands in Corps d'Afrique, New Orleans, 1863 (Partial List)," Bureau of Refugees, Freedmen, and Abandoned Lands, 1865–1869, Records of the New Orleans Field Office, State of Louisiana, National Archives Microfilm Publication no. 1483, at http://www.freedmensbureau.com/louisiana/contrabands.htm, accessed September 25, 2015.

50. John W. Blassingame, *Black New Orleans, 1860–1880* (Chicago: University of Chicago Press, 1973), 30.

51. Darlene Clark Hine and Kathleen Thompson, *A Shining Thread of Hope: The History of Black Women in America* (New York: Broadway Books, 1998), 148.

52. Mary Farmer-Kaiser, *Freedwomen and the Freedmen's Bureau: Race, Gender, and Public Policy in the Age of Emancipation* (Bronx: Fordham University Press, 2010), 30.

53. *The Miscellaneous Documents of the Senate of the United States for the Second Session of the Forty-Fourth Congress*, vol. 2 (Washington, DC: Government Printing Office, 1877), 111.

54. Cross Keys Plantation Records, Manuscripts Collection 918, Manuscripts Department, Tulane University, New Orleans. Anna McCall Watson's diary covers the years 1868 to 1876.

55. Faust, *Mothers of Invention*, 147.

56. Whites and Long, *Occupied Women*, 251.

57. As LeeAnn Whites point outs, some historians, such as Elizabeth Fox-Genovese in her work *Within the Plantation Household*, have argued that gender does not mean as much as class and race because not all women could exert the "rights" and status of womanhood. Linda Kerber even argues that "race trumped gender" for African American women in the postwar South. I seek to show that, while class and race do matter, prosecution for intimate partner violence cut across all lines. While some limits did exist, courts punished the crime, and all women could seek legal redress for abusive partners. As Whites states, clearly "gender matters"; see Whites, *Gender Matters: Civil War, Reconstruction, and the Making of the New South* (New York: Palgrave Macmillan, 2005), 3. See also Linda K. Kerber, *No Constitutional Right to Be Ladies: Women and the Obligations of Citizenship* (New York: Hill and Wang, 1998), 67. Gail Bederman uses the term "manliness" to discuss the social construct of behavioral expectations and expectations for men prior to the 1890s. For more information on southern masculinity immediately after the Civil War, see Ownby, *Subduing Satan*.

58. Nina Silber, "Intemperate Men, Spiteful Women, and Jefferson Davis," in *Divided Houses: Gender and the Civil War*, ed. Catherine Clinton and Nina Silber (New York: Oxford University Press, 1992), 283–305.

59. Ibid.; *Harper's Weekly*, May 27, 1865.

60. Gaines M. Foster, *Ghosts of the Confederacy: Defeat, the Lost Cause, and the Emergence of the New South, 1865–1913* (New York: Oxford University Press, 1987), 26.

61. Ibid., 34.

62. Ibid.

63. Gail Bederman analyzes the invocation of "civilization" to "construct what it meant to be a man," but her focus is on the turn of the twentieth century, particularly the 1880–1917 period. While a remarkable book, her scope does not extend to the period or the region discussed here, but her discussion of masculinity and civilization is an asset in viewing southern masculinity immediately after the Civil War. See Bederman, *Manliness and Civilization*, 24.

64. Historians such as Charles Shindo and Lynn Dumenil have examined the 1920s and the tension over modern change. They have shown how Americans simultaneously clung to the past and yet embraced the future. The same concept in terms of the tension, I argue, could be applied to the South after the Civil War. See Charles J. Shindo, *1927 and the Rise of Modern America* (Lawrence: University Press of Kansas, 2010); and Lynn Dumenil, *The Modern Temper: American Culture and Society in the 1920s* (New York: Hill and Wang, 1995).

65. Edward L. Ayers, *Promise of the New South: Life after Reconstruction* (Oxford: Oxford University Press, 2007), 21.

66. A few examples are the *Columbus (GA) Daily Enquirer*, January 19, 1870; *Morning Republican* (Little Rock), July 26, 1873; *Macon (GA) Weekly Telegraph*, April 8, 1873; and *Morning Republican* (Little Rock), August, 7, 1873.

67. Whites, *Gender Matters*, 16. Some historians, such as Gail Bederman, emphasize careful consideration in phrasing these moments when gender constructs shift. Bederman argues that to imply a crisis in gender means that "manhood is a transhistorical category or fixed essence that has its good moments as well as its bad, rather than an ideological construct which is constantly being remade." I agree with Bederman that gender is a process and not fixed. People were anxious about gender. Their fears, however, express more than anxiety given the changes in the status of African Americans and in the views of southern womanhood. See Bederman, *Manliness and Civilization*, 11.

68. Thelia Bush to Ms. Wilkinson, November 25, 1878, Collinsburg, Louisiana, Micajah Wilkinson Papers, Manuscript Collection 707, Hill Memorial Library, Louisiana State University, Baton Rouge. In the letters from Bush to Wilkinson, Bush stated that the average age of marriage in rural Louisiana was approximately fourteen until after the war, when the lack of men impacted women's ability to marry. A year later, Bush, at the young age of twenty, stated: "[I]f I don't get off pretty soon I will have to take an old bachelor." The pressure to marry soon filled many of her letters to her grandmother.

69. Thelia Bush to Ms. Wilkinson, December 12, 1880, Collinsburg, Louisiana, Micajah Wilkinson Papers, Manuscript Collection 707, Hill Memorial Library, Louisiana State University, Baton Rouge; and O. M. Grisham to Sallie, June 19, 1904, Winnfield, Louisiana, Grisham-Kellogg-Faust Papers, Manuscript Collection 5048, Hill Memorial Library, Louisiana State University, Baton Rouge.

70. Désirée Martin, *Evening Visits with a Sister; or, The Destiny of a Strand of Moss*, trans. Claude L. Remillard and Denise R. Charchere (Manchester, MO: Independent Publishing

Corporation, 2004), 167; first published, New Orleans: Imprimerie Cosmopolite, 1877. Restraint was a component of masculinity in the United States during the nineteenth century. The Victorian Age stressed restraint, particularly for men and emotion. For more information on restraint and manners in the nineteenth century, see John F. Kasson, *Rudeness and Civility: Manners in Nineteenth-Century Urban America* (New York: Hill and Wang, 1990). Also, I use the term "Victorian" to refer to gender expectations of the nineteenth century. See Paul Robinson, *The Modernization of Sex: Havelock Ellis, Alfred Kinsey, William Masters, and Virginia Johnson* (New York: Harper and Row, 1976), 2. Moreover, I want to stress the term "ideal" here and throughout the book. Carl Degler, in "What Ought to Be and What Was," and Helen Lefkowitz Horowitz, in *Rereading Sex*, have been instrumental in showing how Victorian America did not necessarily live up to the widely circulated ideals. However, the enforcement of Victorian ideals by those in power (courts, legislatures, etc.) is key in this book.

71. Désirée Martin worked twenty-seven years as a nun with the Society of the Sacred Heart before retiring and spending her last years with her brother and his twelve children in Grand Point, Louisiana. Martin took special interest in providing moral lessons to her nieces and nephews, but particularly her nieces. The book curiously places emphases on manners and womanhood rather than religious instruction.

72. Martin, *Evening Visits with a Sister.*

73. Aldebert Ames to Blanche Butler, June 28, 1870, Washington, DC, in Blanche Ames and Adelbert Ames, *Chronicles from the Nineteenth Century: Family Letters of Blanche Butler and Adelbert Ames, Married July 21, 1870*, vol. 1 (Clinton, MA: n.p. 1957), 719. Interestingly, Blanche Butler was the daughter of General Benjamin Butler. After Regulators took over the election in 1874, Ames resigned his position as US senator from Mississippi, and the family returned to Massachusetts.

74. Memorandum Book, vol. 50, Daniel Trotter Papers, Manuscript Collection 990, Hill Memorial Library, Louisiana State University, Baton Rouge.

75. Sally G. McMillen, "Antebellum Southern Fathers and the Health Care of Children," *Journal of Southern History* 60, no. 3 (August 1994): 513–32.

76. Dr. M. A. Simmons Medicine Company, *Dr. M.A. Simmons Song, Fortune, Dream, and Cook Book* (St. Louis: Dr. M. A. Simmons Medicine Company, 1901). The company started in Mississippi in 1840 and continued to grow, particularly in the 1870s and 1880s. The tonic appeared to be popular in the South, and other companies tried to copy it. See the *South Western Reporter*, vol. 23 (Saint Paul: West Publishing Company, 1894), 171–72. I cannot find records of the company after 1901 (although that is not to say it did not exist after that year), but it must have closed no later than 1906 with the passage of the Pure Food and Drug Act.

77. Martin, *Evening Visits with a Sister*, 187.

78. Ibid., 158.

79. Ibid., 187.

80. Patmore, *The Angel in the House.*

81. Albert Voorhies, *Revised Laws of Louisiana Approved March 14, 1870, with Copious References to the Acts of the Legislature From and Including the Sessions of 1870, Up To and Including the Session of 1882* (New Orleans: F. F. Hansell, 1884), sections 2177, 2178. For more

information on African Americans and legal changes during Reconstruction, see Charles Vincent, *Black Legislators in Louisiana during Reconstruction* (Baton Rouge: Louisiana State University Press, 1976).

82. Vincent, *Black Legislators in Louisiana*, 32. Recent scholarship has challenged the long-held view that the majority of African Americans sought to legalize their marriages. Rather, some historians claim that African Americans resisted legalizing their marriages in fear of white encroachment in their lives. See Andrew Slap and Michael T. Smith, *This Distracted and Anarchical People: New Answers for Old Questions about the Civil War–Era North* (Bronx: Fordham University Press, 2013).

83. Nancy Bercaw, *Gendered Freedoms: Race, Rights, and the Politics of Household in the Delta, 1861–1875* (Gainesville: University Press of Florida, 2003), 106–7. Although "taking up" and sweethearting were viewed as distinct from marriage, some couples, as Bercaw states, did view those alternative living arrangements as a precursor to marriage. She also uses the term "quitting" to refer to the end of such relationships, which was less formal but easier for African American men and women to obtain than legal divorces.

84. Bercaw, *Gendered Freedoms*, 123.

85. "Briefs," *Savannah Tribune*, December 23, 1876. See Evelyn Brooks Higginbotham, *Righteous Discontent: The Women's Movement in the Black Baptist Church, 1880–1920* (Cambridge, MA: Harvard University Press, 1993), 1.

86. Ibid.

87. Quoted in Blassingame, *Black New Orleans*, 89.

88. "The City," *Daily Picayune*, January 22, 1863.

89. *State v. James Miritare*, First District Court #15945 (January 15, 1864).

90. Farmer-Kaiser, *Freedwomen and the Freedman's Bureau*, 155.

91. Hannah Rosen, *Terror in the Heart of Freedom: Citizenship, Sexual Violence, and the Meaning of Race in the Postemancipation South* (Chapel Hill: University of North Carolina Press, 2009), 225.

92. For more information on the immediate impact on southern manhood after the Civil War, see Foster, *Ghosts of the Confederacy*; and Whites, *Gender Matters*.

Chapter Three

1. *State v. Sylvester Conlon*, CRDC 5573 (1884).

2. Ibid.

3. Linda Gordon, *Heroes of Their Own Lives*, 256. Gordon's section on intimate partner violence focuses on the North and mainly examines child protection agencies rather than the courts. This would account for the difference in women's mentality. New definitions of womanhood in the South, as I have argued, required protection and gave a sense of agency. Moreover, women changed their tactics to appeal to the courts and the Society for the Prevention of Cruelty to Children (SPCC). The SPCC's main goal was to help abused children. Women had to demonstrate that their husbands' abuse toward them also impacted their children. The SPCC could only offer limited help to the abused wife, and this did not include

seeking punishment of the batterer. Consequently, women's approach to the SPCC in the North and courts in the South would not be the same.

4. *State v. George Williams*, CRDC #1304 (1881).

5. Elizabeth Janeway, *Powers of the Weak* (New York: Alfred A. Knopf, 1980), 9.

6. Some more recent studies suggest that while power resides as the central issue in intimate partner violence, abusers who feel disempowered in other areas will be more likely to compensate by engaging in physically or emotionally abusive behaviors. Such factors might have influenced the behavior of men of color or poorer socioeconomic classes in the late nineteenth century (especially considering their lack of legal and social equality as compared to wealthy white men), but ultimately the violence rested on power over their female partner. See Julia C. Babcock, Jennifer Waltz, Neil S. Jacobson, and John M. Gottman, "Power and Violence: The Relation between Communication Patterns, Power Discrepancies, and Domestic Violence," *Journal of Consulting and Clinical Psychology* 61, no. 1 (1993): 40–50.

7. *State v. John Heir*, CRDC #7410 (1885).

8. *State v. Gust Hannewinckle*, CRDC #10128 (1887).

9. Ibid.

10. *State v. Jeffery Hill*, CRDC #7593 (1885).

11. The numbers in table 3.1 reflect findings from the types of plaintiffs in those 225 cases from 1880 to 1889.

12. Karen Lystra, *Searching the Heart: Women, Men, and Romantic Love in Nineteenth-Century America* (New York: Oxford University Press, 1989). For a similar discussion of sentiment in courtship, see Ellen Rothman, *Hands and Hearts: A History of Courtship in America* (New York: Basic Books, 1989).

13. Lystra, *Searching the Heart*, 157–91.

14. This tradition was also mentioned in "Picayunes for the Ladies," *Times-Picayune*, May 16, 1880, 10.

15. Thelia Bush to Ms. Wilkinson, January 29, 1880, Collinsburg, Louisiana, Micajah Wilkinson Papers, Manuscript Collection 707, Hill Memorial Library, Louisiana State University, Baton Rouge.

16. This general argument is expressed in a few historians' works. One frequently used example is Pieter Bruegel the Elder's 1559 painting *The Fight between Carnival and Lent*. Historians claim that, in general, the feast before Lent was an enactment of a "world turned upside down" with the inversion of class-based power, but the day provided an outlet for poorer socioeconomic classes to release their frustrations, thereby maintaining the elite's power and control. See Brian P. Levack, Edward Muir, and Meredith Veldman, *The West: Encounters and Transformations to 1715* (Harlow, Essex, England: Longman, 2007).

17. Ruth McEnery Stuart, "Jessekiah Brown's Courtship," in *A Golden Wedding and Other Tales* (New York: Harper and Brothers, 1893). Although Stuart does not directly mention that the story is situated in Louisiana, it does mention a plantation along a levee and Bayou Teche. Since Bayou Teche is in Louisiana, the story seems to be located there.

18. After the Civil War, the average age at which men married increased to 27.8 and for women, 23.8; however, J. David Hacker, Libra Hilde, and James Holland Jones argue that the Civil War was not solely responsible for the increase in the marrying age. Rather, it was part

of a larger overall trend, similar to what was happening in other industrial countries. See J. David Hacker, Libra Hilde, and James Holland Jones, "The Effect of the Civil War on Marriage Patterns," *Journal of Southern History* 76, no. 1 (February 2010): 39–70.

19. Ibid.

20. Ibid.

21. Robert H. Wiebe, *The Search for Order: 1877–1920* (New York: Hill and Wang, 1967), xii.

22. Kathy L. Peiss, *Cheap Amusements: Working Women and Leisure in Turn-of-the-Century New York* (Philadelphia: Temple University Press, 1986). I avoid the use of the word "dating" for this period, since the modern view of dating did not emerge until the 1920s with the proliferation of cars. See Beth L. Bailey, *From Front Porch to Back Seat: Courtship in Twentieth-Century America* (Baltimore: Johns Hopkins University Press, 1988).

23. *State v. James Davis*, CRDC #3050 (1882).

24. Charles H. Bennett, *The Frog Who Would a Wooing Go* (New York: McLoughlin Brothers, 1875).

25. Lystra, *Searching the Heart*, 9–10.

26. For more information on "treating," see Peiss, *Cheap Amusements*; and Elizabeth Clement, *Love for Sale: Courting, Treating, and Prostitution in New York City, 1900–1945* (Chapel Hill: University of North Carolina Press, 2006).

27. Clement, *Love for Sale*, 3.

28. *State v. Willie Hennessey*, CRDC #9950 (1887).

29. Ibid.

30. *State v. John Green*, CRDC #5627 (1884).

31. *State v. George Samuels and John Schnieder*, CRDC #8592 (1886).

32. Ibid.

33. Ibid.

34. Ibid.

35. Ibid.

36. *State v. Andrew Williams*, CRDC #1805 (1881).

37. Ibid.

38. *State v. Morris Hamilton*, CRDC #10182 (1887).

39. Ibid.

40. Nancy F. Cott, *Public Vows: A History of Marriage and the Nation* (Cambridge, MA: Harvard University Press, 2002), 39.

41. For more information on the social purity movement, see David J. Pivar, *Purity Crusade: Sexual Morality and Social Control, 1868–1900* (Westport, CT: Greenwood Press, 1973). For more information on the progressive movement, see Michael E. McGerr, *A Fierce Discontent: The Rise and Fall of the Progressive Movement in America, 1870–1920* (New York: Free Press, 2003).

42. As cited in Michael Grossberg, *Governing the Hearth: Law and the Family in Nineteenth-Century America* (Chapel Hill: University of North Carolina Press, 1985), 85.

43. Ibid.

44. Ibid., 83–100.

45. Ibid.

46. Bercaw, *Gendered Freedoms*, 106–7. Although taking up and sweethearting were viewed as distinct from marriage, some couples, as Bercaw states, did view those alternative living arrangements as a precursor to marriage.

47. Although states attempted to curb "bad" marriages and rising divorce rates by enacting new legislation, the number of divorces continued to increase. Between 1889 and 1906, the divorce rate grew to fifteen times what it had been prior to the Civil War. See Steven Mintz and Susan Kellogg, *Domestic Revolutions: A Social History of American Family Life* (New York: Free Press, 1988), 109.

48. The State of Louisiana, *Louisiana Legal Archives*, vol. 3, part 1, *Compiled Edition of the Civil Codes of Louisiana* (Baton Rouge: Louisiana State Law Institute, 1940), 51. In 1825 and 1870, a few changes in the punctuation of the description were made, but the content remained the same.

49. Ibid.

50. Ibid.

51. Edmund Augustus Peyroux, *Revised Civil Code of the State of Louisiana to Which Were Added Useful Abundant References to the Decision of the Supreme Court, Annual Reports and also References to the Acts of Legislature Up To and Including the Session of 1882* (New Orleans: Geo Muller Printer, 1885), 133.

52. Goran Lind, *Common Law Marriage: A Legal Institution for Cohabitation* (Oxford: Oxford University Press, 2008), 147.

53. Because common law marriages came under attack during the postbellum era and because some states, such as Louisiana, refused to recognize them, intimate partner violence in common law marriages falls in the nonmarital intimate partner violence category. The court case cited for Louisiana's legal recognition of other states' common law marriages was *Taylor v. Swett*, 3 La. 33 (1831). Also, I use the term "common law marriage" rather than "concubinage" to refer to the committed relationship of two individuals living together regardless of race. Although concubinage refers to a state in which a couple lives together "in a committed relationship without benefit of marriage," common law marriage appears better a term for this discussion. Often, the couple in the court records would refer to each other as husband and wife with the added phrase "although not legally married." To them, they felt married and did not use any other phrase to refer to their arrangement. Sometimes, the couple would eventually seek legal sanction of their marriage. Additionally, other states did and still do recognize common law marriage. Consequently, I have chosen to stay with the phrase "common law marriage" rather than "concubinage" or even "cohabitation." For more information on concubinage in New Orleans, particularly the form called *plaçage*, which involved an interracial relationship, see Long, *The Great Southern Babylon*.

54. *State v. William Anderson*, CRDC #10255 (1888).

55. There are no statistics on intimate partner homicides during the postbellum period. Presently, 75 percent of intimate partner homicides are committed as the victim attempts to leave the relationship. See Hallie Bongar White and James G. White, "Testifying about Lethality Risk Factors," Southwest Center for Law and Policy, and Office on Violence against Women, US Department of Justice, 2005.

56. *State v. William Anderson*, CRDC #10255 (1888). Cotton hooks were found in many court cases involving assault and battery. Since they were common items in areas dependent on cotton as a cash crop, these instruments were accessible and could inflict significant injury, given their sharp end and heavy metal construction.

57. *State v. Major Anderson*, CRDC #8059 (1886).

58. Ibid.

59. Statistics on education in the postbellum era show that roughly half of five- to nineteen-year-olds were enrolled in school. "Rates for males and females were roughly similar throughout the period, but rates for blacks were much lower than for whites. . . . Following the Civil War, enrollment rates for blacks rose rapidly from 10 percent in 1870 to 34 percent in 1880." See Tom Snyder, ed., *120 Years of American Education: A Statistical Portrait* (Washington, DC: US Department of Education, Office of Educational Research and Improvement, National Center for Education Statistics, 1993), chapter 1.

60. *State v. Major Anderson*, CRDC #8059 (1886).

61. Most postmodernist theorists argue that those in power help to formulate or uphold what constitutes "normal" and "not normal." Those considered abnormal are denied access to power. Also, scholarship on disempowered groups has shown how minorities reinterpret and reappropriate these values. See Larry May and Jeff Brown, eds., *Philosophy of Law: Classic and Contemporary Readings* (Oxford: Blackwell, 2010), 133. See also Dianna Taylor and Karen Vintges, eds., *Feminism and the Final Foucault* (Urbana: University of Illinois Press, 2004), 222–23; Michel Foucault, *Discipline and Punish: The Birth of the Prison* (New York: Pantheon Books, 1977); and Keith Jenkins, *The Postmodern History Reader* (London: Routledge, 1997).

62. *State v. Sam Carney*, CRDC #9873 (1887).

63. Ibid.

64. Coverture defined women whose identities were subsumed under their husbands' as "civilly dead." This had been the legal means of identifying women since the colonial era. For more information on coverture in the United States, see Hendrik Hartog, *Man and Wife in America: A History* (Cambridge, MA: Harvard University Press, 2000); Kerber, *No Constitutional Right to Be Ladies*; and Sally Kitch, *The Specter of Sex: Gendered Foundations of Racial Formation in the United States* (Albany: State University of New York Press, 2009).

65. John McKowen to Sallie Henry, December 20, 1895, Wilson, Louisiana, McKowen-Lilley-Stirling Family Papers, Manuscript Collection 4356, Hill Memorial Library, Louisiana State University, Baton Rouge.

66. Carl N. Degler, *At Odds: Women and the Family in America from the Revolution to the Present* (New York: Oxford University Press, 1980), 168. Elaine Tyler May also notices a shift in divorce in the second half of the nineteenth century in her case study of Los Angeles. May says that "the late nineteenth century witnessed a slight straining against the limits of Victorianism" as "altered sex roles" reshaped marital expectations and the courts' response. See Elaine Tyler May, *Great Expectations: Marriage and Divorce in Post-Victorian America* (Chicago: University of Chicago Press, 1980), 49.

67. Of these cases, 146 (65 percent) involved marital intimate partner violence.

68. For more on decoration days, see David W. Blight, *Race and Reunion: The Civil War in American Memory* (Cambridge, MA: Belknap Press of Harvard University Press, 2001); and Foster, *Ghosts of the Confederacy*.

69. John R. Ficklen Papers, Manuscript Collection 144, 209, Louisiana and Lower Mississippi Valley Collections, Louisiana State University, Baton Rouge.

70. Ibid.

71. O. M. Grisham to Sallie, June 19, 1904, Winnfield, Louisiana, Grisham-Kellogg-Faust Papers, Manuscript Collection 5048, Hill Memorial Library, Louisiana State University, Baton Rouge.

72. Peiss, *Cheap Amusements*. Peiss examines working women in a northern urban setting, but her argument can be extended to the South, albeit urban areas like New Orleans.

73. *State v. Mat Lumbardo*, CRDC #9901 (1887).

74. For more information on the history of women and the workforce, see Alice Kessler-Harris, *Out to Work: A History of Wage-Earning Women in the United States* (New York: Oxford University Press, 1982).

75. US Census Bureau, *Statistics of Women at Work*, US Census of 1900, 9, at https://www2.census.gov/prod2/decennial/documents/00779830ch1.pdf, accessed September 10, 2016.

76. Ibid., 132, at https://fraser.stlouisfed.org/scribd/?title_id=296&filepath=/docs/publications/statww/statww_census_1907.pdf, accessed September 10, 2016.

77. *State v. Henry Marks*, CRDC #10180 (1887).

78. *State v. A. Bax*, CRDC #5062 (1884).

79. Ibid.

80. Martin, *Evening Visits with a Sister*.

81. *State v. James Wilson*, CRDC #9856 (1887).

82. *State v. G.C. Shields*, CRDC #9767 (1887).

83. Ibid.

84. Linda Gordon in *Heroes of Their Own Lives* also shows female agency with abused women sometimes fighting back.

85. "An Unhappy Pair," *Daily Picayune*, May 7, 1879.

86. Some claim that women had to play innocent victims before the court. See Beverly J. Schwartzberg, "Grass Widows, Barbarians, and Bigamists: Fluid Marriage in Late Nineteenth-Century America" (PhD diss., University of California, Santa Barbara, 2001), 73–74.

87. In only three cases (1.3 percent) did women express the belief that their husband had some sort of right to beat them. Of thirty-eight nolle prosequi cases, in only three cases (8 percent) did women believed that they were at fault and dropped charges. I think that both statistics are helpful. The first shows how few women viewed intimate partner violence as beyond the reach of the courts. The second shows even among those cases that were dropped, the majority of women did not believe that their husband had the right of chastisement. Nolle prosequi cases, therefore, do not undermine the argument of women's overall agency due to new conceptions of womanhood.

88. *State v. James Gillen*, CRDC #2911 (1882). Mrs. Gillen's first name never appears in the testimony.

89. Ibid.

Chapter Four

1. Hannah Anderson's husband is not referred to or listed in the report by his first name.

2. *State v. James Wilson*, CRDC #9856 (1887).

3. Ibid.

4. Sharon Block, *Rape and Sexual Power in Early America* (Chapel Hill: University of North Carolina Press, 2006). Block also argues that rape, a form of gender-based violence, is based on the issue of gender and power. She uses similar logic to argue for a bottom-up movement addressing the social problem of rape in early American history.

5. *State v. Herman Busch*, CRDC #4192 (1883).

6. *State v. William Joyce*, CRDC #7825 (1885).

7. Ibid.

8. *State v. Ben Lee*, CRDC #5151 (1884); and State v. Ben Lee, CRDC #5421 (1884). Testimony in both cases stated that he had abused her on several previous occasions.

9. *State v. Ben Lee*, CRDC #5421 (1884).

10. "Misdeeds and Mishaps: Domestic Discords," *Daily Picayune*, July 30, 1884.

11. Ibid.

12. "Death Notice," *Wheeling (WV) Register*, July 14, 1891.

13. See Laura F. Edwards, *Gendered Strife and Confusion: The Political Culture of Reconstruction* (Urbana: University of Illinois Press, 1997). As Edwards and other historians have argued, African American households differed from the white ideal before the Civil War, being more matriarchal.

14. *State v. Will Bassinger*, CRDC #9764 (1887).

15. Ibid.

16. Ibid.

17. Ibid.

18. Mary Beth Norton addresses this issue in *Founding Mothers and Fathers: Gendered Power and the Forming of American Society* (New York: Random House, 1996). For more on colonial intimate partner violence, see Elaine Forman Crane, *Witches, Wife Beaters, and Whores: Common Law and Common Folk in Early America* (Ithaca, NY: Cornell University Press, 2011); and Christine Daniels and Michael V. Kennedy, eds., *Over the Threshold: Intimate Violence in Early America* (New York: Routledge, 1999).

19. Norton, *Founding Mothers and Fathers*, 78.

20. Historians often discuss this loss of status, particularly legal status, as feme covert.

21. Some historians discuss the notion of paternal benevolence as simply justification for the continuation of slavery. Viewing slavery as "best" for the slave—a system in which the owner was kind and treated slaves as part of his family—ideally mitigated the harsh view of abolitionists and books like *Uncle Tom's Cabin*. See Lacy K. Ford, *Deliver Us from Evil: The Slavery Question in the Old South* (Oxford: Oxford University Press, 2009); and Edlie L. Wong, *Neither Fugitive nor Free: Atlantic Slavery, Freedom Suits, and the Legal Culture of Travel* (New York: New York University Press, 2009).

22. The South generally disapproved of intimate partner homicide, while spousal abuse was broadly accepted. Although two southern states did pass laws against wife abuse prior to

the Civil War (Tennessee in 1850 and Georgia in 1857), other southern states, such as North Carolina, upheld the right of chastisement (*State v. Jesse Black*, 1 Winston 266).

23. "Recorder's Court, Second Municipality," *Daily Picayune*, March, 19, 1840. A similar case in which both the husband and wife were arrested is discussed in "Local Matters," *Baltimore Sun*, October 21, 1852.

24. American Statistical Association, *Publications of the American Statistical Association*, vol. 1: *1888–1889* (Boston: W. J. Schofield, 1889), 46.

25. Ibid.

26. John Smith Kendall, *History of New Orleans*, vol. 2 (Chicago: Lewis Publishing Company, 1922), 683.

27. American Statistical Association, *Publications*, 1:58–59.

28. *State v. William Teal*, CRDC #1786 (1881).

29. Ibid.

30. *State v. Martin Johnson*, CRDC #8652 (1886).

31. Nancy Willard to Ms. Wilkinson, August 13, 1877, Collinsburg, Louisiana, Micajah Wilkinson Papers, Manuscript Collection 707, Hill Memorial Library, Louisiana State University, Baton Rouge; and Nancy Willard to Ms. Wilkinson, October 22, 1877, Collinsburg, Louisiana, Micajah Wilkinson Papers, Manuscript Collection 707, Hill Memorial Library, Louisiana State University, Baton Rouge.

32. Nancy Willard to Ms. Wilkinson, October 22, 1877, Collinsburg, Louisiana, Micajah Wilkinson Papers, Manuscript Collection 707, Hill Memorial Library, Louisiana State University, Baton Rouge.

33. Ibid.

34. Ibid.

35. *State v. James Gillen*, CRDC #2911 (1882).

36. Ibid.

37. Alecia Long's *The Great Southern Babylon*, for example, examines the shift from relative tolerance for "sex across the color line" in New Orleans immediately following the war to a more rigid definition of white and black by 1910. C. Vann Woodward, in *The Strange Career of Jim Crow* (New York: Oxford University Press, 1974), also explores the role of race and its increasing importance during the postbellum era. By 1882, race, although categories such as "octoroon" had been abandoned, generally mattered in most aspects of life. The social view of intimate partner violence, however, broke down racial barriers, allowing for temporary cross-racial alliances.

38. Long, *The Great Southern Babylon*; and Woodward, *The Strange Career of Jim Crow*.

39. *State v. William Hines*, CRDC #8841 (1886).

40. Prosecution of intimate partner violence by witnesses accounted for 16 of the 225 court cases examined (7 percent); of the 16, only 2 were dropped (12.5 percent). More generally, cases that ended nolle prosequi accounted for 17 percent of all intimate partner violence charges. The small sample size for witnesses notwithstanding, the percentage of dropped cases is similar regardless of who filed, showing a high prosecution rate overall. Testimony from the court cases and newspaper accounts shows a high level of public intervention, but overwhelmingly it was the female victims who filed suit for assault and battery.

41. Some feminists, legal scholars, and sociologists have examined the unintended negative consequences of mutual arrest and mandatory arrest laws. See Susan L. Miller, *Victims as Offenders: The Paradox of Women's Violence in Relationships* (New Brunswick, NJ: Rutgers University Press, 2005); and Meloy and Miller, *The Victimization of Women*.

42. *State v. John Traylor*, CRDC #8758 (1886).

43. *State v. Warren Powell*, CRDC #10434 (1888).

44. *State v. Louis Mayfield*, CRDC #9643 (1887).

45. Ibid.

46. Ibid.

47. Ibid.

48. Dewey W. Grantham, *Southern Progressivism: The Reconciliation of Progress and Tradition* (Knoxville: University of Tennessee Press, 1983), 111.

49. Wiebe, *The Search for Order.*

Chapter Five

1. James Schouler, *A Treatise on the Law of the Domestic Relations: Embracing Husband and Wife, Parent and Child, Guardian and Ward, Infancy, and Master and Servant* (Boston: Little, Brown, 1870). Aside from William Blackstone's *Commentaries*, Schouler's various works were among the most cited legal tracts of the time. *A Treatise on the Law of the Domestic Relations* was Schouler's first publication on any topic, and it was reprinted (and circulated more widely) in 1874, 1882, 1889, and 1895.

2. Siegel, "The Rule of Love." Reva Siegel is the foremost legal scholar on intimate partner violence and the law, and she discusses the legal shifts in dealing with the problem. Also, historians generally recognize that companionate marriages became the predominant form of marital union after 1900, but emotional expectations in marriage (marrying for love) gained ground in the late 1800s, as evidenced by Schouler's work. Peter Bardaglio also notices this "growing emphasis on affectionate love between husband and wife" in the late 1800s; see Peter W. Bardaglio, *Reconstructing the Household: Families, Sex, and the Law in the Nineteenth-Century South* (Chapel Hill: University of North Carolina Press, 1995), xiii. For more information on the emergence of companionate marriage, see Stephanie Coontz, *Marriage, a History: How Love Conquered Marriage* (New York: Penguin, 2006); and Rebecca L. Davis, "'Not Marriage at All, but Simple Harlotry': The Companionate Marriage Controversy," *Journal of American History* 94, no. 4 (March 2008): 1137–63.

3. Siegel, "The Rule of Love."

4. Pleck, "Wife Beating in Nineteenth-Century America," 56.

5. Ibid.

6. Harriet S. Daggett, *Louisiana Statutes Related to the Civil Code* (New Orleans: Louisiana Law Institute, 1943).

7. *Margaret Moclair v. James Leahy*, 36 La. Ann. 583, 1884 WL 8065 (La.).

8. Ibid.

9. *Macado v. Bonet*, 39 La. Ann. 475, 2 So. 49.

10. For more information on the issues victims face when they fight back, see Miller, *Victims as Offenders*; and Meloy and Miller, *The Victimization of Women*.

11. *Macado v. Bonet*, 39 La. Ann. 475, 2 So. 49.

12. *Fulgham v. the State*, 46 Ala. 143 (1871).

13. Ibid. Since George and Matilda Fulgham were African American, some scholars contend that the courts sought to regulate the "lower classes" and people of color; however, in the trial court, Judge Peters cut across class and race lines in his ruling, denying any "special privilege" before the eyes of the law. He argued: "The law for one rank is the law for all ranks of the people, without regard to station." The Supreme Court of Alabama upheld the lower court judge's opinion. Southern courts, while concerned with class and race, did extend protection, rights, and the status of womanhood to abused wives. For arguments about *Fulgham* as a means of social control over lower socioeconomic classes and people of color, see Siegel, "The Rule of Love"; Bardaglio, *Reconstructing the Household*; and Edwards, "Women and Domestic Violence."

14. *Fulgham v. the State*, 46 Ala. 143 (1871).

15. Pleck, "Wife Beating in Nineteenth-Century America."

16. Richard H. Clark, *The Code of the State of Georgia*, 2nd ed. (Macon, GA: John H. Seals, 1873), 825.

17. While some states did pass legislation around the turn of the twentieth century criminalizing what they termed "wife beating," most did not. The general belief in the United States held spousal abuse to be illegal after 1871 (see Pleck, *Domestic Tyranny*), but courts were left to interpret the law as it stood to include intimate partner violence. In Louisiana, for instance, W. S. Posey, a Democratic legislator, proposed a law to define and punish wife beating in 1886, but it never made it to the House floor. However, not all states uniformly ruled on the issue. Louisiana had no law on wife beating, but criminal court dockets on assault and battery indicate that husbands were routinely arrested and tried for beating their wives. See also Pleck, "Wife Beating in Nineteenth-Century America." As I seek to show in this book, the country generally tried to prosecute abusive men under assault and battery charges during the postbellum period. The current legal system does define a separate criminal statute for "domestic violence," but those changes stem more from the mass consciousness–raising efforts of the women's movement in the 1960s and 1970s. Louisiana's most current statute is based on legislative changes made in 2000.

18. Most cases in the Orleans Parish criminal court for assault and battery used Section 796; for example, *State v. Thomas Coffey*, CRDC #5211 (1884), and *State v. George Blancque*, CRDC #5251 (1884).

19. *State v. Ben Lee*, CRDC #5421 (1884).

20. Ibid.

21. Ibid.

22. Ibid.

23. Ibid.

24. Republican Office, *Revised Laws of Louisiana, Containing the Revised Statutes of the State as Amended by Acts of the Legislature from the Session of 1870 to That of 1896, Inclusive and All Other Acts of General Nature for the Same Period, All Annotated with the Decisions*

of the Supreme Court of Louisiana Contained in Annuals 39 to 48 and a Part of 49 (New Orleans: Republican Office, 1870), 337.

25. Some 5,344 of 13,215 court cases during the 1880–1889 period in Orleans Parish criminal courts involved charges of simple assault, assault and battery, assault by wounding and cutting, assault with a dangerous weapon, inflicting a wound, assault by willfully shooting at a victim, assault with intent to commit murder, and assault with intent to rape. Assault cases, then, accounted for 40.4 percent of the total number of criminal cases during the period.

26. For this reason, I refer to various assault cases as well as the assault and battery incidents under the collective phrase "assault and battery." The courts seemed to view assault only cases as assault and battery in their sentencing. The punishments for assault cases and assault and battery cases were generally the same, with only the intent to murder leading to a more severe fine or longer jail time. Moreover, often the assault only cases involved bodily damage, so differentiating between assault only and assault and battery cases is problematic and confusing to those accustomed to the current legal system's definitions of criminal charges.

27. Intimate partner violence included courtship violence, abuse against a common law wife, and wife beating.

28. Cases increased from 25 antebellum cases to 225 cases during the 1880–1889 period.

29. Louisiana, Orleans Parish, 1880 Census, population schedule by race, sex, and nativity.

30. For the majority of cases in this book, I do not discuss the race of the defendants and plaintiffs, primarily because such information is lacking in the records. The courts were not required to report the race or ethnicity of the people involved in any of the documents. Sometimes I could tease out the race based on testimony, but there were no other clues. Only the addresses and names of the people involved were recorded. I tried to match these against census records, but the limited information prevented me from definitively establishing the race of the vast majority of people in question. From those cases in which I was able to establish race, I did not see a difference in how judges ruled during the 1870s and 1880s. Other historians, such as Bertram Wyatt-Brown, and legal scholars, such as Carolyn Ramsey, have noted that wealthy white men were frequently the defendants in wife-beating cases during this period. See Ramsey, "A Diva Defends Herself"; and Wyatt-Brown, *Southern Honor*.

31. *State v. Ben Lee*, CRDC #5151 (1884).

32. *State v. Nicholas Seldner*, CRDC #8916 (1886).

33. Ibid.

34. Ibid.

35. Ibid.

36. Ibid. Works discussing women having to fulfill the role of passive victim to get successful prosecution include Edwards, "Women and Domestic Violence"; May, *Great Expectations*; Ann Lloyd, *Doubly Deviant, Doubly Damned: Society's Treatment of Violent Women* (London: Penguin, 1995); and Siegel, "The Rule of Love." Moreover, Emma Seldner did not deny or justify her attempt to choke her husband, although she claimed not to have had a brick in her possession. Moreover, Sophie Langs pushed him off her porch during the incident. Neither Langs nor Emma sought to cover up, deny, or justify that action either. Still, the court convicted the husband for assault and battery. While gender expectations as well

as racial and socioeconomic class bias played into courtroom decisions, judges seemed more preoccupied with punishing abusive husbands than enforcing a rigid hierarchy of class, race, and gender. Also, the decision suggests that the courts seemed less influenced by paternalism and more by, as I argue, the necessity to punish "uncivilized" men.

37. *State v. Nicholas Seldner*, CRDC #8916 (1886).

38. From 1880 to 1889, 146 cases (65 percent) involved marital intimate partner violence. Marital intimate partner violence nolle prosequi cases totaled 30 out of 38 cases, or 79 percent.

39. From 1880 to 1889, seventy-nine intimate partner violence cases (35 percent) involved unmarried couples (common law marriage, courting violence, etc.). Nonmarital intimate partner violence cases accounted for eight of the thirty-eight nolle prosequi and not-guilty cases, or 21 percent.

40. Bastardy cases could hold fathers in relationships outside of legal marriage accountable, but men often escaped these suits. See Edward J. Blum and W. Scott Poole, eds., *Vale of Tears: New Essays on Religion and Reconstruction* (Macon, GA: Mercer University Press, 2005), 30.

41. Siegel, "The Rule of Love," 2163.

42. *State v. William Green*, CRDC #7194 (1885).

43. Ibid.

44. Ibid.

45. *State v. Henry Gibbons*, CRDC #8845 (1886).

46. *State v. Richard Sheldon*, CRDC #8776 (1886).

47. *State v. Richard Sheldon*, CRDC #7353 (1885). The formal punishment was ten days in the Orleans Parish prison, but Sheldon had not made bail and had remained in jail for a few weeks before the trial date and sentencing.

48. *State v. Gerhart Koester*, CRDC #10213 (1887). The closest census records to match the couple are from the 1880 census. A "G. Koester Jr." lived in New Orleans and was married to an Ellen Koester in 1880. They inhabited a mixed neighborhood with immigrants from Italy and England as well as whites and African Americans. The Koester name appears to be of German origin, but "G. Koester Jr." from the 1880 census listed his race as white and his birthplace as Louisiana, making him at the very least a second-generation immigrant if he was German at all.

49. *State v. Gerhart Koester*, CRDC #10213 (1887).

50. For example, *State v. J. O. C. Wallis*, CRDC #11094 (1888); *State v. Richard Sheldon*, CRDC #8776 (1886); and *State v. Martin Johnson*, CRDC #8562 (1886).

51. For more information on whipping post regulations, see Pleck, "Wife Beating in Nineteenth-Century America"; and Pleck, *Domestic Tyranny*. Delaware and Oregon also passed whipping post legislation during the first decade of the twentieth century, but it was, like Maryland's law, rarely used.

52. As early as 1876, state legislatures in North Carolina and Indiana proposed whipping post legislation. In 1877, Nevada passed a bill that punished men who beat women (whether a wife or not) by tying them to a post for two to ten hours while they wore a sign saying "Woman Beater" or "Wife Beater." The Nevada law, however, was not used. See Pleck, *Domestic Tyranny*, 110.

53. "Wife Beating," *Wheeling (WV) Register*, March 21, 1877.

54. Kessler-Harris, *Out to Work*, 301. For more on women in the workforce, see Alice Kessler-Harris, *In Pursuit of Equity: Women, Men, and the Quest for Economic Citizenship in 20th-Century America* (Oxford: Oxford University Press, 2001); and Boydston, *Home and Work*.

55. *Daily Picayune*, March 14, 1881; and *Daily Capitolian-Advocate* (Baton Rouge), May 11, 1886.

56. By the mid-1880s, states such as Massachusetts, Pennsylvania, and New Hampshire were debating whipping post legislation. See Pleck, *Domestic Tyranny*, 113. In Louisiana, a state legislator (Charles Cordill) announced that he would propose whipping post legislation, but he never did. See "The Legislative Journal," *Daily Capitolian-Advocate* (Baton Rouge), May 11, 1886.

57. "The Whipping Post: Fifteen Lashes in Sixteen Seconds for Wife Beating," *Baltimore Sun*, June 16, 1885.

58. "A Wife Beater Flogged," *New Haven Evening Register*, June 16, 1885.

59. Ibid.

60. "The Whipping Post: Fifteen Lashes in Sixteen Seconds for Wife Beating," *Baltimore Sun*, June 16, 1885.

61. Ibid.

62. "Mr. Adams: Senate," *Philadelphia Inquirer*, January 24, 1885.

63. Ibid.

64. In the 1880s, charges were dropped in 38 of the 225 cases examined.

65. *State v. Gust Hannewinckle*, CRDC #10128 (1887).

66. Ibid.

67. Mrs. Blondeau was illiterate and had to sign documents with an *X* instead of a proper signature. The letterhead of her letter was that of the city court, indicating that she had dictated her letter to a clerk, who handwrote it and then submitted it to the district attorney.

68. *State v. Gaston Blondeau*, CRDC #8757 (1886). She was fourth months pregnant at the time of the abuse. Her first name was never used in any of the documents, where she was constantly referred to as Mrs. Blondeau.

69. *State v. Ike Carter*, CRDC #10995 (1888).

70. *State v. J. O. C. Wallis*, CRDC #11094 (1888).

71. *State v. Augustus Richards*, CRDC #4703 (1884). For more information on Kate Townsend, see James Gill, *Lords of Misrule: Mardi Gras and the Politics of Race in New Orleans* (Jackson: University Press of Mississippi, 1997), 138.

72. *State v. Augustus Richards*, CRDC #4703 (1884). Typically, bail for assault and battery fell at $250; $500 usually meant that the assailant had attacked with a dangerous weapon or had the intent to murder. Richards did not make bail from a lending agency but rather from a friend, Charles Fox. Given Richards's connection to someone with the means to raise $500, Martha's ability to read and write, and their household at 1922 Tchoupitoulas Street near Henry Clay Avenue (a nicer neighborhood in New Orleans during the 1880s), the Richards household was arguably at least of middling means, and certainly not within the poorer socioeconomic class.

73. Ramsey, "A Diva Defends Herself."

74. Ibid.

75. Ibid.

76. See Walker, *The Battered Woman*; and Lenore Walker, *The Battered Woman Syndrome* (New York: Springer, 1984).

77. Such apologizing is commonly recognized as part of the cycle of intimate partner violence and partially explains why the victim has a difficult time leaving a violent relationship. For more information, see Walker, *The Battered Woman*. Nineteenth-century Americans held a basic grasp of the pattern of violence, as shown in "Legislative Acts and Legal Proceedings," *Daily Picayune*, April 3, 1872.

78. *State v. Henry Gasper*, CRDC #9114 (1887).

79. Henry to Odelia Nelson, February 17, 1887, *State v. Henry Gasper*, CRDC #9114 (1887).

80. Henry to Odelia Nelson, February 22, 1887, *State v. Henry Gasper*, CRDC #9114 (1887).

81. In only three cases, roughly 1.5 percent of intimate partner violence cases from the 1880s, did the woman express the belief that her husband had some sort of right to abuse her. In thirty-eight nolle prosequi cases, three cases (8 percent) had women who believed that they had done something wrong (one of those cases still resulted in a conviction). Both statistics are helpful. The first demonstrates how few women viewed intimate partner violence as beyond the reach of the courts. The second demonstrates that, even among the cases dropped, the majority of women did not believe that their husbands had the right of chastisement. Nolle prosequi cases, therefore, do not undermine the argument of women's overall agency due to new views of womanhood.

82. *State v. James Gillen*, CRDC #2911 (1882). Mrs. Gillen's first name never appears in the testimony.

83. Ibid.

84. *State v. George Clark*, CRDC #9946 (1887).

85. Ibid.

86. *State v. Warren Powell*, CRDC #10434 (1888).

87. Ibid.

88. *State v. Sarah Hodges*, CRDC #5051 (1884).

89. *State v. Jennie Robinson*, CRDC #11236 (1888).

90. Schouler, *A Treatise on the Law of the Domestic Relations*.

91. A total of 184 cases resulted in a full trial. Only 14 of the defendants in assault and battery cases tried were found to be not guilty, leaving 170 defendants (92 percent) with a guilty verdict.

Chapter Six

1. In this chapter's epigraph, Vardaman writes in the *Greenwood (MS) Commonwealth*, July 15, 27, 1897; as quoted in Michael Newton, *The Ku Klux Klan in Mississippi: A History* (Jefferson, NC: McFarland, 2010), 62.

2. The role of populism in the rise of the Jim Crow era is addressed, for example, in Ayers, *The Promise of the New South*.

3. Leanna Keith, *The Colfax Massacre: The Untold Story of Black Power, White Terror, and the Death of Reconstruction* (Oxford: Oxford University Press, 2008), 76.

4. *United States v. Cruikshank*, 92 U.S. 542 (1875).

5. United States Congress, *Report and Testimony of the Select Committee of the United States Senate to Investigate the Causes of the Removal of the Negroes from the Southern States to the Northern States*, Senate Report 693, 46th Cong., 2nd Sess., part 2, 89.

6. Windom was a Radical Republican from Minnesota. For more information, see "Windom, William (1827–1891)," Biographical Directory of the United States Congress, at http://bioguide.congress.gov/scripts/biodisplay.pl?index=W000629.

7. United States Congress, *Report and Testimony*, 91. Other whites testified that there was no racial strife in the South; W. P. Ford, for example, claimed that "as a whole, great friendliness of feeling exists between the colored and the white men. . . . [T]hey live on the most amicable terms." See United States Congress, *Report and Testimony*, 166.

8. "A Queer Southern Outrage," *Daily Picayune*, November 26, 1878.

9. Edward Ayers in *The Promise of the New South* estimates that from 25 percent to more than 50 percent of rural southerners over twenty-one years of age (varying based on state) joined the Populist Party.

10. Several historians argue the presidential election of 1896 and the fusion between Democrats and Populists ended the Populist Party. See, for example, Lawrence Goodwyn, *The Populist Moment: A Short History of the Agrarian Revolt in America* (Oxford: Oxford University Press, 1978).

11. Thomas E. Watson, "The Negro Question in the South," *Arena* 6 (October 1892): 540–50.

12. Woodward, *The Strange Career of Jim Crow*; and Ayers, *The Promise of the New South*.

13. Woodward, *The Strange Career of Jim Crow*.

14. US Census Bureau, *Report on Population of the United States at the Tenth Census: 1880* (Washington, DC: Government Printing Office, 1885).

15. US Census Bureau, *Report on Population of the United States at the Eleventh Census: 1890* (Washington, DC: Government Printing Office, 1896).

16. An anti-miscegenation law was first created in Louisiana in 1808; see Louisiana Civil Code, art. 8 (1808). The new 1870 Civil Code altered the reasons justifying nullification of a marriage, leaving out interracial unions. See Louisiana Civil Code, art. 94 (1870). The code was then amended in 1894; see Louisiana Acts 1894, no. 54. For the law on concubinage, see Act no. 87 of 1908; see also Frank W. Sweet, *Legal History of the Color Line: The Rise and Triumph of the One-Drop Rule* (Palm Coast, FL: Backintyme, 2000), 494.

17. US Census Bureau, *Report on Population of the United States at the Eleventh Census*, xciii.

18. Mary E. Frederickson, *Looking South: Race, Gender, and Transformation of Labor from Reconstruction to Globalization* (Gainesville: University Press of Florida, 2011).

19. *Plessy v. Ferguson*, 163 U.S. 537 (1896). For more information, see Klarman, *From Jim Crow to Civil Rights*; and Blair Murphy Kelley, *Right to Ride: Streetcar Boycotts and African American Citizenship in the Era of Plessy v. Ferguson* (Chapel Hill: University of North Carolina Press, 2010). Louisiana legally enshrined the "one-drop rule" with *Lee v. New Orleans Great Northern Railroad*, 125 La. 236, 51 So. 182 (1910).

20. Mississippi Constitution of 1890, art. 12, sec. 240, 243, 244.

21. Andrew L. Shapiro, "Challenging Criminal Disenfranchisement under the Voting Rights Act: A New Strategy," *Yale Law Journal* 103, no. 2 (November 1993): 538.

22. "Colored Americans: The National Organization Issues an Address," *Knoxville Journal*, February 7, 1890.

23. *Williams v. Mississippi*, 170 U.S. 213 (1898).

24. State of Alabama, *Journal Proceedings of the Constitutional Convention of the State of Alabama Held in the City of Montgomery* (Montgomery, AL: Brown Printing Company, 1901).

25. Ibid., 9.

26. Ibid., 13.

27. As quoted in Jason Schall, "The Consistency of Felon Disenfranchisement with Citizenship Theory," *Harvard Blackletter Law Journal* 22 (2006): 59.

28. State of Virginia, *Proceedings on the Debates of the Constitutional Convention of the State of Virginia Held in the City of Richmond*, vol. 1 (Richmond: Hermitage Press, 1906), 1678.

29. Charles W. Chesnutt, *The Disenfranchisement of the Negro* (New York: Patt, 1903), 83–84.

30. Springing up around the same time, different people used the phrase "the New Negro Crime." See "Some Fresh Suggestions on the New Negro Crime," *Harper's Weekly*, January 23, 1904, 120–21; "The Negro Problem and the New Negro Crime," *Harper's Weekly*, June 20, 1903, 1050–51; and Mrs. W. H. Felton, "From a Southern Woman," *Harper's Weekly*, November 14, 1903, 1830.

31. "Negro Rapist Captured," *Weekly Times-Herald* (Dallas), February 1, 1890; "An Arkansas Young Lady Assaulted, Mutilated, and Murdered; Her Slayer Lynched," *Duluth Daily Tribune*, February 14, 1890; "Ravisher Lynched, Swung to a Telegraph Pole—Riddled with Bullets," *Daily Herald* (Grand Forks, ND), February 28, 1890; and "A Rape Fiend Lynched," *Omaha Daily World-Herald*, March 1, 1890.

32. "An Arkansas Young Lady Assaulted, Mutilated, and Murdered; Her Slayer Lynched," *Duluth Daily Tribune*, February 14, 1890.

33. Ibid.

34. For more information on these racial stereotypes, see Bederman, *Manliness and Civilization*; Donna J. Haraway, *Primate Visions: Gender, Race, and Nature in the World of Modern Science* (New York: Routledge, 1989); and White, *Ar'n't I a Woman?*

35. W. Fitzhugh Brundage, *Lynching in the New South: Georgia and Virginia, 1880–1930* (Urbana: University of Illinois Press, 1993), 7, 19. Brundage focuses on Virginia and Georgia as case examples of southern lynchings, but his findings on the types of lynchings bare similarities to the rest of the South (20).

36. Ibid., 8.

37. W. E. B. Du Bois specifically tried to combat images of "negro criminality" in his photographic exhibit at the Paris Exposition in 1900.

38. As quoted in Martha E. Hodes, *White Women, Black Men: Illicit Sex in the Nineteenth-Century South* (New Haven, CT: Yale University Press, 1997), 193. Crystal Feimster, in *Southern Horrors*, also discusses the lynchings of women (both white and black). She argues that most had committed a violent crime or were deemed guilty of immorality. Lynching these

women showed that black women were "unwomanly" and further served as a means of terror to "remake lower-class white women into self-disciplined 'southern ladies' worthy of protection" (Feimster, *Southern Horrors*, 180). Ultimately, lynching black women helped uphold
white male dominance.

39. Feimster, *Southern Horrors*. See also LeeAnn Whites, "Rebecca Latimer Felton and the
Wife's Farm: The Class and Racial Politics of Gender Reform," *Georgia Historical Quarterly*
76, no. 2 (Summer 1992): 354–72.

40. "Raped: A Colored School Teacher—The Way White Men Do Things in the
South," *Washington Bee*, January 11, 1890; at Chronicling America: Historic American Newspapers, Library of Congress, at http://chroniclingamerica.loc.gov/lccn/
sn84025891/1890–01–11/ed–1/seq–1/, accessed November 13, 2013. Another discussion of
rape is found in Kidada E. Williams, *They Left Great Marks on Me: African American
Testimonies of Racial Violence from Emancipation to World War I* (New York: New York
University Press, 2012), 107–8.

41. For more information on miscegenation, see Peggy Pascoe, *What Comes Naturally: Miscegenation Law and the Making of Race in America* (Oxford: Oxford University Press, 2009).

42. Ibid., 6.

43. *Scott v. Georgia*, 39 Ga. 321, 323 (1869).

44. *State v. George Adams*, CRDC #15081 (1891).

45. Ibid.

46. "Is Wife Beating Still in Vogue?," *State* (Columbia, SC), June 22, 1903.

47. Ibid.

48. "Debates and Proceedings on the Constitutional Convention," *Richmond Dispatch*,
September 6, 1901.

49. "The News in Georgia," *Macon (GA) Weekly Telegraph*, September 10, 1884.

50. "Beat His Wife with a Club," *Wheeling (WV) Register*, November 26, 1893; "A Wife's
Complaint: Archie Barry Charged with Beating His Wife," *Daily Picayune*, November 6, 1895;
"Southern States Items of Interest," *Daily Picayune*, July 9, 1896; and "A Blood Thirsty Negro
Attempts to Kill His Wife," *Daily Advocate* (Baton Rouge), August 15, 1896.

51. Documented cases of white intimate partner violence after 1890 are found in the
annual reports of the Louisiana Society for the Prevention of Cruelty to Children from 1893
onward as well as in local newspapers such as the *Daily Picayune*, September 13, 1895.

52. "White Wife Beater," *Sunday State* (Columbia, SC), October 16, 1898. This newspaper's
readership was white and conservative and not African American, which makes the motive
for the application of the word "white" less circumspect. See Lynn Salsi and Margaret Sims,
Columbia: History of a Southern Capital (Charleston, SC: Arcadia, 2003), 103–8.

53. "Alleged Wife Beaters Arrested on Warrants Sworn Out by Wives—Said to Have Been
Drunk," *Lexington (KY) Herald*, October 15, 1904.

54. "A Bad Wife Beater: Negro Convict Made an Assault on the Guard," *State* (Columbia,
SC), January 1, 1905.

55. *Idaho Daily Statesman* (Boise), October 13, 1893. Other articles on the David Jackson
lynching include "Southern States Items of Interest Gleaned by the Picayune's Corps of
Special Correspondents; Covington Enlivened," *Daily Picayune*, October 11, 1893; "Jackson

Was Not Lynched, but His Career of Crime Will Be Cut Short by a Term in the Penitentiary," *Daily Picayune*, October 13, 1893; "Thrown in the Tchefuncta [*sic*]: The Negro Dave Jackson Hanged by Unknown Parties," *Daily Picayune*, October 29, 1893; and "Coroner's Inquest on Dave Jackson's Body, Cook's Disappearance," *Daily Picayune*, October 31, 1893.

56. "Coroner's Inquest on Dave Jackson's Body, Cook's Disappearance," *Daily Picayune*, October 31, 1893.

57. Ida B. Wells-Barnett, *The Red Record: Tabulated Statistics and Alleged Causes of Lynching in the United States, 1892, 1893, 1894* (Chicago: Donohue and Henneberry, 1895), at http://www.gutenberg.org/files/14977/14977-h/14977-h.htm, accessed December 10, 2012.

58. Ibid.

59. "A Negro, Supposed to Have Been a Wife Beater, Lynched," *Daily Picayune*, October 11, 1893.

60. Schall, "The Consistency of Felon Disenfranchisement," 58–59.

61. South Carolina Code, sec. 7-5-120 (proviso).

62. As quoted in Siegel, "The Rule of Love," 2140.

63. "The Alabama Convention: Former Governor Oates Proposes a Suffrage Scheme," *Daily Picayune*, June 5, 1901.

64. "Annual Report of the Chief of Police," *Columbus (GA) Enquirer-Sun*, December 12, 1896.

65. Louisiana, Orleans Parish, 1880 Census, population schedule by race, sex, and nativity.

66. Louisiana, Orleans Parish, 1900 Census, population schedule by sex, general nativity, and color. Due to the loss of many of the 1890 census, the 1900 census records were used.

67. *Daily Advocate* (Baton Rouge), August 15, 1896; *Daily Advocate* (Baton Rouge), August 7, 1895; *Daily Picayune*, July 9, 1896; *Daily Picayune*, November 6, 1895; *Daily Picayune*, March 23, 1895; *Daily Advocate* (Baton Rouge), December 8, 1900; *Age Herald* (Birmingham), October 7, 1900; *Weekly Advocate* (Baton Rouge), July 29, 1899; *Charlotte Observer*, August 25, 1896; *Birmingham Herald*, September 15, 1895; *Daily Advocate* (Baton Rouge), June 16, 1895; *Wheeling (WV) Register*, November 26, 1893; *Charlotte News*, July 17, 1893; *Columbus (GA) Daily Enquirer*, June 28, 1893; *Charlotte Observer*, October 8, 1892; *Columbus (GA) Daily Enquirer*, June 12, 1892; *Knoxville Journal*, November 3, 1891; *Columbus (GA) Daily Enquirer*, August 8, 1891 (two articles); and *Charlotte News*, January 17, 1891.

68. *Ratliff v. Beale*, 20 So. 865, 868 (Miss. 1896).

69. Schall, "The Consistency of Felon Disenfranchisement," 58–59; and South Carolina Code sec. 7-5-120 (proviso).

70. *Commonwealth v. Sapp*, 12 Ky. L. Rptr. 484 (1890). The conservative ruling of *Sapp* is discussed in *Indiana Law Journal*, "Evidence—Privileged Communications—Husband and Wife," *Indiana Law Journal* 10, no. 3 (1934), at http://www.repository.law.indiana.edu/ilj/vo110/iss3/8, accessed June 25, 2013.

71. *Commonwealth v. Sapp*, 12 Ky. L. Rptr. 484 (1890).

72. *State v. Hussey*, 44 N.C. (Busb.) 123 (1852).

73. *Fightmaster v. Fightmaster*, 22 Ky. L. Rptr. 1512 (1901).

74. *Alexander v. Alexander*, 165 N.C. 45 (1914). *Alexander*, like *Sapp*, cited an older case to support protection of the privilege of chastisement. In *Alexander*, the judges used *Joyner v.*

Joyner, 52 N.C. 322 (1862), which stated that "the law gives the husband power to use such a degree of force as is necessary to make the wife behave herself and know her place."

75. Alice Ruth Moore Dunbar-Nelson, *The Goodness of St. Rocque and Other Stories* (New York: Dodd, Mead and Company, 1899), 22.

76. Ibid., 23.

77. Ibid., 25.

78. Ibid., 33.

79. For information on African American women and rape, particularly a culture of dissemblance, see Hine, "Rape and the Inner Lives of Black Women," 912–20; and Eleanor Alexander, *Lyrics of Sunshine and Shadow: The Tragic Courtship and Marriage of Paul Laurence Dunbar and Alice Ruth Moore* (New York: New York University Press, 2001).

80. For more on the shift to the SPCC and family courts, see Pleck, *Domestic Tyranny*, 126, 136.

81. "Whipping Post for Wife Beaters," *Biloxi Daily Herald*, May 23, 1904.

Epilogue

1. Louisiana Society for the Prevention of Cruelty to Children, *3rd Annual Report* (New Orleans: Hopkins' Printing Office, 1895). The quotation in the epigraph is from page 20.

2. George MacAdam, "Feminist Revolutionary Principle Is Biological Bosh," *New York Times*, January 18, 1914.

3. Ibid.

4. Abraham Myerson, *The Nervous Housewife* (Boston: Little, Brown, 1920).

5. Ibid.

6. "Votes for Women Put Temporarily in the Background: Whether to Beat or Not to Beat Your Wife Is the Latest Controversy in Order," *Angelica (NY) Advocate*, August 21, 1913. A similar article was published in the *Sunday Oregonian* (Portland), August 10, 1913, 3.

7. "Votes for Women Put Temporarily in the Background: Whether to Beat or Not to Beat Your Wife Is the Latest Controversy in Order," *Angelica (NY) Advocate*, August 21, 1913.

8. Gail Bederman provides an excellent discussion of G. Stanley Hall and his psychological theories in her book *Manliness and Civilization*, 77–120. Neurasthenia has been largely debunked by the psychiatric profession, and the American Psychiatric Association's authoritative *Diagnostic and Statistical Manual of Mental Disorders* no longer lists the affliction as a diagnosis.

9. "Jealous Women Need Whipping," *Chicago Daily Tribune*, August 11, 1912.

10. For a comprehensive discussion of the professionalization of medicine in the United States and the resultant internal conflicts, such as between psychologists and psychiatrists, see Paul Starr, *The Social Transformation of American Medicine* (New York: Basic Books, 1982). For a history of American psychotherapy in particular, see John Norcross, Gary VandenBos, and Donald Freedheim, *History of Psychotherapy: Continuity and Change* (Washington, DC: American Psychological Association, 2011).

11. Ernest R. Mowrer and Harriet R. Mowrer, *Domestic Discord: Its Analysis and Treatment* (Chicago: University of Chicago Press, 1928), 4–5.

12. Ibid.

13. Ibid., 25.

14. Ibid, 89. The cases discussed are all reports from the caseworkers and not interpretations of the Mowrers.

15. *Thompson v. Thompson*, 218 U.S. 611 (1910).

16. Ibid.

17. Ibid.

18. Ibid.

19. *Thompson v. Thompson* was cited by no fewer than 296 cases that followed, from 1921 to the present.

20. *Virginia Law Review*, "Husband and Wife: Right of Husband to Enjoin 'Nagging' by Wife," *Virginia Law Register*, n.s. 6, no. 12 (April 1921): 946–48.

21. *Drake v. Drake*, 177 N.W. 624, 625 (Minn. 1920).

22. Ibid.

23. By 1923, every state except Wyoming and Connecticut had juvenile courts. See Albert R. Roberts, *Juvenile Justice Sourcebook: Past, Present, and Future* (Oxford: Oxford University Press, 2004), 168.

24. Pleck, *Domestic Tyranny*, 126.

25. Both *Drake v. Drake* and *Thompson v. Thompson* explicitly labeled intimate partner violence as unimportant.

26. The Mowrer sample focused on data from the United Charities of Chicago and the Jewish Social Service Bureau of Chicago. Abuse topped the list of diagnostic factors in 41 percent of all cases. See Mowrer and Mowrer, *Domestic Discord*, 40.

27. Ibid., 152.

28. Ibid., 169.

29. Ibid.

30. Historically, psychotherapy has had what some professionals call a "gender gap," in which man is held as the standard of mental health. This immediately categorizes woman as "other" and more often than not "abnormal." See Jean Baker Miller, "The Effects of Inequality on Psychology," in *The Gender Gap in Psychotherapy: Social Realities and Psychological Processes*, edited by Patricia Perri Rieker and Elaine Hilberman Carmen (New York: Plenum Press, 1984), 5–16.

31. Harriet R. Mowrer, *Personality Adjustment and Domestic Discord* (New York: American Book Company, 1935), 5.

32. Whites, *Gender Matters*.

Bibliography

Primary Sources

Books, Articles, and Reports

Addams, Jane. *The Child, the Clinic, and the Court: A Group of Papers.* New York: New Republic, 1925.

Alabama, State of. *Journal Proceedings of the Constitutional Convention of the State of Alabama Held in the City of Montgomery.* Montgomery, AL: Brown Printing Company, 1901.

American Statistical Association. *Publications of the American Statistical Association.* Vol. 1, *1888–1889.* Boston: W. J. Schofield, 1889.

Ames, Blanche, and Adelbert Ames. *Chronicles from the Nineteenth Century: Family Letters of Blanche Butler and Adelbert Ames, Married July 21, 1870.* Vol. 1. Clinton, MA: n.p., 1957.

Bennett, Charles H. *The Frog Who Would a Wooing Go.* New York: McLoughlin Brothers, 1875.

Broughton, Virginia E. W. *Twenty Years' Experience of a Missionary.* Chicago: Pony Press, 1907.

Campbell, Helen, Colonel Thomas W. Knox, and Thomas Byrnes. *Darkness and Daylight; or, Light sand Shadows of New York Life: A Pictorial Record of Personal Experiences by Day and Night in the Great Metropolis.* Hartford: Hartford Publishing Company, 1896.

Cavan, Ruth S., and Katherine H. Tinker. *The Family and the Depression: A Study of One Hundred Chicago Families.* Chicago: University of Chicago Press, 1938.

Chesnutt, Charles W. *The Disenfranchisement of the Negro.* New York: Patt, 1903.

Children's Aid Society. *Annual Report of the Children's Aid Society.* Vols. 21–30. New York: Wynkoop and Hallenbeck, 1883.

Clark, Richard H. *The Code of the State of Georgia.* 2nd ed. Macon, GA: John H. Seals, 1873.

Cory, Marielou Armstrong. *The Ladies' Memorial Association of Montgomery, Alabama: The Origin and Organization, 1860–1870.* Montgomery: Alabama Printing Company, 1902.

Cumming, Kate. *Kate: The Journal of a Confederate Nurse.* Edited by Richard Barksdale Harwell. Baton Rouge: Louisiana State University Press, 1959.

Daggett, Harriet S. *Louisiana Statutes Related to the Civil Code.* New Orleans: Louisiana Law Institute, 1943.

Daniels, W. H. *The Temperance Reform and Its Great Reformers: An Illustrated History*. New York: Nelson and Philips, 1878.

Davis, Paulina. *A History of the National Woman's Rights Movement, for Twenty Years with the Proceedings of the Decade Meeting Held . . . October 20, 1870, from 1850 to 1870*. New York: Journeymen Printers' Co-operative Association, 1871.

Dawson, Sarah Morgan. *A Confederate Girl's Diary*. New York: Houghton Mifflin, 1913.

De Bow, J. D. B., ed. *De Bow's Commercial Review of the South and West: A Monthly Journal of Trade, Commerce, Commercial Polity, Agriculture, Manufactures, Internal Improvements and General Literature*. New Orleans: Weld and Company, 1850.

Dennett, Mary W. *The Sex Side of Life: An Explanation for Young People*. N.p.: n.p., 1919.

Dimitry, Adelaide Stuart. *War-Time Sketches, Historical and Otherwise*. New Orleans: Louisiana Printing Company Press, 1911.

Dr. M. A. Simmons Medicine Company. *Dr. M. A. Simmons Song, Fortune, Dream, and Cook Book*. St. Louis: Dr. M. A. Simmons Medicine Company, 1901.

Dunbar-Nelson, Alice Ruth Moore. *The Goodness of St. Rocque and Other Stories*. New York: Dodd, Mead and Company, 1899.

Felton, Rebecca Latimer. *My Memoirs of Georgia Politics*. Atlanta: Index Printing Company, 1911.

———. *The Romantic Story of Georgia's Women*. Atlanta: Atlanta Georgian Sunday American, 1930.

Fitzhugh, George. *Cannibals All! or, Slaves without Masters*. Richmond: A. Morris, 1857.

———. *Sociology for the South; or, The Failure of Free Society*. Richmond: A. Morris, 1854.

Friedan, Betty. *The Feminine Mystique*. New York: W. W. Norton, 1963.

———. "The National Organization for Women's 1966 Statement of Purpose." National Organization for Women, First National Conference, Washington, DC, October 29, 1966.

Grattan, Peachy R. *Reports of Cases Decided in Supreme Court of Appeals in Virginia*. Vol. 22. Richmond: R. F. Walker, 1873.

Hennen, William D. *A Digest of the Reported Decisions of the Superior Court of the Late Territory of Orleans; the Late Court of Errors and Appeals; and the Supreme Court of the State of Louisiana*. Vol. 2. Boston: Little, Brown, 1852.

Kanin, Eugene J. "Male Aggression in Dating-Courtship Relations." *American Journal of Sociology* 63, no. 2 (September 1957): 197–204.

Kendall, John Smith. *History of New Orleans*. Vol. 2. Chicago: Lewis Publishing Company, 1922.

Louisiana, State of. *Louisiana Legal Archives*. Vol. 3, part 1, *Compiled Edition of the Civil Codes of Louisiana*. Baton Rouge: Louisiana State Law Institute, 1940.

———. *Official Journal of the Proceedings of the Constitutional Convention of the State of Louisiana, Held in New Orleans, Monday, April 21, 1879*. New Orleans: James H. Cosgrove, 1879.

Louisiana Society for the Prevention of Cruelty to Children. *3rd Annual Report*. New Orleans: Hopkins' Printing Office, 1895.

———. *20th Annual Report*. New Orleans: Hopkins' Printing Office, 1911.

Makepeace, James M. "Courtship Violence among College Students." *Family Relations* 30, no. 1 (January 1981): 97–102.

Marr, Robert. *Annotated Revised Statutes of Louisiana*. Vol. 1. New Orleans: F. F. Hansell, 1916.

Martin, Désirée. *Evening Visits with a Sister; or, The Destiny of a Strand of Moss*. Translated by Claude L. Remillard and Denise R. Charchere. Manchester, MO: Independent Publishing Corporation, 2004. First published, New Orleans: Imprimerie Cosmopolite, 1877.

Massachusetts Society for the Prevention of Cruelty to Children. *Thirty-Second Annual Report*. Boston: Berkeley Press, 1912.

———. *Annual Report*. Vols. 1–18. Boston: Wright and Potter, 1900.

———. *Thirty-Sixth Annual Report*. Boston: Griffith Stillings, 1916.

———. *Fortieth Annual Report*. Boston: Griffith Stillings, 1920.

Mitchell, Silas Weir. *Fat and Blood: And How to Make Them*. Philadelphia: J. B. Lippincott, 1877.

Moore, Marinda Branson. *The First Dixie Reader: Designed to Follow the Dixie Primer*. Raleigh: Branson, Farrar and Company, 1863.

Mowrer, Ernest R., and Harriet R. Mowrer. *Domestic Discord: Its Analysis and Treatment*. Chicago: University of Chicago Press, 1928.

Mowrer, Harriet R. *Personality Adjustment and Domestic Discord*. New York: American Book Company, 1935.

Myerson, Abraham. *The Nervous Housewife*. Boston: Little, Brown, 1920.

Nation, Carry A. *The Use and Need of the Life of Carry A. Nation*. N.p.: n.p., 1905.

National Women's Christian Temperance Union. *Minutes of the National Women's Christian Temperance Union at the Twelfth Annual Meeting in Philadelphia, PA, October 30, 31, and November 2, 3, with Addresses, Reports, and Constitutions*. Brooklyn: Martin and Niper, 1885.

New Orleans Temperance Society. *An Address to the Citizens of New Orleans on the Subject of Temperance*. New Orleans: Toy, Printer, Office of the Lafayette City Advertiser, 1841.

Parton, James. *General Butler in New Orleans: History of the Administration of the Department of the Gulf in the Year 1862*. New York: Mason Brothers, 1864.

Patmore, Coventry. *The Angel in the House*. London: Macmillan, 1863.

Peyroux, Edmund Augustus. *Revised Civil Code of the State of Louisiana to Which Were Added Useful Abundant References to the Decision of the Supreme Court, Annual Reports and also References to the Acts of Legislature Up To and Including the Session of 1882*. New Orleans: Geo Muller Printer, 1885.

Phinney, Mary, Baroness von Olnhausen. *Adventures of an Army Nurse in Two Wars*. Boston: Little, Brown, 1903.

Powdermaker, Hortense. *After Freedom: A Cultural Study in the Deep South*. New York: Viking, 1939.

Powell, Aaron M. *The National Purity Congress: Its Papers, Addresses, and Portraits*. New York: American Purity Alliance, 1896.

Rabbino, Bernhard. *Back to the Home*. New York: Court Press, 1933.

Republican Office. *Revised Laws of Louisiana, Containing the Revised Statutes of the State as Amended by Acts of the Legislature from the Session of 1870 to That of 1896, Inclusive and All Other Acts of General Nature for the Same Period, All Annotated with the Decisions of the Supreme Court of Louisiana Contained in Annuals 39 to 48 and a Part of 49*. New Orleans: Republican Office, 1870.

Roberts, Giselle, ed. *The Correspondence of Sarah Morgan and Francis Warrington Dawson, with Selected Editorials Written by Sarah Morgan for the Charleston News Courier*. Athens: University of Georgia Press, 2004.

Robinson, William J. *Sex Morality: Past, Present, and Future*. New York: Critic and Guide Company, 1912.

Schouler, James. *A Treatise on the Law of the Domestic Relations: Embracing Husband and Wife, Parent and Child, Guardian and Ward, Infancy, and Master and Servant*. Boston: Little, Brown, 1870.

Solomon, Clara. *The Civil War Diary of Clara Solomon: Growing Up in New Orleans, 1861–1862*. Baton Rouge: Louisiana State University Press, 1995.

Souder, Emily Bliss Thacher. *Leaves from the Battlefield of Gettysburg: A Series of Letters from a Field Hospital and National Poems*. Philadelphia: C. Sherman, Son and Company, 1864.

South Western Reporter. Vol. 23. Saint Paul: West Publishing Company, 1894.

Stanton, Elizabeth Cady, Susan B. Anthony, Matilda Joslyn Gage, and Ida Husted Harper. *History of Woman Suffrage, 1861–1876*. Vol. 2, *Susan B. Anthony*. Rochester, NY: n.p., 1881.

Stuart, Ruth McEnery. "Jessekiah Brown's Courtship." In *A Golden Wedding and Other Tales*. New York: Harper and Brothers, 1893.

United States Census Bureau. *Report on Population of the United States at the Tenth Census: 1880*. Washington, DC: Government Printing Office, 1885.

———. *Report on Population of the United States at the Eleventh Census: 1890*. Washington, DC: Government Printing Office, 1896.

———. "Statistics of Women at Work." At http://www.census.gov/prod/www/abs/decennial/1900.html.

United States Congress. *The Miscellaneous Documents of the Senate of the United States for the Second Session of the Forty-Fourth Congress*. Vol. 2. Washington, DC: Government Printing Office, 1877.

———. *Report and Testimony of the Select Committee of the United States Senate to Investigate the Causes of the Removal of the Negroes from the Southern States to the Northern States*, Senate Report 693, 46th Cong., 2nd Sess., part 2.

———. *Testimony Taken by the US Congress Joint Select Conditions of Affairs in the Late Insurrectionary States*, Senate Report, 42nd Cong., no. 41, 1872.

Upton, Wheelock. *Civil Code of the State of Louisiana with Annotations*. New Orleans: E. Johns and Stationer's Hall, 1838.

Virginia, State of. *Proceedings on the Debates of the Constitutional Convention of the State of Virginia Held in the City of Richmond*. Vol. 1. Richmond: Hermitage Press, 1906.

Virginia Law Review. "Husband and Wife: Right of Husband to Enjoin 'Nagging' by Wife." *Virginia Law Register*, n.s. 6, no. 12 (April 1921): 946–48.

Voorhies, Albert. *Revised Laws of Louisiana Approved March 14, 1870, with Copious References to the Acts of the Legislature From and Including the Sessions of 1870, Up To and Including the Session of 1882*. New Orleans: F. F. Hansell, 1884.

———. *A Treatise on the Criminal Jurisprudence of Louisiana, Embracing the Criminal Statutes of the Territory of Orleans, and of the State of Louisiana, from the Year 1805 to the Year 1858, Inclusively, and Having Copious References to the Decisions of the Late Court* of Errors and Appeals, and of the Present Supreme Court, Up To the Thirteenth Volume of Louisiana Annual Reports, Inclusively. New Orleans: Bloomfield and Steel, 1860.

Waitz, Julia Ellen LeGrand, Kate Mason Rowland, and Agnes E. Browne Croxall. *The Journal of Julia LeGrand, New Orleans, 1862–1863*. Richmond: Everett Waddey, 1911.

Watkins, Samuel Rush. *Memoir of Samuel Rush Watkins*. Chattanooga: Times Printing Company, 1900.

Watson, Thomas E. "The Negro Question in the South." *Arena* 6 (October 1892): 540–50.

Watterson, Henry. "Major Jones's Courtship." In *Oddities in Southern Life and Character*. Boston: Houghton Mifflin, 1883.

Wells-Barnett, Ida B. *The Red Record: Tabulated Statistics and Alleged Causes of Lynching in the United States, 1892, 1893, 1894*. Chicago: Donohue and Henneberry, 1895.

———. *Southern Horrors: Lynch Law in All Its Phases*. New York: New York Age, 1892.

Willard, Frances. *Address before the Second Biennial Convention of the World's Woman's Christian Temperance Union*. Chicago: Women's Temperance Publishing Association, 1893.

Woodhull, Victoria. *The Principles of Social Freedom Delivered in New York City, November 20, 1871*. New York: Woodhull, Claflin and Company, 1871.

———. "The Speech of Victoria C. Woodhull before the National Women's Suffrage Convention at Apollo Hall, May 11, 1871." In *The Argument for Women's Electoral Rights under Amendments XIV and XV of the Constitution of the United States: A Review of My Work at Washington, D.C., in 1870–1871*. London: G. Norman and Son, 1887.

Wright, Almroth. *The Unexpurgated Case against Woman Suffrage*. London: Constable, 1913.

Newspapers and Periodicals

Age Herald (Birmingham)

Angelica (NY) Advocate

Baltimore Sun

Biloxi Daily Herald

Birmingham Herald

Charlotte News

Charlotte Observer

Chicago Daily Tribune

Cleveland Gazette

Columbus (GA) Daily Enquirer

Columbus (GA) Enquirer-Sun

Daily Advocate (Baton Rouge)

Daily Capitolian-Advocate (Baton Rouge)

Daily Delta (New Orleans)

Daily Herald (Grand Forks, ND)

Daily Picayune

Duluth Daily Tribune

Greenwood (MS) Commonwealth

Harper's Weekly
Idaho Daily Statesman (Boise)
Knoxville Journal
Lexington (KY) Herald
Macon (GA) Weekly Telegraph
Morning Republican (Little Rock)
Nation, The
New Haven Evening Register
New Orleans Times
New York Herald
New York Times
Omaha Daily World-Herald
Philadelphia Inquirer
Richmond Dispatch
Richmond Examiner
Savannah Tribune
State (Columbia, SC)
Sunday Oregonian (Portland)
Sunday State (Columbia, SC)
Telegraph (Macon, GA)
Times-Picayune
Washington Bee
Washington Post
Weekly Advocate (Baton Rouge)
Weekly Times-Herald (Dallas)
Wheeling (WV) Register

Court Cases

Alexander v. Alexander, 165 N.C. 45 (1914).
Bailey v. Bailey, 21 Gratt. (62 Virginia), 43 (1871).
Bienvenu v. Buisson, 14 La. Ann. 386, 1859 WL 6096.
Bradley v. State, Mississippi (I Walker) 156 (1824).
Commonwealth v. McAfee, 108 Mass. 458 (1871).
Commonwealth v. Sapp, 12 Ky. L. Rptr. 484 (1890).
Drake v. Drake, 177 N.W. 624, 625 (Minn. 1920).
Fightmaster v. Fightmaster, 22 Ky. L. Rptr. 1512 (1901).
Fleytas v. Pigneguy, 9 La. Reports 419 (1836).
Fulgham v. the State, 46 Ala. 143 (1871).
Joyner v. Joyner, 52 N.C. 322 (1862).
Knight v. Knight, 31 Iowa 451 (1871).
Lee v. New Orleans Great Northern Railroad, 125 La. 236, 51 So. 182 (1910).
Macado v. Bonet, 39 La. Ann. 475, 2 So. 49.
Mack v. Handy, 39 La. Ann. 491, 2 So. 181 (1887).

Margaret Moclair v. James Leahy, 36 La. Ann. 583, 1884 WL 8065 (La.).

Plessy v. Ferguson, 163 U.S. 537 (1896).

Ratliff v. Beale, 20 So. 865, 868 (Miss. 1896).

Scott v. Georgia, 39 Ga. 321, 323 (1869).

Shackett v. Shackett, 49 Vt. 195 (1876).

State v. Huntley, 91 N.C. 617 (1884).

State v. Rhodes, 61 N.C. 453 (1868).

State v. Peter Molloy (1852), FDC #7987.

State v. John George Mayers (1854), FDC #9229.

State v. Xavier Simeon (1860), FDC #14520.

State v. Anthony Howe (1861), FDC #15177.

State v. Sandberschwartz (1861), FDC #15483.

State v. John Mooney (1862), FDC #15758.

State v. James Miritare (1864), FDC #15945.

State v. Dennis Henderson (1880), CRDC #366.

State v. James Kenney (1881), CRDC #1243.

State v. Alfred Basile (1881), CRDC #1272.

State v. George Williams (1881), CRDC #1304.

State v. William Coyle (1881), CRDC #1447.

State v. Charles (Chas) Fletcher (1881), CRDC #1770.

State v. William Teal (1881), CRDC #1786.

State v. Andrew Williams (1881), CRDC #1805.

State v. James Gillen (1882), CRDC #2911.

State v. James Davis (1882), CRDC #3050.

State v. Herman Busch (1883), CRDC #4192.

State v. Augustus Richards (1884), CRDC #4703.

State v. Sarah Hodges (1884), CRDC #5051.

State v. A. Bax (1884), CRDC #5062.

State v. Louis Mayfield (1884), CRDC #5149.

State v. Ben Lee (1884), CRDC #5151.

State v. Thomas Coffey (1884), CRDC #5211.

State v. George Blancque (1884), CRDC #5251.

State v. Ben Lee (1884), CRDC #5421.

State v. Sylvester Conlon (1884), CRDC #5573.

State v. John Green (1884), CRDC #5627.

State v. William Green (1885), CRDC #7194.

State v. Richard Sheldon (1885), CRDC #7353.

State v. John Heir (1885), CRDC #7410.

State v. Jeffery Hill (1885), CRDC #7593.

State v. William Joyce (1885), CRDC #7825.

State v. Major Anderson (1886), CRDC #8059.

State v. Martin Johnson (1886), CRDC #8562.

State v. George Samuels and John Schnieder (1886), CRDC #8592.

State v. Gaston Blondeau (1886), CRDC #8757.

State v. John Traylor (1886), CRDC #8758.

State v. Richard Sheldon (1886), CRDC #8776.

State v. William Hines (1886), CRDC #8841.

State v. Henry Gibbons (1886), CRDC #8845.

State v. Nicholas Seldner (1886), CRDC #8916.

State v. Henry Gasper (1887), CRDC #9114.

State v. George Gill (1887), CRDC #9741.

State v. Louis Mayfield (1887), CRDC #9643.

State v. Will Bassinger (1887), CRDC #9764.

State v. G. C. Shields (1887), CRDC #9767.

State v. James Wilson (1887), CRDC #9856.

State v. Sam Carney (1887), CRDC #9873.

State v. Mat Lumbardo (1887), CRDC #9901.

State v. George Clark (1887), CRDC #9946.

State v. Willie Hennessey (1887), CRDC #9950.

State v. Gust Hannewinckle (1887), CRDC #10128.

State v. William Meyers (1887), CRDC #10179.

State v. Henry Marks (1887), CRDC #10180.

State v. Morris Hamilton (1887), CRDC #10182.

State v. Gerhart Koester (1887), CRDC #10213.

State v. William Anderson (1888), CRDC #10255.

State v. Warren Powell (1888), CRDC #10406.

State v. Warren Powell (1888), CRDC #10434.

State v. Ike Carter (1888), CRDC #10995.

State v. J. O. C. Wallis (1888), CRDC #11094.

State v. Jennie Robinson (1888), CRDC #11236.

State v. William Dreux (1888), CRDC #11291.

State v. Jefferson Green (1891), CRDC #14826.

State v. George Adams (1891), CRDC #15081.

State v. James Reynolds (1891), CRDC #17008.

State v. Jesse Black, 1 Winston 266.

State v. Hussey, 44 N.C. (Busb.) 123 (1852).

Taylor v. Swett, 3 La. 33 (1831).

Thompson v. Thompson, 218 U.S. 611 (1910).

Trowbridge v. C. T. Carlin, 12 La. Ann. 882 (1857).

United States v. Cruikshank, 92 U.S. 542 (1875).

Williams v. Mississippi, 170 U.S. 213 (1898).

Manuscript and Archival Collections

American Song Sheets, Duke Digital Collections, Duke University Libraries, Durham, NC.

Bureau of Refugees, Freedmen, and Abandoned Lands, 1865–1869, Records of the New Orleans Field Office, State of Louisiana, National Archives Microfilm Publication no. 1483.

Civil War Era NC, North Carolina State University, Raleigh.

Cross Keys Plantation Records, Manuscripts Collection 918, Manuscripts Department, Tulane University, New Orleans.

John R. Ficklen Papers, Manuscript Collection 144, 209, Louisiana and Lower Mississippi Valley Collections, Louisiana State University, Baton Rouge.

Gras-Lauzin Family Papers, ms.5, Louisiana and Lower Mississippi Valley Collections, Hill Memorial Library, Louisiana State University, Baton Rouge.

Grisham-Kellogg-Faust Papers, Manuscript Collection 5048, Hill Memorial Library, Louisiana State University, Baton Rouge.

James Knapp Papers, Manuscript Collection 880, Hill Memorial Library, Louisiana State University, Baton Rouge.

Gilder Lehrman Collection, Gilder Lehrman Institute of American History, New York.

McKowen-Lilley-Stirling Family Papers, Manuscript Collection 4356, Hill Memorial Library, Louisiana State University, Baton Rouge.

Daniel Trotter Papers, Manuscript Collection 990, Hill Memorial Library, Louisiana State University, Baton Rouge.

Micajah Wilkinson Papers, Manuscript Collection 707, Hill Memorial Library, Louisiana State University, Baton Rouge.

Secondary Sources

Books and Book Chapters

Abel, Emily K. *Hearts of Wisdom: American Women Caring for Kin, 1850–1940*. Cambridge, MA: Harvard University Press, 2000.

Alexander, Eleanor. *Lyrics of Sunshine and Shadow: The Tragic Courtship and Marriage of Paul Laurence Dunbar and Alice Ruth Moore*. New York: New York University Press, 2001.

Allured, Janet, and Judith F. Gentry. *Louisiana Women: Their Lives and Times*. Athens: University of Georgia Press, 2009.

Ayers, Edward L. *The Promise of the New South: Life After Reconstruction*. New York: Oxford University Press, 2007.

Bailey, Beth L. *From Front Porch to Back Seat: Courtship in Twentieth-Century America*. Baltimore: Johns Hopkins University Press, 1988.

Bardaglio, Peter W. *Reconstructing the Household: Families, Sex, and the Law in the Nineteenth-Century South*. Chapel Hill: University of North Carolina Press, 1995.

Bederman, Gail. *Manliness and Civilization: A Cultural History of Gender and Race in the United States, 1880–1917*. Chicago: University of Chicago Press, 1995.

Bellesiles, Michael A., ed. *Lethal Imagination: Violence and Brutality in American History*. New York: New York University Press, 1999.

Bercaw, Nancy. *Gendered Freedoms: Race, Rights, and the Politics of Household in the Delta, 1861–1875*. Gainesville: University Press of Florida, 2003.

Berger, Maurice, Brian Wallis, and Simon Watson, eds. *Constructing Masculinity*. New York: Routledge, 1995.

Bergeron, Arthur W., Jr. "Louisiana's Free Men of Color in Gray." In *Louisianians in the Civil War*, edited by Lawrence Lee Hewitt and Arthur W. Bergeron Jr. Columbia: University of Missouri Press, 2002.

Blassingame, John W. *Black New Orleans, 1860–1880*. Chicago: University of Chicago Press, 1973.

Bleser, Carol, ed. *In Joy and in Sorrow: Women, Family, and Marriage in the Victorian South, 1830–1900*. New York: Oxford University Press, 1991.

Blight, David W. *Race and Reunion: The Civil War in American Memory*. Cambridge, MA: Belknap Press of Harvard University Press, 2001.

Block, Sharon. *Rape and Sexual Power in Early America*. Chapel Hill: University of North Carolina Press, 2006.

Blum, Edward J., and W. Scott Poole, eds. *Vale of Tears: New Essays on Religion and Reconstruction*. Macon, GA: Mercer University Press, 2005.

Bordin, Ruth B. A. *Woman and Temperance: The Quest for Power and Liberty, 1873–1900*. Philadelphia: Temple University Press, 1981.

Boswell, Angela. *Her Act and Deed: Women's Lives in a Rural Southern County*. College Station: Texas A&M University Press, 2001.

Boydston, Jeanne. *Home and Work: Housework, Wages, and the Ideology of Labor in the Early Republic*. New York: Oxford University Press, 1990.

Bruce, Dickson D., Jr. *Violence and Culture in the Antebellum South*. Austin: University of Texas Press, 1979.

Brundage, W. Fitzhugh. *Lynching in the New South: Georgia and Virginia, 1880–1930*. Urbana: University of Illinois Press, 1993.

Butler, Judith. "Imitation and Gender Insubordination." In *The Judith Butler Reader*, edited by Sara Salih, 119–37. Malden, MA: Blackwell, 2003.

Bynum, Victoria E. *Unruly Women: The Politics of Social and Sexual Control in the Old South*. Chapel Hill: University of North Carolina Press, 1992.

Campanella, Richard. *Bourbon Street: A History*. Baton Rouge: Louisiana State University Press, 2014.

Carnes, Mark C., and Clyde Griffen, eds. *Meanings for Manhood: Constructions of Masculinity in Victorian America*. Chicago: University of Chicago Press,1980.

Cash, W. J. *The Mind of the South*. New York: Alfred A. Knopf, 1941.

Celello, Kristin. *Making Marriage Work: A History of Marriage and Divorce in the Twentieth-Century United States*. Chapel Hill: University of North Carolina Press, 2009.

Chauncey, George. *Gay New York: Gender, Urban Culture, and the Making of the Gay Male World, 1890–1940*. New York: Basic Books, 1994.

Clark, Emily. *The Strange History of the American Quadroon: Free Women of Color in the Revolutionary Atlantic World*. Chapel Hill: University of North Carolina Press, 2013.

Clayton, Bruce, and John A. Salmond. *"Lives Full of Struggle and Triumph": Southern Women, Their Institutions, and Their Communities*. Gainesville: University Press of Florida, 2003.

Clement, Elizabeth. *Love for Sale: Courting, Treating, and Prostitution in New York City, 1900–1945*. Chapel Hill: University of North Carolina Press, 2006.

Clinton, Catherine. *Half Sisters of History: Southern Women and the American Past*. Durham, NC: Duke University Press, 1994.

———. *The Plantation Mistress: Woman's World in the Old South.* New York: Pantheon Books, 1984.

Clinton, Catherine, and Nina Silber, eds. *Divided Houses: Gender and the Civil War.* New York: Oxford University Press, 1992.

Coleman, Kenneth. *A History of Georgia.* Athens: University of Georgia Press, 1977.

Coontz, Stephanie. *Marriage, a History: How Love Conquered Marriage.* New York: Penguin, 2006.

Cott, Nancy F. *The Bonds of Womanhood: "Woman's Sphere" in New England, 1780–1835.* New Haven, CT: Yale University Press, 1977.

———. *Public Vows: A History of Marriage and the Nation.* Cambridge, MA: Harvard University Press, 2002.

Crane, Elaine Foreman. *Witches, Wife Beaters, and Whores: Common Law and Common Folk in Early America.* Ithaca, NY: Cornell University Press, 2011.

Culpepper, Marilyn M. *All Things Altered: Women in the Wake of Civil War and Reconstruction.* Jefferson, NC: McFarland, 2002.

Daniels, Christine, and Michael V. Kennedy, eds. *Over the Threshold: Intimate Violence in Early America.* New York: Routledge, 1999.

Davis, Rebecca L. *More Perfect Unions: The American Search for Marital Bliss.* Cambridge, MA: Harvard University Press, 2010.

Davis, Richard L. *Domestic Violence: Facts and Fallacies.* Westport, CT: Praeger, 1998.

Dayton, Cornelia Hughes. *Women before the Bar: Gender, Law, and Society in Connecticut, 1639–1789.* Chapel Hill: University of North Carolina Press, 1995.

Dean, Eric T., Jr. *Shook Over Hell: Post-Traumatic Stress, Vietnam, and the Civil War.* Cambridge, MA: Harvard University Press, 1997.

Degler, Carl N. *At Odds: Women and the Family in America from the Revolution to the Present.* New York: Oxford University Press, 1980.

Donzelot, Jacques, and Robert Hurley. *The Policing of Families.* Baltimore: Johns Hopkins University Press, 1997.

Dorson, Richard. *American Negro Folktales.* Greenwich, CT: Fawcett Publications, 1967.

Duggan, Lisa. *Sapphic Slashers: Sex, Violence, and American Modernity.* Durham, NC: Duke University Press, 2001.

Dumenil, Lynn. *The Modern Temper: American Culture and Society in the 1920s.* New York: Hill and Wang, 1995.

Edwards, Laura F. *Gendered Strife and Confusion: The Political Culture of Reconstruction.* Urbana: University of Illinois Press, 1997.

———. *The People and Their Peace: Legal Culture and the Transformation of Inequality in the Post-Revolutionary South.* Chapel Hill: University of North Carolina Press, 2009.

———. *Scarlett Doesn't Live Here Anymore: Southern Women in the Civil War Era.* Urbana: University of Illinois Press, 2000.

———. "Women and Domestic Violence in Nineteenth-Century Carolina." In *Lethal Imagination: Violence and Brutality in American History,* edited by Michael A. Bellesiles, 114–36. New York: New York University Press, 1999.

Enstad, Nan. *Ladies of Labor, Girls of Adventure: Working Women, Popular Culture, and Labor Politics at the Turn of the Twentieth Century.* New York: Columbia University Press, 1999.

Epstein, Barbara Leslie. *The Politics of Domesticity: Women, Evangelism, and Temperance in Nineteenth-Century America*. Middletown, CT: Wesleyan University Press, 1981.

Farmer-Kaiser, Mary. *Freedwomen and the Freedmen's Bureau: Race, Gender, and Public Policy in the Age of Emancipation*. Bronx: Fordham University Press, 2010.

Faust, Drew Gilpin. *Mothers of Invention: Women of the Slaveholding South in the American Civil War*. Chapel Hill: University of North Carolina Press, 1996.

———. *This Republic of Suffering: Death and the American Civil War*. New York: Vintage Books, 2008.

Feimster, Crystal Nicole. *Southern Horrors: Women and the Politics of Rape and Lynching*. Cambridge, MA: Harvard University Press, 2009.

Fernandez, Mark F. *From Chaos to Continuity: The Evolution of Louisiana's Judicial System, 1712–1862*. Baton Rouge: Louisiana State University Press, 2001.

Foner, Eric. *Reconstruction: America's Unfinished Revolution, 1863–1877*. New York: Harper and Row, 1988.

Ford, Lacy K. *Deliver Us from Evil: The Slavery Question in the Old South*. Oxford: Oxford University Press, 2009.

Foster, Gaines M. *Ghosts of the Confederacy: Defeat, the Lost Cause, and the Emergence of the New South, 1865–1913*. New York: Oxford University Press, 1987.

———. *Moral Reconstruction: Christian Lobbyists and the Federal Legislation of Morality, 1865–1920*. Chapel Hill: University of North Carolina Press, 2002.

Foucault, Michel. *Discipline and Punish: The Birth of the Prison*. New York: Pantheon Books, 1977.

Fox, Richard Wightman, and T. J. Jackson Lears, eds. *The Power of Culture: Critical Essays in American History*. New York: Routledge, 1996.

Fox-Genovese, Elizabeth. *Within the Plantation Household: Black and White Women of the Old South*. Chapel Hill: University of North Carolina Press, 1988.

Frank, Lisa Tendrich. *The Civilian War: Confederate Women and Union Soldiers during Sherman's March*. Baton Rouge: Louisiana State University Press, 2015.

Frank, Stephen M. *Life with Father: Parenthood and Masculinity in the Nineteenth-Century American North*. Baltimore: Johns Hopkins University Press, 1998.

Frankel, Noralee. *Freedom's Women: Black Women and Families in Civil War Era Mississippi*. Bloomington: Indiana University Press, 1999.

Franklin, John Hope. *The Militant South, 1800–1861*. Cambridge, MA: Belknap Press of Harvard University Press, 1956.

Frederickson, Mary E. *Looking South: Race, Gender, and the Transformation of Labor from Reconstruction to Globalization*. Gainesville: University Press of Florida, 2011.

Friend, Craig Thompson. *Southern Masculinity: Perspectives on Manhood in the South since Reconstruction*. Athens: University of Georgia Press, 2009.

Friend, Craig Thompson, and Lorri Glover, eds. *Southern Manhood: Perspectives on Masculinity in the Old South*. Athens: University of Georgia Press, 2004.

Gallman, J. Matthew. *The North Fights the Civil War: The Home Front*. Chicago: Ivan R. Dee, 1994.

Geertz, Clifford. *Local Knowledge: Further Essays in Interpretive Anthropology*. New York: Basic Books, 1983.

Genovese, Eugene D. *Roll, Jordan, Roll: The World Slaves Made*. New York: Pantheon Books, 1974.

Giesberg, Judith A. *Civil War Sisterhood: The U.S. Sanitary Commission and Women's Politics in Transition*. Boston: Northeastern University Press, 2000.

Gill, James. *Lords of Misrule: Mardi Gras and the Politics of Race in New Orleans*. Jackson: University Press of Mississippi, 1997.

Gilmore, Glenda Elizabeth. *Gender and Jim Crow: Women and the Politics of White Supremacy in North Carolina, 1896–1920*. Chapel Hill: University of North Carolina Press, 1996.

Ginzberg, Lori D. *Women and the Work of Benevolence: Morality, Politics, and Class in the 19th-Century United States*. New Haven, CT: Yale University Press, 1990.

Goodwyn, Lawrence. *The Populist Moment: A Short History of the Agrarian Revolt in America*. Oxford: Oxford University Press, 1978.

Gordon, Linda. *Heroes of Their Own Lives: The Politics and History of Family Violence; Boston, 1880–1960*. New York: Viking, 1988.

Grantham, Dewey W. *Southern Progressivism: The Reconciliation of Progress and Tradition*. Knoxville: University of Tennessee Press, 1983.

Greenberg, Amy S. *Manifest Manhood and the Antebellum American Empire*. Cambridge: Cambridge University Press, 2005.

Greenberg, Kenneth S. *Honor and Slavery: Lies, Duels, Noses, Masks, Dressing as a Woman, Gifts, Strangers, Humanitarianism, Death, Slave Rebellions, the Proslavery Argument, Baseball, Hunting, and Gambling in the Old South*. Princeton, NJ: Princeton University Press, 1996.

Grimsley, Mark. *The Hard Hand of War: Union Military Policy toward Southern Civilians, 1861–1865*. Cambridge: Cambridge University Press, 1995.

Griswold, Robert L. *Fatherhood in America: A History*. New York: Basic Books, 1993.

Gross, Ariela Julie. *Double Character: Slavery and Mastery in the Antebellum Southern Courtroom*. Princeton, NJ: Princeton University Press, 2000.

Gross, Kali N. *Colored Amazons: Crime, Violence, and Black Women in the City of Brotherly Love, 1880–1910*. Durham, NC: Duke University Press, 2006.

Grossberg, Michael. *Governing the Hearth: Law and the Family in Nineteenth-Century America*. Chapel Hill: University of North Carolina Press, 1985.

Gutman, Herbert. *Black Family in Slavery and Freedom, 1750–1925*. New York: Vintage, 1976.

Hale, Grace Elizabeth. *Making Whiteness: The Culture of Segregation in the South, 1890–1940*. New York: Vintage Books, 1999.

Hale, Nathan G. *The Rise and Crisis of Psychoanalysis in the United States: Freud and the Americans, 1917–1985*. New York: Oxford University Press, 1995.

Hall, Jacquelyn D. *Revolt against Chivalry: Jessie Daniel Ames and the Women's Campaign against Lynching*. New York: Columbia University Press, 1979.

Haraway, Donna J. *Primate Visions: Gender, Race, and Nature in the World of Modern Science*. New York: Routledge, 1989.

Hartog, Hendrik. *Man and Wife in America: A History*. Cambridge, MA: Harvard University Press, 2000.

Hearn, Chester G. *When the Devil Came Down to Dixie: Ben Butler in New Orleans*. Baton Rouge: Louisiana State University Press, 1997.

Hewitt, Lawrence Lee, and Arthur W. Bergeron Jr., eds. *Louisianians in the Civil War*. Columbia: University of Missouri Press, 2002.

Hewitt, Nancy A., and Suzanne Lebsock. *Visible Women: New Essays on American Activism*. Urbana: University of Illinois Press, 1993.

Higginbotham, Evelyn Brooks. *Righteous Discontent: The Women's Movement in the Black Baptist Church, 1880–1920*. Cambridge, MA: Harvard University Press, 1993.

Hine, Darlene Clark, and Earnestine Jenkins, eds. *A Question of Manhood: A Reader in U.S. Black Men's History and Masculinity*. Bloomington: Indiana University Press, 1999.

Hine, Darlene Clark, and Kathleen Thompson. *A Shining Thread of Hope: The History of Black Women in America*. New York: Broadway Books, 1998.

Hirsch, Arnold R., and Joseph Logsdon. *Creole New Orleans: Race and Americanization*. Baton Rouge: Louisiana State University Press, 1992.

Hodes, Martha E. *White Women, Black Men: Illicit Sex in the Nineteenth-Century South*. New Haven, CT: Yale University Press, 1997.

Hoff, Joan. *Law, Gender, and Injustice: A Legal History of U.S. Women*. New York: New York University Press, 1991.

Hoffert, Sylvia D. *When Hens Crow: The Woman's Rights Movement in Antebellum America*. Bloomington: Indiana University Press, 1995.

Hogue, James K. *Uncivil War: Five New Orleans Street Battles and the Rise and Fall of Radical Reconstruction*. Baton Rouge: Louisiana State University Press, 2011.

Hollandsworth, James G. *Louisiana Native Guards: The Black Military Experience during the Civil War*. Baton Rouge: Louisiana State University Press, 1995.

———. *Pretense of Glory: The Life of General Nathaniel P. Banks*. Baton Rouge: Louisiana State University Press, 1998.

Horowitz, Helen Lefkowitz. *Rereading Sex: Battles over Sexual Knowledge and Suppression in Nineteenth-Century America*. New York: Alfred A. Knopf, 2002.

Hunter, Tera W. *To 'Joy My Freedom: Southern Black Women's Lives and Labors after the Civil War*. Cambridge, MA: Harvard University Press, 1997.

Isenberg, Nancy. *Sex and Citizenship in Antebellum America*. Chapel Hill: University of North Carolina Press, 1998.

Janeway, Elizabeth. *Powers of the Weak*. New York: Alfred A. Knopf, 1980.

Jenkins, Keith. *The Postmodern History Reader*. London: Routledge, 1997.

Johansen, Shawn. *Family Men: Middle-Class Fatherhood in Industrializing America*. New York: Routledge, 2001.

Jones, Jacqueline. *Labor of Love, Labor of Sorrow: Black Women, Work, and the Family from Slavery to the Present*. New York: Basic Books, 1985.

Kasson, John F. *Houdini, Tarzan, and the Perfect Man: The White Male Body and the Challenge of Modernity in America*. New York: Hill and Wang, 2001.

———. *Rudeness and Civility: Manners in Nineteenth-Century Urban America*. New York: Hill and Wang, 1990.

Kein, Sybil, ed. *Creole: The History and Legacy of Louisiana's Free People of Color*. Baton Rouge: Louisiana State University Press, 2000.

Keith, Leanna. *The Colfax Massacre: The Untold Story of Black Power, White Terror, and the Death of Reconstruction*. Oxford: Oxford University Press, 2008.

Kelley, Blair Murphy. *Right to Ride: Streetcar Boycotts and African American Citizenship in the Era of Plessy v. Ferguson.* Chapel Hill: University of North Carolina Press, 2010.

Kennedy, Leslie W., and Vincent Sacco. *Crime Victims in Context.* Los Angeles: Roxbury, 1998.

Kerber, Linda K. *No Constitutional Right to Be Ladies: Women and the Obligations of Citizenship.* New York: Hill and Wang, 1998.

Kessler-Harris, Alice. *In Pursuit of Equity: Women, Men, and the Quest for Economic Citizenship in 20th-Century America.* Oxford: Oxford University Press, 2001.

———. *Out to Work: A History of Wage-Earning Women in the United States.* New York: Oxford University Press, 1982.

Kimmel, Michael S. *Manhood in America: A Cultural History.* New York: Free Press, 1996.

King, Wilma. *The Essence of Liberty: Free Black Women during the Slave Era.* Columbia: University of Missouri Press, 2006.

Kitch, Sally. *The Specter of Sex: Gendered Foundations of Racial Formation in the United States.* Albany: State University of New York Press, 2009.

Klarman, Michael J. *From Jim Crow to Civil Rights: The Supreme Court and the Struggle for Racial Equality.* Oxford: Oxford University Press, 2004.

Krafft-Ebing, Richard von. *Psychopathia Sexualis.* Translated by Charles G. Chaddock. Philadelphia: F. A. Davis, 1892.

Landes, Alison, Nancy R. Jacobs, and Mark A. Siegel. *Violent Relationships.* Wylie, TX: Information Plus, 1995.

LaRossa, Ralph. *The Modernization of Fatherhood: A Social and Political History.* Chicago: University of Chicago Press, 1997.

Lawson, Kate, and Lynn Shakinovsky. *The Marked Body: Domestic Violence in Mid-Nineteenth-Century Literature.* Albany: State University of New York Press, 2002.

Lazarus-Black, Mindie, and Susan F Hirsch, eds. *Contested States: Law, Hegemony, and Resistance.* New York: Routledge, 1994.

Lemisch, Jesse. *Jack Tar in the Streets: Merchant Seamen in the Politics of Revolutionary America.* Manchester, NH: Irvington Publishers, 1968.

Lerner, Gerda. *The Creation of Patriarchy.* New York: Oxford University Press, 1986.

Levack, Brian P., Edward Muir, and Meredith Veldman. *The West: Encounters and Transformations to 1715.* Harlow, Essex, England: Longman, 2007.

Lind, Goran. *Common Law Marriage: A Legal Institution for Cohabitation.* Oxford: Oxford University Press, 2008.

Link, William A. *The Paradox of Southern Progressivism, 1880–1930.* Chapel Hill: University of North Carolina Press, 1992.

Lloyd, Ann. *Doubly Deviant, Doubly Damned: Society's Treatment of Violent Women.* London: Penguin, 1995.

Long, Alecia P. *The Great Southern Babylon: Sex, Race, and Respectability in New Orleans, 1865–1920.* Baton Rouge: Louisiana State University Press, 2005.

———. "(Mis)Remembering General Order no. 28: Benjamin Butler, the Woman Order, and Historical Memory." In *Occupied Women: Gender, Military Occupation, and the American Civil War,* edited by LeeAnn Whites and Alecia P. Long, 17–32. Baton Rouge: Louisiana State University Press, 2009.

Lystra, Karen. *Searching the Heart: Women, Men, and Romantic Love in Nineteenth-Century America*. New York: Oxford University Press, 1989.

Martin, John P. *Violence and the Family*. Chichester, West Sussex, England: John Wiley, 1978.

Martin, Sara Hines. *More Than Petticoats: Remarkable Georgia Women*. Guilford, CT: Two Dot Press, 2003.

May, Elaine Tyler. *Great Expectations: Marriage and Divorce in Post-Victorian America*. Chicago: University of Chicago Press, 1980.

May, Larry, and Jeff Brown, eds. *Philosophy of Law: Classic and Contemporary Readings*. Oxford: Blackwell, 2010.

McBeth, Leon. *Women in Baptist Life*. Nashville: Broadman Press, 1979.

McCurry, Stephanie. *Masters of Small Worlds: Yeoman Households, Gender Relations, and the Political Culture of the Antebellum South Carolina Low Country*. New York: Oxford University Press, 1995.

McGerr, Michael E. *A Fierce Discontent: The Rise and Fall of the Progressive Movement in America, 1870–1920*. New York: Free Press, 2003.

Meloy, Michelle L., and Susan L. Miller. *The Victimization of Women: Law, Policies, and Politics*. Oxford: Oxford University Press, 2011.

Miller, Jean Baker. "The Effects of Inequality on Psychology." In *The Gender Gap in Psychotherapy: Social Realities and Psychological Processes*, edited by Patricia Perri Rieker and Elaine Hilberman Carmen. New York: Plenum Press, 1984.

Miller, Susan L. *Victims as Offenders: The Paradox of Women's Violence in Relationships*. New Brunswick, NJ: Rutgers University Press, 2005.

Mills, Gary B. *The Forgotten People: Cane River's Creoles of Color*. Baton Rouge: Louisiana State University Press, 1977.

Mintz, Steven. *Moralists and Modernizers: America's Pre-Civil War Reformers*. Baltimore: Johns Hopkins University Press, 1995.

Mintz, Steven, and Susan Kellogg. *Domestic Revolutions: A Social History of American Family Life*. New York: Free Press, 1988.

Muncy, Robyn. *Creating a Female Dominion in the Age of Reform, 1890–1935*. New York: Oxford University Press, 1991.

Newton, Michael. *The Ku Klux Klan in Mississippi: A History*. Jefferson, NC: McFarland, 2010.

Norcross, John, Gary VandenBos, and Donald Freedheim. *History of Psychotherapy: Continuity and Change*. Washington, DC: American Psychological Association, 2011.

Norton, Mary Beth. *Founding Mothers and Fathers: Gendered Power and the Forming of American Society*. New York: Random House, 1996.

Ownby, Ted. *Subduing Satan: Religion, Recreation, and Manhood in the Rural South, 1865–1920*. Chapel Hill: University of North Carolina Press, 1990.

Paludan, Phillip Shaw. *"A People's Contest": The Union and the Civil War, 1861–1865*. New York: Harper and Row, 1988.

Pascoe, Peggy. *What Comes Naturally: Miscegenation Law and the Making of Race in America*. Oxford: Oxford University Press, 2009.

Pateman, Carole, and Elizabeth Grosz, eds. *Feminist Challenges: Social and Political Theory*. Boston: Northeastern University Press, 1986.

Peiss, Kathy L. *Cheap Amusements: Working Women and Leisure in Turn-of-the-Century New York*. Philadelphia: Temple University Press, 1986.

Perman, Michael. *Struggle for Mastery: Disfranchisement in the South, 1888–1908*. Chapel Hill: University of North Carolina Press, 2001.

Peterson del Mar, David. *Physically Violent Husbands of the 1890s and Their Resources*. New York: Plenum Press, 1991.

———. *What Trouble I Have Seen: A History of Violence against Wives*. Cambridge, MA: Harvard University Press, 1996.

Pivar, David J. *Purity Crusade: Sexual Morality and Social Control, 1868–1900*. Westport, CT: Greenwood Press, 1973.

Pleck, Elizabeth H. *Domestic Tyranny: The Making of Social Policy against Family Violence from Colonial Times to the Present*. New York: Oxford University Press, 1987.

Polenberg, Richard. *Fighting Faiths: The Abrams Case, the Supreme Court, and Free Speech*. Ithaca, NY: Cornell University Press, 1987.

Rambo, Kirsten S. *"Trivial Complaints": The Role of Privacy in Domestic Violence Law and Activism in the U.S.* New York: Columbia University Press, 2009.

Reesman, Jeanne Campbell, ed. *Trickster Lives: Culture and Myth in American Fiction*. Athens: University of Georgia Press, 2001.

Roberts, Albert R. *Juvenile Justice Sourcebook: Past, Present, and Future*. Oxford: Oxford University Press, 2004.

Roberts, John W. *From Trickster to Badman: The Black Folk Hero in Slavery and Freedom*. Philadelphia: University of Pennsylvania Press, 1989.

Robinson, Paul. *The Modernization of Sex: Havelock Ellis, Alfred Kinsey, William Masters, and Virginia Johnson*. New York: Harper and Row, 1976.

Robinson, Sally. *Marked Men: White Masculinity in Crisis*. New York: Columbia University Press, 2000.

Rosen, Hannah. *Terror in the Heart of Freedom: Citizenship, Sexual Violence, and the Meaning of Race in the Postemancipation South*. Chapel Hill: University of North Carolina Press, 2009.

Rothman, Ellen. *Hands and Hearts: A History of Courtship in America*. New York: Basic Books, 1989.

Sabin, Robin C. *Marital Cruelty in Antebellum America*. Baton Rouge: Louisiana State University Press, 2016.

Sager, Robin C. *Marital Cruelty in Antebellum America*. Baton Rouge: Louisiana State University Press, 2016.

Salsi, Lynn, and Margaret Sims. *Columbia: History of a Southern Capital*. Charleston, SC: Arcadia, 2003.

Sarat, Austin, and Thomas R. Kearns. "Beyond the Great Divide: Forms of Legal Scholarship and Everyday Life." In *Law and Everyday Life*, edited by Austin Sarat and Thomas R. Kearns, 21–62. Ann Arbor: University of Michigan Press, 1993.

Schafer, Judith Kelleher. *Becoming Free, Remaining Free: Manumission and Enslavement in New Orleans, 1846–1862*. Baton Rouge: Louisiana State University Press, 2003.

———. *Slavery, the Civil Law, and the Supreme Court of Louisiana*. Baton Rouge: Louisiana State University Press, 1994.

Schuster, David G. *Neurasthenic Nation: America's Search for Health, Happiness, and Comfort, 1869–1920*. New Brunswick, NJ: Rutgers University Press, 2011.

Schwalm, Leslie A. *A Hard Fight for We: Women's Transition from Slavery to Freedom in South Carolina*. Chicago: University of Illinois Press, 1997.

Schweninger, Loren. *Families in Crisis in the Old South: Divorce, Slavery, and the Law*. Chapel Hill: University of North Carolina Press, 2012.

Scott, Anne Firor. *The Southern Lady: from Pedestal to Politics, 1830–1930*. Chicago: University of Chicago Press, 1970.

Scott, Joan Wallach. *Feminism and History*. Oxford: Oxford University Press, 1996.

———. *Gender and the Politics of History*. New York: Columbia University Press, 1988.

Shindo, Charles J. *1927 and the Rise of Modern America*. Lawrence: University Press of Kansas, 2010.

Silber, Nina. "Intemperate Men, Spiteful Women, and Jefferson Davis." In *Divided Houses: Gender and the Civil War*, edited by Catherine Clinton and Nina Silber, 283–305. New York: Oxford University Press, 1992.

Simmons, LaKisha Michelle. *Crescent City Girls: The Lives of Young Black Women in Segregated New Orleans*. Chapel Hill: University of North Carolina Press, 2015.

Sims, Anastatia. *The Power of Femininity in the New South: Women's Organizations and Politics in North Carolina, 1880–1930*. Columbia: University of South Carolina Press, 1997.

Sklar, Kathryn K. *Catharine Beecher: A Study in American Domesticity*. New Haven, CT: Yale University Press, 1973.

Slap, Andrew, and Michael T. Smith. *This Distracted and Anarchical People: New Answers for Old Questions about the Civil War–Era North*. Bronx: Fordham University Press, 2013.

Snyder, Tom, ed. *120 Years of American Education: A Statistical Portrait*. Washington, DC: US Department of Education, Office of Educational Research and Improvement, National Center for Education Statistics, 1993.

Spruill, Marjorie J. *New Women of the New South: The Leaders of the Woman Suffrage Movement in the Southern States*. New York: Oxford University Press, 1993.

Stansell, Christine. *City of Women: Sex and Class in New York, 1789–1860*. New York: Alfred A. Knopf, 1986.

Starr, Paul. *The Social Transformation of American Medicine*. New York: Basic Books, 1982.

Sterkx, H. E. *The Free Negro in Ante-Bellum Louisiana*. Rutherford, NJ: Fairleigh Dickinson University Press, 1972.

Sterling, Dorothy. *We Are Your Sisters: Black Women in the Nineteenth Century*. New York: W. W. Norton, 1984.

Straus, Murray A., Richard J. Gelles, and Christine Smith. *Physical Violence in American Families: Risk Factors and Adaptations to Violence in 8,145 Families*. New Brunswick, NJ: Transaction Publishers, 1990.

Sweet, Frank W. *Legal History of the Color Line: The Rise and Triumph of the One-Drop Rule*. Palm Coast, FL: Backintyme, 2000.

Talmadge, John E. *Rebecca Latimer Felton: Nine Stormy Decades*. Athens: University of Georgia Press, 1960.

Taylor, Dianna, and Karen Vintges, eds. *Feminism and the Final Foucault*. Urbana: University of Illinois Press, 2004.

Thorne-Finch, Ron. *Ending the Silence: The Origins and Treatment of Male Violence against Women*. Toronto: University of Toronto Press, 1992.

Tice, Karen. *Tales of Wayward Girls and Immoral Women: Case Records and the Professionalization of Social Work*. Urbana: University of Illinois Press, 1998.

Towers, Frank. *The Urban South and the Coming of the Civil War*. Charlottesville: University of Virginia Press, 2004.

Trelease, Allen W. *White Terror: The Ku Klux Klan Conspiracy and Southern Reconstruction*. New York: Harper and Row, 1971.

Tunnell, Ted. *Crucible of Reconstruction: War, Radicalism, and Race in Louisiana, 1862–1877*. Baton Rouge: Louisiana State University Press, 1984.

Turner, Elizabeth H. *Women and Gender in the New South: 1865–1945*. Wheeling, IL: Harlan Davidson, 2009.

Tyrrell, Ian R. *Sobering Up: From Temperance to Prohibition in Antebellum America, 1800–1860*. Westport, CT: Greenwood Press, 1979.

Ulrich, Laurel Thatcher. *Good Wives: Image and Reality in the Lives of Women in Northern New England, 1650–1750*. New York: Alfred A. Knopf, 1982.

Vincent, Charles. *Black Legislators in Louisiana during Reconstruction*. Baton Rouge: Louisiana State University Press, 1976.

Waldrep, Christopher, and Donald G. Nieman. *Local Matters: Race, Crime, and Justice in the Nineteenth-Century South*. Athens: University of Georgia Press, 2001.

Walker, Lenore E. *The Battered Woman*. New York: Harper and Row, 1979.

———. *The Battered Woman Syndrome*. New York: Springer, 1984.

Weiner, Marli F. *Mistresses and Slaves: Plantation Women in South Carolina, 1830–1880*. Urbana: University of Illinois Press, 1997.

White, Deborah Gray. *Ar'n't I a Woman? Female Slaves in the Plantation South*. New York: W. W. Norton, 1985.

———. *Too Heavy a Load: Black Women in Defense of Themselves, 1894–1994*. New York: W. W. Norton, 1999.

Whites, LeeAnn. *Gender Matters: Civil War, Reconstruction, and the Making of the New South*. New York: Palgrave Macmillan, 2005.

Whites, LeeAnn, and Alecia P. Long, eds. *Occupied Women: Gender, Military Occupation, and the American Civil War*. Baton Rouge: Louisiana State University Press, 2009.

Wiebe, Robert H. *The Search for Order, 1877–1920*. New York: Hill and Wang, 1967.

Wiener, Jonathan M. *Social Origins of the New South: Alabama, 1860–1885*. Baton Rouge: Louisiana State University Press, 1978.

Williams, Jack Kenny. *Dueling in the Old South: Vignettes of Social History*. College Station: Texas A&M University Press, 1980.

Williams, Kidada E. *They Left Great Marks on Me: African American Testimonies of Racial Violence from Emancipation to World War I*. New York: New York University Press, 2012.

Wong, Edlie L. *Neither Fugitive nor Free: Atlantic Slavery, Freedom Suits, and the Legal Culture of Travel*. New York: New York University Press, 2009.

Woodward, C. Vann. *Origins of the New South, 1877–1913*. Baton Rouge: Louisiana State University Press, 1951.

———. *The Strange Career of Jim Crow*. New York: Oxford University Press, 1974.

Wyatt-Brown, Bertram. *Honor and Violence in the Old South*. New York: Oxford University Press, 1986.

———. *The House of Percy: Honor, Melancholy, and Imagination in a Southern Family*. New York: Oxford University Press, 1994.

———. *Southern Honor: Ethics and Behavior in the Old South*. New York: Oxford University Press, 1982.

Journal Articles

Adler, Jeffrey S. "'Bessie Done Cut Her Old Man': Race, Common-Law Marriage, and Homicide in New Orleans, 1925–1945." *Journal of Social History* 44, no. 1 (Fall 2010): 123–43.

Babcock, Julia C., Jennifer Waltz, Neil S. Jacobson, and John M. Gottman. "Power and Violence: The Relation between Communication Patterns, Power Discrepancies, and Domestic Violence." *Journal of Consulting and Clinical Psychology* 61, no. 1 (1993): 40–50.

Baker, Paula. "The Domestication of Politics: Women and American Political Society, 1780–1920." *American Historical Review* 89, no. 3 (June 1984): 620–47.

Cairns, John W. "The de la Vergne Volume and the Digest of 1808." *Tulane European and Civil Law Forum* 24, no. 1 (2009): 31–81.

Cott, Nancy. "What's in a Name? The Limits of 'Social Feminism'; or, Expanding the Vocabulary of Women's History." *Journal of American History* 76, no. 3 (1989): 809–29.

Custer, Joseph A. "The Three Waves of Married Women's Property Acts in the Nineteenth Century with a Focus on Mississippi, New York, and Oregon." *Ohio Northern University Law Review* 40 (2013–2014): 395–440.

Davis, Rebecca L. "'Not Marriage at All, but Simple Harlotry': The Companionate Marriage Controversy." *Journal of American History* 94, no. 4 (March 2008): 1137–63.

Degler, Carl. "What Ought to Be and What Was: Women's Sexuality in the Nineteenth Century." *American Historical Review* 79 (1974): 1467–90.

Edwards, Laura F. "Law, Domestic Violence, and the Limits of Patriarchal Authority in the Antebellum South." *Journal of Southern History* 65, no. 4 (November 1999): 733–70.

Elliot, Pam. "Shattering Illusions." *Journal of Gay and Lesbian Social Services* 4, no. 1 (1996).

Franke, Katherine M. "Becoming a Citizen: Reconstruction Era Regulation of African American Marriages." *Yale Journal of Law and the Humanities* 11 (1999): 251–309.

Haag, Pamela. "The 'Ill-Use of a Wife': Patterns of Working-Class Violence in Domestic and Public New York City, 1860–1880." *Journal of Social History* 25, no. 3 (Spring 1992): 447–77.

Hacker, J. David. "A Census-Based Count of the Civil War Dead." *Civil War History* 57, no. 4 (December 2011): 306–47.

Hacker, J. David, Libra Hilde, and James Holland Jones. "The Effect of the Civil War on Marriage Patterns." *Journal of Southern History* 76, no. 1 (February 2010): 39–70.

Hennessey, Melinda Meek. "Racial Violence during Reconstruction: The 1876 Riots in Charleston and Cainhoy." *South Carolina Historical Magazine* 86, no. 2 (April 1985): 100–112.

Higginbotham, Evelyn Brooks. "African-American Women's History and the Metalanguage of Race." *Signs* 17, no. 2 (Winter 1992): 251–74.

Hine, Darlene Clark. "Rape and the Inner Lives of Black Women in the Middle West." *Signs* 14, no. 4 (Summer 1989): 912–20.

Indiana Law Journal. "Evidence—Privileged Communications—Husband and Wife." *Indiana Law Journal* 10, no. 3 (1934).

Lebsock, Suzanne D. "Radical Reconstruction and the Property Rights of Southern Women." *Journal of Southern History* 43 (1977): 195–209.

McClintock, Megan J. "Civil War Pensions and the Reconstruction of Union Families." *Journal of American History* 83, no. 2 (September 1996): 456–80.

McMillen, Sally G. "Antebellum Southern Fathers and the Health Care of Children." *Journal of Southern History* 60, no. 3 (August 1994): 513–32.

Meyerowitz, Joanne. "A History of 'Gender.'" *American Historical Review* 113, no. 5 (December 2008): 1346–56.

Moore, R. Lawrence. "Religion, Secularization, and the Shaping of the Culture of Industry in Antebellum America." *American Quarterly* 41, no. 2 (June 1989): 216–42.

Nadelhaft, Jerome. "'The Public Gaze and the Prying Eye': The South and the Privacy Doctrine in Nineteenth-Century Wife Abuse Cases." *Cardozo Journal of Law and Gender* 14, no. 3 (2008): 549–607.

———. "Wife Torture: A Known Phenomenon in Nineteenth-Century America." *Journal of American Culture* 10 (Fall 1987): 39–59.

Neuhaus, Jessamyn. "The Way to a Man's Heart: Gender Roles, Domestic Ideology, and Cookbooks in the 1950s." *Journal of Social History* 32 (Spring 1999): 529–55.

Parise, Agustín. "A Constant Give and Take: Tracing Legal Borrowings in the Louisiana Civil Law Experience." *Seton Hall Legislative Journal* 35, no. 1 (2010): 1–35.

Peterson, David. "Wife Beating: An American Tradition." *Journal of Interdisciplinary History* 23, no. 1 (Summer 1992): 97–118.

Pleck, Elizabeth. "Wife Beating in Nineteenth-Century America." *Victimology: An International Journal* 4 (1979): 60–74.

Ramsey, Carolyn B. "A Diva Defends Herself: Gender and Domestic Violence in an Early Twentieth-Century Headline Trial." *St. Louis University Law Journal* 55 (2011): 1347–67. University of Colorado Law Legal Studies Research Paper no. 12-12. At http://ssrn.com/abstract=2096360.

Reinders, Robert. "The Free Negro in the New Orleans Economy, 1850–1860." *Louisiana History* 6 (1965): 273–85.

Schall, Jason. "The Consistency of Felon Disenfranchisement with Citizenship Theory." *Harvard Blackletter Law Journal* 22 (2006): 58–59.

Schweninger, Loren. "Antebellum Free Persons of Color in Postbellum Louisiana." *Louisiana History* 30 (1989): 345–64.

Scott, Joan Wallach. "Gender: A Useful Category of Historical Analysis." *American Historical Review* 91, no. 5 (December 1986): 1053–75.

Shapiro, Andrew L. "Challenging Criminal Disenfranchisement under the Voting Rights Act: A New Strategy." *Yale Law Journal* 103, no. 2 (November 1993).

Siegel, Reva B. "'The Rule of Love': Wife Beating as Prerogative and Privacy." Yale Law School, Faculty Scholarship Series, no. 1092, 1996. At http://digitalcommons.law.yale.edu/fss_papers/1092.

Smith, J. Denson. "How Louisiana Prepared and Adopted a Criminal Code." *Journal of Criminal Law and Criminology* 41, no. 2 (July–August 1950): 125–35.

Smith-Rosenberg, Carroll. "The Female World of Love and Ritual: Relations between Women in Nineteenth-Century America." *Signs* 1, no. 1 (1975): 1–29.

Summers, Gertrude, and Nina Feldman. "Blaming the Victim vs. Blaming the Perpetrator: An Attributional Analysis of Spouse Abuse." *Journal of Social and Clinical Psychology* 2, no. 4 (1984): 339–47.

Tyrrell, Ian R. "Drink and Temperance in the Antebellum South: An Overview and Interpretation." *Journal of Southern History* 48, no. 4 (December 1988): 485–510.

Waller, Altina L. "Community, Class, and Race in the Memphis Race Riot of 1866." *Journal of Social History* 18 (Winter 1984): 233–46.

Welter, Barbara. "The Cult of True Womanhood, 1820–1860." *American Quarterly* 18, no. 2 (Summer 1966): 151–74.

White, Hallie Bongar, and James G. White. "Testifying about Lethality Risk Factors." *Southwest Center for Law and Policy, and Office on Violence against Women*, US Department of Justice, 2005.

Whites, LeeAnn. "Rebecca Latimer Felton and the Wife's Farm: The Class and Racial Politics of Gender Reform." *Georgia Historical Quarterly* 76, no. 2 (Summer 1992): 354–72.

Dissertations

Roberts, Kodi. "Voodoo and the Promise of Power: The Racial, Gender, and Economic Politics of Religion in New Orleans, 1881–1940." PhD diss., University of Chicago, 2012.

Schwartzberg, Beverly J. "Grass Widows, Barbarians, and Bigamists: Fluid Marriage in Late Nineteenth-Century America." PhD diss., University of California, Santa Barbara, 2001.

Index

CPSIA information can be obtained
at www.ICGtesting.com
Printed in the USA
BVOW09*0224210917
494862BV00002B/4/P